Hope Is a Good Breakfast

Hope Is a Good Breakfast

and other humble thoughts on my cancer journey

by Tara Anne Shuman

WP

Wildewood Press
Boston, Massachusetts

ISBN-10: 0692365494
ISBN-13: 978-0-692-36549-6

10 9 8 7 6 5 4 3 2

Front-cover photograph by Jennifer Davidson
Back-cover photograph by Erica Shea
Cover design by Mark Abair

The author has used pseudonyms
to protect the privacy of certain individuals.

Dedication

_____

For those who have nourished me with hope.

Foreward

by Karen Fasciano, PsyD

For the past two decades, I have worked as a psychologist with adults and children facing cancer. Most recently I have spent the majority of my professional time directing a psychosocial program for young-adult cancer patients. Since the emotional distress of cancer can rival the physical challenges, I think passionately about how my work can validate the complexity of human emotions, teach new ways of coping, deepen existential exploration, and ultimately facilitate resilience.

Over the years I have found that my patients' experiences often raise the same types of questions: *Why me? How do I cope with change and uncertainty? How do I communicate with others about my cancer? How do I disempower fears about the future? How do I give meaning to this experience? And how do I accept what I cannot change?* While medical science continues to provide new and improved treatments and even cures for cancer, questions like these remain.

Coping with cancer is about so much more than the biology of a tumor, the mechanism of treatment, and the management of symptoms and side effects. A whirlwind of emotion accompanies every cancer diagnosis and the ups and downs of cancer treatment. Some of those emotions are familiar and some are foreign. Some are treasured and others are indescribably painful.

Every day I see the unwelcome effects of cancer. Every day I also see personal discovery in my patients and their loved ones despite illness, or perhaps because of it. *Hope Is a Good Breakfast* is an extraordinary example of such personal discovery and resilience. It's a brilliant memoir that explores the many complexities of hope, and the role that hope plays in what we can and cannot control. *Hope Is a Good Breakfast* explores many of the difficult questions facing young adults with cancer, in a way that unifies people of all ages who face a variety of different challenges.

A cancer diagnosis in one's twenties or thirties presents its own unique trials and tribulations. Young adulthood is a time of planning for the future, establishing a profession, developing and deepening intimate relationships, and solidifying personal values and goals. It's a time when we move from dependence on family of origin, to independence, to interdependence with our chosen families and communities. However, illness changes a young person's life course. What was once certain becomes uncertain. What was a plan becomes a possibility.

It is exceedingly difficult for anyone—never mind a young adult—to tackle the complexities of cancer with grace. With this book, Tara has managed to do just that. Her honest and keen insight gives all of us the opportunity to examine our own lives. That opportunity affords us the time to recognize and to celebrate so much of what before may have been invisible.

As Tara writes in her Prologue, "…it's not enough to be full of hope…" Indeed it isn't, and fortunately this memoir is about so much more than hope. It is about a young woman's journey of self-discovery. That discovery forces Tara (and all of us) to confront many contradictory emotions—joy and pain, sorrow and gratitude, anger and acceptance, fear and hope. This memoir is about the societal and personal expectations we have for our lives. It's about how we struggle to adjust when something unexpected and out of our control threatens to dismantle our sense of security. Finally, *Hope Is a Good Breakfast* is a beautiful depiction of the knowledge we gain from recognizing our own mortality.

Rarely are we blessed with a young writer's insights that help us—regardless of our age or situation—find a deeper understanding of what it means to embrace the complexities of human life. *Hope Is a Good Breakfast* is one such gift.

Karen Fasciano, PsyD
Dana-Farber / Brigham and Women's Cancer Center
Harvard Medical School
Boston, Massachusetts

Prologue

Hope is a good breakfast,
but it is a bad supper.

Francis Bacon
(philosopher, scientist, author)

Somehow Coexisting

I never understood the concept until I got cancer.

Hope.

I had heard about it quite a bit, in quotes and on *Oprah*. I had observed how important *hope* was to people who were going through hard times. But I had no clue of its significance until I was 32 years old, diagnosed with an aggressive form of breast cancer. No family history. No reason. No words. At least, not at first.

It was August 2012. I had just celebrated my sister Rachel's wedding and, the day after, my sixth wedding anniversary to my college sweetheart, Brian. We had two children—Teddy who was four and Annabel who was one. Brian and I both had full-time jobs, a mortgage on an imperfect house that we thought was perfect, and an assumption that we would grow old together. We may have even felt entitled to the growing-old part.

Then a radiologist told me I had cancer. My world froze in a hellish sort of way.

Darkness set in.

In that cold and lonely place, I felt too sick with worry to eat. My relationship with eating and exercising had been rocky for years, but this had nothing to do with body image. This had to do with the fact that I was so nauseated with fear that I couldn't stomach the thought of so much as a cracker.

I started to shed weight almost immediately. As I watched my body shrink, I figured that cancer was killing me.

Cancer equals death. At least, that's what I thought when I was diagnosed.

More darkness. Then…a light.

A few days after my diagnosis, I felt something I had never felt before:

Hope.

As I write about herein, I found hope in my sister's tearless eyes and in the empathy of two nurses at the breast cancer center of the community hospital where my mother worked.

It will be okay. You will fight this.

That hope—that despite cancer, I still had a life to live—was one of the most precious gifts I have ever received.

It will be okay. I will fight this.

The night after I found hope—after I *tasted* it—I ate a small dinner. I don't even remember what it was. But I know it was more than I had eaten in days.

* * *

In the darkest times of my cancer journey, many of which I write about in the pages before you, I clung to hope with white, shivering knuckles. I also came to realize that I needed more than hope to find peace with what was then happening to me, and even more so, with what could happen down the road.

I came to agree with Francis Bacon, a sixteenth-century English philosopher, scientist, author, and the father of empiricism:

Hope is a good breakfast, but it is a bad supper.

* * *

I originally conceived of this book as a way to spread a message of hope. I wanted to share with others, particularly those who have been thrown into a dark cave by cancer or by any other cruel reality, the possibility that they could still have light; that what we thought was our end may not be our end after all.

You will fight this.

I wanted to write a book that would leave readers with an implicit and humble message that *I did it* and *others can do it* and *with enough hope, we could all find happiness beyond the darkness of a really shitty time.*

We can beat cancer.

I wanted to believe it.

I *had* to believe it.

Over time, however, something in me changed. What it meant to *beat cancer* changed.

Maybe I'm not a fighter after all.

The evolution happened slowly and inadvertently. It happened as I observed, with a keener eye than ever before, life around me—the mundane, the extraordinary, the struggles, the beauty, the tragedy. All the intersections, rotaries, and detours those phenomena take.

It happened as I watched my friends and family help to make me well again. It happened as I watched old friends and new ones face metastatic disease with grace that both inspired me to be strong and crumbled me into a heap of uncontrollable tears. It happened as I watched people I cared about pass on from not only cancer, but from heart attack, ALS, and complications due to cystic fibrosis.

The evolution of my hope came into focus as I watched my daughter learn to sing and make jokes, and my son hug her every morning before he got on the school bus. It intensified as I fell in love with my husband more than ever before, and as I witnessed a strength in my mother that may go forever unmatched.

Maybe part of fighting means accepting.

At 32 years old, I started the long journey of accepting the harsh and liberating reality—that no one's life, including my own, would last forever. I felt fear and freedom in the realization that I couldn't control how I died. But I could control, at least in part, how I lived.

An odd and unexpected understanding.

And so beating cancer evolved into something more than a medical update about how a tumor had or had not progressed. Beating cancer became less about the physical and more about the spiritual. It became less about tomorrow, and more about today.

* * *

Cancer has shown me that sometimes, a moment is so heavy with fear and worry that one can't bear the thought of the future, not even the very next split-second. Since hope is innately forward-looking, sometimes it was no help—at least not on its own. What *did* help was the simple mantra that I arrived at soon after my diagnosis:

I am here now.

In my moments of panic, I found myself repeating those four words over and over again in my head, even whispering them out loud to myself.

I am here now.

When I heard them (*really* heard them), my mind and my body existed in the same place for a moment.

No fighting. No surrendering. Just being.

* * *

For me, at the end of the day, it's not enough to be full of hope for something to happen—or not happen—in the future. Better also to work hard to affect positive change. Better to be in the moment that *is*. Better to live without feeling entitled to anything—particularly tomorrow.

Please don't get me wrong. I still believe deeply in the power of hope. I feed off of hope every day—hope that modern medicine can one day treat or cure all cancer. Hope that pain will subside. But we can't stop there. We can't go a whole day on breakfast alone.

In the end, this isn't simply a book about hope, or a book about cancer for that matter. This is about book about life and love, fear and fragility. It's a book about what I found, in myself and in those around me, not only as I battled cancer, but as I learned to accept it as something more than an enemy.

This book is one story. My story. I don't claim that it will do anything for anyone. Nevertheless I hope that somehow my story helps others cope with and appreciate the innately intertwined tragedy and beauty that exists in every precious opportunity we get to live another day. And in every precious chance we get to eat another meal of whatever it is that makes our spirit feel full. Filled with hope, perhaps. Or better yet, filled with peace.

* * *

Peace.
In a fighter.
Somehow coexisting.

Part One
Diagnosis

There will come a time
when you believe
everything is finished.
That will be the beginning.

Louis L'Amour
(writer)

An Unlikely Lump

I felt my tumor for the first time on Friday, August 3, 2012. It was a beautiful night in our Boston suburb, which was a relief, because we hosted a barbecue and our house isn't big enough to fit everyone if it were to have rained.

My husband Brian is a dedicated public high-school teacher and a passionate boys' varsity ice hockey coach. Every summer we invite his alumni players to our house for burgers, hot dogs, and an inevitable game or two of wiffle ball. Brian does all of the cooking and grilling. I help serve the food, clean up, and comfort our little ones when they self-destruct at sunset.

One of our guests that summer night was Corey, Brian's good friend, colleague, and fellow coach. When Corey came around to the backyard with his two-year-old in tow, I gave Corey a hug and asked him the question I always ask when I first see him—"How's Kristin doing?"

Kristin is Corey's wife, and one of our dear friends. At the time, she was a few weeks into her chemotherapy treatment for breast cancer, so Brian and I were thinking of her often. Corey gave me a quick update and while he talked, I realized it had been way too long since I'd last seen Kristin. I made a mental note to see her soon.

Over an hour later, Annabel was fast asleep in her crib and Teddy was getting cranky. I decided that Teddy and I would drive Corey's son home so that I could visit with Kristin while Corey and Brian enjoyed a rare chance to sit down and relax. It was a last minute, life-changing decision, as decisions often can be.

I drove over to Kristin and Corey's house enjoying the playful chatter of the boys in the back seat. I couldn't help but smile at how cute they were, although I pretended not to hear them so they wouldn't stop.

As we got closer to the house, I began to fret about how strange and uncomfortable it could be to see Kristin bald. Prior to the chemo, Kristin had gorgeous, thick, reddish-brown hair and I hadn't seen her since she lost all of it. I hoped I could fake a positive reaction if, in fact, it made me scared or sad.

After pulling into the driveway and unbuckling the boys, Kristin came to the front door. She had a pink scarf on her head and I was relieved to see that there was nothing strange or uncomfortable about her appearance. Without an ounce of makeup, Kristin looked beautiful, even healthy and strong. I didn't know that cancer patients could look so good, perhaps because at the time I didn't know any other cancer patients.

Kristin and I watched our sons run around her house together while we talked and drank ice water. Kristin told me about her treatment, and, as she was wont to do, downplayed her own strength and courage. I reminded her of how incredible she was, but I knew that she was too modest and humble to really see it.

When I left Kristin's house that night, I was angry that she had to endure what she did, all while teaching kindergarten and raising two young children. I also felt grateful to call such a remarkable woman my friend.

After "the hockey guys" (as Teddy calls them) left the barbecue, Brian and I cleaned up a bit, then settled on the sofa in our living room to watch the Summer Olympics.

While we sat there, I considered my visit with Kristin. I thought about how young she was to have breast cancer. I always assumed breast cancer was a disease that affected mostly older women, but Kristin was only 42. I was even younger—just 32—but still, I decided to feel my own breasts for cancer.

I didn't lie down or use a circular motion with my fingers like a formal breast self-exam suggests. I just reached under my t-shirt and poked around.

I felt the lump in my left breast almost immediately. It wasn't big or especially apparent, but what I felt in the left one I didn't feel in the right.

A few minutes later, I told Brian that I felt something. I lifted up my shirt, took Brian's hand, and placed it on the lump. He looked away, as if that would help him focus. When he looked back at me, I saw fear in his eyes. He told me I should make an appointment to have it checked out.

Disclaimer: I have always been somewhat of a hypochondriac, and a strange one at that. I usually assume the worst, but I don't rush to the doctor with my symptoms. I just torture myself internally, and usually the symptoms subside. In the instances when they haven't, I reluctantly carved out a morning to visit my doctor. Inevitably my worries would turn out to be nothing serious. Although I worried that a lump in my boob could be breast cancer, I figured that since none of my many other worries ever turned out to be significant, this would be no different.

If left alone, I would have made an appointment a few weeks or a month down the road. But Brian quietly worries more than I do, and he insisted that I schedule an appointment as soon as possible.

When I reached my office on Monday morning, I called my primary care physician. "She's out this week," her secretary told me without offering any more detail.

"Is there someone else I can see? I don't really want to wait until she gets back." There was a long pause and I could hear computer keys clicking.

"Dr. Nell can see you Friday afternoon," the secretary explained apathetically. I put it in my calendar, which usually made me feel better, and almost always helped to control the symptoms. But that scheduled appointment didn't make the lump disappear.

I returned to the lump while watching TV later that night. I kept wondering why there was a lump on one side and not the other.

On Tuesday morning, August 7, 2012, I called the doctor again. I explained that I had an appointment for the upcoming Friday but that I was really nervous about the lump. "Does any doctor have time to see me today?" I asked. I pulled out my commuter train schedule while the secretary clicked away again.

"Can you be here at two?" she asked, still as apathetic as before. I ran my finger over the tiny print on the train schedule. The 1:20 PM train out of South Station would get me there just in time.

"Yes, I'll be there," I responded.

I don't remember asking Brian to come with me, but he did, and I definitely wanted him to be there. He sat quietly in the small exam room while the doctor massaged my pathetic excuse for a boob.

"Does this hurt when I press on it?" she asked while bearing down on the lump.

"Kind of," I answered.

"Good. I'm pretty sure it's just a cyst," she explained. "It wouldn't hurt if it were a tumor." Brian and I smiled at each other when we heard that.

"You're so young, no family history," she explained while typing something into the computer and avoiding eye contact with me and Brian.

Once the doctor said "cyst," I was fine. No cancer. No worries. Just something to add to the list of false alarms. I was going to be okay and I celebrated that for a minute or two in order to wash away the embarrassment that I felt for my overreaction. Then I got impatient and wanted to go home.

"I'm still going to schedule a mammogram since you've never had one," the doctor explained. I was surprised, but not nervous. *She's just being extra careful*, I thought. Then I started to wonder about the recent health care cost-containment reform bill that the governor of Massachusetts had signed just two days earlier, and how it may or may not have affected the doctor's decision to send me for more tests. I was a health care attorney, so it wasn't as random a thought as it may seem.

After I got dressed, Brian and I walked down to the radiology department. I was reluctant to schedule another appointment because I was convinced that it would be a complete waste of time and money. However, I'm a rule-follower, so I followed the rules.

The scheduler at the radiology desk was new to his position. When I handed him the little card that the doctor gave me, he told me that I would need to schedule an ultrasound, too. I didn't remember the doctor saying anything about an ultrasound and I became annoyed at the thought of missing even more work for a useless test.

He managed to schedule my mammogram with ease—for the very next morning—but the ultrasound gave him some trouble. I was getting antsy and I told him to not bother with the ultrasound. "If they see anything in the mammogram, I'll book an ultrasound," I told him, trying to push my rudeness back down to its hiding place. But the scheduling guy was a rule-follower, too, and he told me that he had to schedule the two appointments together.

About 10 minutes later, the scheduler had my ultrasound set for just after the mammogram. I thanked him (unable to fake a smile) and said I'd be there. He didn't know that I planned on ditching the second appointment if the train schedule wouldn't accommodate it. (Even rule-followers sometimes break the rules.)

Brian and I left the doctor's office that day holding hands and talking about what he would make us for dinner. I didn't worry about the stupid lump for another minute that night. I even considered, albeit not seriously, skipping the mammogram altogether. I thank my lucky stars every single day that I didn't.

My First (and Last) Mammogram

Brian spends the summers home with the kids and he often plans mini-adventures to keep the days exciting and him from going insane. The morning after my it's-just-a-cyst appointment, Brian took the kids to a small zoo just north of the Rhode Island border. He asked me if I wanted him to cancel the zoo trip and come with me to the follow-up appointments, but I insisted that it would be a waste of his time. I didn't really know what a mammogram was, but I figured it would be quick and painless. There was no need for anyone to hold my hand while the radiologist confirmed that I had a stupid little cyst in my breast.

My mammogram was scheduled for 9:30 AM, so I planned on catching the 10:30 AM train to Boston in order to be at my desk just after 11.

Being 32 with no family history of cancer and no risk factors, that August 8 mammogram was my first one. I undressed and put my clothes in a tiny locker by the internal waiting area. I was cold, but not scared.

At the time, I thought mammograms were like ultrasounds—performed with a wand while the patient is lying down. I had no idea that a mammogram was done standing up, or that it would involve propping my pancake of a boob on a metal plate and pressing another plate down on it. The machine reminded me of a big, cold panini press.

The mammogram didn't hurt, although I won't claim that it tickled to have my breast placed in a panini-maker. It was kind of like a seat belt—a small inconvenience for something much bigger: Life.

I followed directions the technician (Jean) gave me, lifted my arms when instructed, and held still while she snapped my glamour shots. But as Jean repeatedly repositioned my left pancake between the plates, I started to feel like something may be wrong. I asked her if she saw anything bad. Jean hesitated, then gave me a vague response.

When we were done, Jean lead me back to the waiting room. I heard her talking to the radiologist, Dr. Redmond, in his windowless office nearby. I could tell that Dr. Redmond was showing her something on the image. I heard him say that he wanted more pictures.

The plates felt much colder the second time. By then, I was most definitely scared. Jean tried to comfort me, but I could tell in her voice that she saw something. She asked me if I had any family history of breast cancer and when I said no, she said that was great news. After additional photos, I sat shivering in my johnny in the waiting area by the lockers.

About 10 minutes later, Jean came back to retrieve me. She whispered that Dr. Redmond wanted to do the ultrasound right away.

Within minutes I was lying on the ultrasound table, trying to stop my world from spinning. I remembered that machine from the joyful days of seeing my two babies in my belly. I used to love the feel of the cool gel because it meant I was about to see our unborn child. This time, what was growing in me would not bring us joy. The gel was just cold goop—an informidable weapon used to hunt down an intruder.

Dr. Redmond told me that he saw cancer within minutes of placing the wand on my chest. At the time, the words he used were completely foreign to me but I know now exactly what he saw and what he said—invasive ductal carcinoma, as well as ductal carcinoma in situ (DCIS). The "invasive" part was the 1.2-centimeter-in-diameter tumor. The DCIS was a four-inch-in-diameter blanket of cancer that had not yet broken out of the ducts.

I can recall precisely the first thought I had after Dr. Redmond told me he saw cancer: *If this is only breast cancer, I will survive.* At the time, I didn't understand breast cancer that has reached the chest or the bones or the brain is still breast cancer. What I meant in my head was, *If this hasn't spread, I will beat it.* Since then, I have heard amazing stories of men and women who lived many years with cancer that has spread (also known as metastatic cancer), but I know that for most of those people, the fight is an uphill battle.

Within a split second after that initial thought, I started to feel cancer all over. I tend to have an overactive imagination and a lot of very bad dreams. I wondered if maybe I was in the middle of one of them. But I couldn't shake myself out of it. This was real. *I had cancer.*

Dr. Redmond tried to comfort me with words like "treatable" and "best care in the world." But in my mental disarray, I only had one question for him.

"Will I see my kids grow up?" I blurted out, perhaps more than once. He said yes, but his eyebrows were raised, and he didn't sound very convincing.

The Biopsy

I always thought that a biopsy came before a cancer diagnosis. In my case, however, the experienced radiologist treated the biopsy as something my cancer doctors were going to need in my medical record before they would meet with me. He had no doubt about what he saw and it turned out that he was exactly right.

After the ultrasound, Dr. Redmond told me that he had to gather some materials for the biopsy. While I waited, Jean let me use her office to call Brian.

Foolishly, I thought I could tell Brian the news without crying. The moment I sent the words, "He thinks he saw cancer," from my brain to my mouth, the tears poured out. I was in shock, trying hard to stay standing on a ground that felt like it had fallen out from under me.

Brian told me he would be home as soon as he could. I don't remember anything else that he said although he always ends his calls with "Love you," so I'm certain he said that too.

I sat back down in the small internal waiting area. At one point I started crying again, and a young blond woman seated next to me asked me if I had ever had a mammogram before. I could barely respond and I definitely couldn't look her in the eyes. "I have a family history so I've gotten lots of them. Don't worry, it's not that scary," she explained, trying to comfort me.

"Thank you—I know. It's the hearing-you-have-cancer part that's scary," I laughed and cried in response. She apologized, stunned. That was the first time (but not the last) that I saw that holy-shit shocked look on someone's face. Later, I worried that I had been flippant to a kind woman who was just trying to be nice.

The biopsy part was messy…literally. Dr. Redmond numbed the area and then used some sort of device that made loud clicks and spit out tiny globs of some liquid (blood?) or solid (chest flesh?). It didn't hurt at all, but it was terrifying because it hit me then and there that I wasn't going to be catching my train to work that day. As Dr. Redmond extracted pieces of my cancer, I realized my whole life was about to change.

I don't remember getting dressed. I just remember standing in Dr. Redmond's dark office afterward while he explained to me some vague timeline of events, which I wouldn't remember either. He handed me a small, white appointment card with a phone number for new breast-cancer patients.

I walked to my car and called Mark—my colleague, mentor, and friend—to tell him that I wouldn't be coming into the office that day, or probably for the rest of the week. I told him that I had a lump checked and the doctor thought it was breast cancer. There's no easy way to deliver that news, no preface that can make it easier to say or hear. I felt so badly that I had to tell Mark something that would upset him, but there was really no way around it.

Then I drove home. I remember very little about that ride. I remember feeling adrenaline, or something like it, coursing through my body. I remember that when I pulled into the driveway, I realized I hadn't turned on any music. I *always* play music in the car.

My Angels Fly In

Brian and the kids returned from the zoo within minutes of me arriving home from the doctor's office. Teddy could tell that something was wrong, but he wasn't that worried about it. "That was a small zoo!" he exclaimed when I asked him how his trip had been. I love that kid; he always tells it like it is.

My mother was on a business trip in Nashville, Tennessee during this time. Despite her cell phone's voice mail greeting warning callers that she never checks her messages, I left one. I told her, "Don't worry, everyone is fine, but please call me back as soon as you can." As I said, "Everyone is fine," I wondered if I were lying.

My mom called back almost immediately, and I told her what the doctor told me. *Breast cancer. Treatable. Treatable. Treatable.* She said she would be home as soon as she could; that we would figure everything out; that she loved me and was so sorry that I had to go through the morning's appointments alone.

Not to exaggerate or anything, but my mom has superpowers. Those powers aren't based on invisibility or scaling skyscrapers, but on intelligence, patience, empathy, generosity, and the ability to get shit done. She was home from Nashville within hours of our conversation and in between her hectic travels, she managed to speak with my father, sister, and brother to make sure that everyone was aware of the news and was handling it alright.

My mom works in health care, so she also touched base with a few friends and colleagues who were connected to the world-renowned Dana-Farber Cancer Institute in Boston. Within hours of being blindsided by a cancer diagnosis in her 32-year-old daughter, my mother had stabilized a family, hopped on a plane, and started to plug me into a group of the best cancer doctors on the planet. As I said, superpowers.

Meanwhile, my best friend of 20 years, Brianne, and her husband Seamus, scooped up Teddy for an indoor mini-golf adventure to allow Brian and I time to process everything while Annabel napped. It turned out that processing everything was far too ambitious of a goal. A more reasonable one was simply to keep breathing.

In an unusually quiet house, Brian and I sat close on the sofa, trying to convince ourselves that *cancer* didn't mean *death*. That's not an easy thing to do when cancer is in the room too.

As I sat there, I thought about the people that I knew, or knew of, who were cancer victims and survivors. My mind went immediately to a young female attorney at my prior law firm who lost her cancer battle in 2002. The firm named their annual Outstanding Pro Bono Service Award in honor of her memory and I always thought the people who won that award were the most important attorneys at the firm. Was that my destiny? Would there be an award or a golf tournament or a scholarship named after me? I tried really hard to not vomit from thoughts like these.

In my brainstorming, I also remembered that one of my dear friends, Sara, had a brother who had fought and beat leukemia several years before. I decided not to tell anyone else about the cancer until we had the biopsy results, but I couldn't stop myself from calling her.

Sara is an oncology nurse in Boston. She is also one of the most caring people I've ever met. I don't even know what I said to her, but I remember precisely where I was sitting (our porch) and what I was staring at (the wood floor planks). I also remember exactly how Sara responded when I told her. "Oh my goodness, my friend Maggie is going through the exact same thing."

Sara told me that Maggie graduated from Bowdoin four years after I had. That made her 28 years old. Maggie married her college sweetheart just like I did. Sara went on to tell me about Maggie's diagnosis and treatment. She said she could put me in touch with Maggie and I said that would be great. But truthfully, I was just trying to be nice. I knew I wasn't ready to talk to anyone who was also dealing with this nightmare. I could barely comprehend my own.

By dinnertime, my angels had assembled in a loyal group around our dinner table. My mom was home safe from Nashville and my sister and her husband had arrived from Virginia. My dad, brother, and my brother's fiancé gathered with us too.

My mom's reaction was exactly as I would have suspected—she wished she could take my place. When she arrived at my front door she cried a bit, hugged me tight, then got down to business. Without the biopsy results, she couldn't get me formally connected to the system at Dana-Farber just yet, but she had everything lined up so that when the results arrived, we would have a great starting point.

My dad's reaction was also as I may have expected—a threat against his family is simply unacceptable. He arrived at our house soon after he heard the news and I met him outside, mainly so that we could have a moment away from the kids. He hugged me tighter than he ever had, and cried like I had never seen. He gritted his teeth, and with a tone intertwined with love and anger, he declared, "We'll throw the world at this thing. It has no chance. We will fight it. You will beat it. We will fight, fight, fight, you got that?" I didn't feel that fire myself just yet, but I appreciated his comforting hug, and the fact that I had another fighter in my corner.

My sister was different. She strolled in without a tear in her eye. She hugged me, totally sympathetic, but oddly relaxed. When we got a minute alone, she looked me in the eye and told me that she was upset that I would have to go through some grueling treatment, but she wasn't *really* upset because she knew in her heart and soul that everything was going to be fine. For the first time since my mammogram, I felt an ounce of peace. I made her repeat it over and over—that I was going to be okay—until somehow, part of me started to believe it.

My sister and I have always had a connection whereby we instinctively know things about one another before we even talk. Rachel was 100% sure that Annabel was a girl and even called the baby "Annabel" when she was no bigger than a lima bean, despite that everyone else (except Teddy) was convinced that we were having another boy. Oddly, on the day of my mammogram, Rachel hadn't gone to work. She had no reason not to, simply a feeling that she should work from home that day. When my mom called mid-afternoon, Rachel was packed in minutes and on the next flight to Boston.

Then there was my brother, "Un-coe," as Annabel constantly repeats. Un-coe Sean cleaned our house from top to bottom that night, and took care of me as if I were his little sister. He knows exactly how to make me feel better, and his fiancé Lauren, who is a nurse, is just the kind of caregiver any patient would want at his or her bedside.

That night we all huddled in our house, so closely and nervously that it felt as if a war were raging outside. Even the Olympics, my ultimate pick-me-up, provided only a mild distraction. But somehow, amidst the utter terror we all felt inside, I started to feel twinges of a sense of safety—an odd type of comfort that we were all gearing up for a battle we would win.

The First and Worst Night

The first night after my diagnosis was the worst night of my life. I was not strong, not a fighter, not anyone's inspiration. I fell asleep around 11 PM, snuggled next to Brian and completely spent, but at 1 AM I woke as if bombs were falling outside. I didn't want to wake up Brian, who deserved his sleep more than anyone, and I wouldn't dream of bothering my mother, even though she insisted that I do so.

So I just lay there, wondering about how our house would feel without me in it. I wondered about whether my family could enjoy a summer vacation or a Christmas morning if I weren't there. I hoped that there would be another woman to treat Brian like the most wonderful man that he is, and I felt anger that I couldn't be the one to enjoy his company. I lay there weak and so indescribably scared that something would steal me away from the people I loved. I was bursting at the seeming injustice that I wouldn't hurt a soul, but some nasty disease was tearing mine apart.

In that first night after my diagnosis, I felt cancer crawling up and down my body like poisonous spiders. Worst of all, I kept thinking I heard the kids cry for me, but it was just the air conditioner humming.

Then I shook uncontrollably, despite my body feeling like cold stone. I could barely breathe. I was starved, but couldn't eat. I needed to vomit, but lacked the strength to do it. Needless to say, it was one fucking awful night. (Apologies—I swear when I get really upset.)

I had lived with some anxiety prior to cancer, and I always resisted medication for it. I didn't want a pill to change me; I wanted to do it myself. But on August 9, 2012, I realized that there are some things I just can't do myself, like sleep through the night after a cancer diagnosis.

When my mom offered to call my doctor for a sleep aid and anxiety prescription, I didn't say yes or no, which meant *yes*. If there were a pill that would make sure a night like that never happened again, I was going to take it—even if the side effects included growing a tail.

The Results

The biopsy results took only a day to process. I don't know how that happened so fast, but I'm sure my mom's persistence had something to do with it.

It was a very strange experience, to wait for the biopsy results. On the one hand, I wanted to be hopeful. *Maybe the radiologist was wrong*, I thought every now and then. On the other hand, he was very confident about what he saw, so I knew I had to prepare myself for the official news that it was, in fact, cancer.

I was lying down when the phone rang. The caller ID showed the number of my doctor's office. I answered it because the phone was right by my side. A nurse that I didn't know was on the line. She asked for Tara Shuman.

"Yes, I'm here but can you please wait a second?" I handed the phone to my mother. I couldn't do it. I couldn't hear the words. My mom took the phone and I went into the other room. Brian followed.

It was clear by my mom's reaction that the biopsy showed what we hoped it would not. I wasn't surprised, and I don't even think I cried at the news. I actually felt some relief; like I had been given the green light to start fighting this thing.

Brian, however, had a difficult time with the results. He told me later that he had hung onto hope that the results would have been negative, that the radiologist made a big mistake. My poor husband was crushed, and I was too. I just happened to be a day or so ahead of him in processing it.

With the biopsy results, and my first (of several) pathology reports, my mom was armed and ready to assemble my team. I didn't even know what she was doing; I was too weak and too scared to help. Now I know that she was busy getting my pathology report to Dana-Farber and figuring out who would be the best oncologist to guide us.

After hours of my mom's research and investigation, I got an appointment for the following week with Dr. Denver. Dr. Denver is a pretty big deal at Dana-Farber, but far more importantly, we heard that he was great with people and he was taking new patients. Having an appointment at one of the best cancer institutes in the world was a big first-step forward. And that day, forward progress was something we all needed.

Breaking the News

Thanks to Ativan, the second night after my diagnosis did not include a total mind-and-body meltdown. I did, however, wake up around 3 AM knowing there was no way I would ever be able to get back to sleep.

I lay in bed trying to protect my body from violent shakes, and wondered what I could do to pass the time. Eventually I decided to go downstairs and, finding my way to the computer, began to compose an email to family and friends about my diagnosis. I strung together some seemingly coherent thoughts and by the time the kids got up a few hours later, I was pretty sure that I would send it.

On Friday, August 10, 2012, after those who were able to eat had eaten breakfast, I sent the following email to relatives, friends, and colleagues:

Hello All,

I'm so sorry to be the bearer of bad news, and I also apologize in advance for doing it over email. I would much rather talk to you in person about this, but that's not quite possible right now.

This week I was diagnosed with breast cancer. To say it was a total shock is more than an understatement. I have no history in my family and am only 32. Luckily, I'm also hypochondriacal enough to feel a lump and head to the doctor. Just never thought it would be cancer.

Nonetheless, here we are. As you'd expect, Brian and my family are incredible—so strong and so productive even when we all just want to sit and cry and hit something. Since many of us work in health care and have a take-no-prisoners attitude at this point, it looks like we'll have Dana-Farber shaken down before Monday. After that, I should know more about where the cancer has gone. Even as I type this, I can't believe it's real.

I am terribly sorry if this upsets you but each of you (and probably so many others that I haven't even added yet) mean so much to me and I wanted you to know. I also know that most of you will first respond by asking what you can do. Truthfully, the most helpful thing for me is just words of encouragement, stories you know of people who have fought this, and lots of praying and hoping. Most of all, I want everyone to know that as hard as this is on me, it is equally hard on Brian—maybe even worse—because he wants to help so much more can even be possible.

Please feel free to pass this to others I may have missed. As you know I'm a kind of tell-it-like-it-is person, so this isn't a big secret—it's just life.

Thank you so much for all of the kindness and love you share with me and my family.

* * *

When I sent that email, I was in crisis. I wasn't brave, nor strong, nor even considerate of the emotional waves the virtual message may cause. I was just trying to breathe, to fill the hours before the rest of the world awoke, and remove as much of a terrible burden off of my loved ones as I possibly could. In those dark moments, I simply trusted what my instincts told me to do. And they told me to write that email.

Finding Hope

A few hours after I sent the email, I got dressed in my comfy clothes that had already grown baggy on my sick-with-worry frame. My mom, Brian, and I dragged ourselves into the car for a trip to Winchester Hospital, the community hospital where my mother worked for 15 years. My mom had scheduled us to meet two nurses at the hospital's breast care center. The purpose of the appointment was to get our bearings in the world of breast cancer, a world completely foreign to all of us.

I became so nauseated on the way to the appointment that I spent the first few minutes after we arrived bent over the toilet, waiting to throw up. I didn't, probably because I had barely eaten anything in days.

A short while later, we floated into a small, comfortable conference room, so dazed and devastated that we barely knew our own names. Then Christine, one of the nurses, took my hand. I'm not a religious person, but the only word I can think of to describe her is an angel. An angel is someone who picks you up from the darkest place and puts you in a more comfortable one, right? Then Christine is an angel, because that's what she did for me.

I can barely remember what Christine said. All I remember is that she gave me something indescribably precious; something that I had never felt before. She gave me hope.

While my mind had gone as far as to wonder where I wanted my ashes scattered, Christine brought me back with the pep talk of my life. She told me with words, and emphasized with the look in her eye, that I would beat this. She gave me a sense of hope so powerful that I felt it *physically*. Brian and my mom felt it too. It was almost magical.

In that hour, Christine and Pat, the other nurse-angel, somehow found the perfect balance of medical information, compassion, empathy, and encouragement. Most importantly though, they helped me with a paradigm shift I didn't even know I needed. They helped me realize that this was going to be a journey. I would get answers I wouldn't like, maybe even a higher stage of cancer than I would appreciate. (I really wanted no stage of cancer so I already had to stomach that one.) But those answers would all become part of the plan, the counterattack. We would adjust better than the enemy could, and we would defeat it.

I felt the weight of the world partially lifted in that appointment. Even if this proved to be a complicated fight, it would be a fight nonetheless, and I would have a say in the outcome. I would have a team of some of the best doctors in the world, and I would have my family and friends by my side. Together, we would have some control of my destiny. For the first time in days, I felt like I landed back on planet Earth. I felt like I was me again, albeit, a nervous and shaky version of me.

Dr. Lui, a surgeon, joined us an hour or so later and helped me with my fear that cancer had invaded my whole body. Dr. Lui explained that years ago she thought she had bed bugs and she itched for days. After she confirmed that there were no bed bugs, the itching immediately subsided and she realized the true power of her imagination. This analogy gave me hope that the cancer I felt all over my body since my diagnosis was a figment of my imagination.

When I got home, my in-laws came over. Janice and Paul are two of the most caring, comforting people I've ever met. I cried when I hugged them, but it was a different cry than the cries from the last few days—it was one less full of fear and more full of thanks.

By later that afternoon, my email inbox and my cell phone had collected messages from so many good people in my life. Those messages gave me my life back. They brought more clarity to what I started to realize at the hospital that day—that I was still here. Still a mom and a wife and a daughter and a sister. I still had a house, a job, a life. I was still a force to be reckoned with.

A Blog Is Born

Hours before sunrise the next morning, I was once again wide awake and far too terrified to close my eyes. Clearly, my sleep problems were not going away any time soon. Remembering that the predawn hours of the morning prior had passed more quickly and less painfully because I drafted the email to family and friends, I decided to write an update.

I quickly realized that I didn't want to clog anyone's inbox with information that he or she may not have wanted. I needed a way to write about my medical updates, but in a way that didn't force anything onto anybody.

I had never read a blog, but I had heard of them. I loved the Meryl

Streep and Amy Adams movie *Julie & Julia,* and the true story it depicted about an unlikely blogger's adventure through a Julia Child cookbook. As cliché as it sounded, I was a young woman in crisis and I needed a blog.

Sometime around 4 AM, I googled, "Start a blog." The heading of the first hit explained, "Create a blog. It's free." So I did, and it was.

Just before 7 AM that morning, I published my first post.

As I wrote those five short paragraphs, I fought an intense darkness that came with the cancer diagnosis. I learned immediately that writing helped me breathe, think, and remember that I was still alive, despite the intruder that was trying to kill me. I was thankful for this light. In fact, I was so thankful that the following morning I returned to my computer again when that fear started to strangle me.

The fear and darkness were indescribably powerful. Any moment that I stopped fighting them, they would start to make me think that this was it. This was my end.

Months later, I found this quote by Louis L'Amour: "There will come a time when you believe everything is finished. That will be the beginning."

That quote reached me. The first part hit home so hard. Out of nowhere, I was forced to face the time when I believed that everything was finished. But I had no idea how the second part was relevant. This was the beginning? Of what? I had no idea. In the meantime, I kept writing.

Gradually, I figured it out. My cancer battle was indeed the beginning of something. That something is this book.

Meeting My Team

The first logical step of any calculated fight is to study the enemy and learn its game. While I got my bearings, pathologists in labs somewhere dissected slices of my tumor and tested them to determine the type of breast cancer I had. I didn't even know that there *were* different types of breast cancer, but I soon learned that the variations matter because they determine the course of treatment.

Did the cancer power off of estrogen? Yes, mine did. Did it power off of another hormone, progesterone? Yes, mine did that, too. Finally, for perhaps the most significant question, did it carry with it the HER2 protein? More on this later, but in time, I would discover that yes, my tumor also carried the infamous human epidermal growth factor receptor 2 (HER2) protein, which often indicates an aggressive form of breast cancer.

In addition to discovering what type of cancer I had, we obviously needed to know if it had traveled beyond the breast and, if so, where and how far. At the time, that was the scariest step, considering that since

August 8, 2012, I felt cancer everywhere.

I tried to convince myself that the pain I felt all over was due to something other than cancer. Perhaps my back hurt because Teddy weighed 50 pounds and I had to drag him up to his room for a time-out when he tackled Annabel for trying to borrow his, or better yet, *her* ride-along Winnie the Pooh truck. Annabel stood her ground, and since time-outs pretty much meant nothing to Teddy, it really just served as a way to get a few minutes of peace downstairs and give Annabel an uninterrupted turn on her toy. Bad parenting? Perhaps. An explanation for my backache? I sure as hell hoped so.

* * *

On the Monday morning after my diagnosis, Brian, my mom, and I pulled into the parking lot at the Dana-Farber Cancer Institute. We laughed nervously and remarked about how we all used to marvel at the strength of people who had to walk into that building. Now it was us: nauseated and petrified, and on a mission like never before.

We spent over six hours at Dana-Farber that day, visited two different buildings, traveled to five different floors, and spoke with nine different clinicians.

The real answers came from the two and a half hours we spent with my breast surgeon, Dr. Nadia, and my medical oncologist, Dr. Denver.

The way I saw it from my perch, Dr. Nadia would remove the cancer's command center and Dr. Denver would hunt down any stragglers in the field to ensure that they never have a chance to regroup. A one-two punch, and, may I say, a good-looking one at that.

After a good cry at the start of the first appointment, I surprised myself and found a way to listen, and later even take notes, as Dr. Nadia explained my cancer. Like Dr. Redmond had suspected, I had two different types of breast cancer—invasive ductal carcinoma and ductal carcinoma in situ (DCIS). As one may guess, the cancer started in the milk ducts. I knew I hated those damn ducts the very first time I tried to breastfeed Teddy, thus perpetuating my desire to start a "Breastfeeding Sucks" campaign.

I've since learned that the "in situ" part of ductal carcinoma in situ means that it's still hanging out in the milk ducts. I don't like any kind of cancer, but if I had to pick one type, I'd choose the lazy, in situ kind.

The invasive kind, however, I will always hate. "Invasive" sounds energetic, vengeful, mean. It's mobile, and when an enemy can move, it's generally a lot stronger. This is why I had a chest X-ray and blood draw at the end of that first long day at Dana-Farber—to see if there were any obvious signs that the cancer had infiltrated other parts of my body. My family and I erupted in cheers, hugs, and cries at dinner later that night when Dr. Denver called to say there weren't any obvious signs that it had.

At my first appointment with her, Dr. Nadia talked a lot about the invasive tumor. She explained that from what they had seen, it looked to be about a centimeter in diameter. She told us that my lymph node in the "bad boob" tested negative for cancer. I didn't even know that I had lymph nodes in my boobs.

Dr. Nadia explained that we wouldn't know if my cancer spread until she removed the sentinel lymph node from under my left arm. That would happen in my first surgery, which had yet to be scheduled, and was still a month or two away. The thought of that surgery made me want to vomit. Thankfully, the morsels of food I was able to eat that morning stayed put because of Dr. Nadia's confidence that even if the cancer had spread, she could still remove all of the poisoned nodes. The invasive cancer sure wasn't good news, but Dr. Nadia made me feel good about my chances at beating it.

Once we were finished talking about the tumor, Dr. Nadia lowered her tone as if she had to deliver some really bad news. *Adrenaline rush. Gulp.* The DCIS, she said, was "widespread." I had "calcifications" all over my breast, and there was "no way to save it."

"Save it?" I almost yelled back, "Hell, chop that thing off today if you can!" I'm sure every woman has a different reaction when told that she will need to have her breast removed. I didn't know what my own reaction would be, but when it happened, it was clear. I wanted the surgeon to take that saggy boob and all the cancer with it!

Dr. Nadia clearly was expecting more of a discussion on the topic of the unavoidable mastectomy, because we could all tell that she had to skip ahead in her mental agenda when I had nothing to discuss on the issue.

Next we talked about "reconstruction," which I previously would have guessed was a term used by general contractors at a building site. I learned, however, that reconstruction is the process of making fake boobs where the old ones had been. I explained to Dr. Nadia that I didn't care about what my chest looked like when everything was over. "I just want to live," I told her. She smiled and said that I was going to be okay. I wanted to ask her, "So does that mean I'm going to live?" But I just let it be, in case she hadn't meant it in such a literal way.

My next appointment was with Dr. Denver. He told us that my cancer was receptor positive to estrogen and progesterone, two hormones that a woman's body produces naturally. Dr. Denver explained that given those test results, I would be prescribed a drug called Tamoxifen for the next five years. Tamoxifen is a small pill taken daily. It is considered a hormone therapy in that it suppresses the hormones in order to lower the risk of cancer recurrence. That didn't sound so bad.

The third of the main characteristics of breast cancer (at least, the ones discovered thus far) made the hair on the back of my neck stand up. It involved the HER2 protein.

When Dr. Denver first mentioned HER2, he explained that we would hear back on the results in the next day or two. All he initially told me was that if the test results came back as "HER2 positive," I would need a relatively new drug called Herceptin (drug name trastuzumab) to treat it. Dr. Denver described Herceptin as the biggest breakthrough in breast cancer treatment since chemotherapy. Dr. Denver wouldn't prescribe Herceptin without chemotherapy so a positive HER2 result meant that chemo would also be necessary.

We were completely exhausted by the time we left Dana-Farber that first day. We learned a lot, which helped, but there were still so many unknowns that I can't say I felt much consolation. What I did feel though was the beginning of something that would eventually bring me a heightened sense of peace. Over a year later, I would come to realize that the first day of appointments, tests, and talk about scary proteins was the beginning of a brand-new faith—a faith in my doctors, and in the science that could treat and maybe even cure my cancer.

Dr. Schmidt

Less than a week after we learned I had cancer, Brian and I found ourselves huddled close in a small office at Brigham and Women's Hospital. Seated behind the messy desk was a fertility doctor, Dr. Schmidt. Dr. Denver referred us to this specialist to discuss our options if we wanted to have another biological child. We *did* want to have another child, just not anytime soon, so this appointment felt terribly uncomfortable before it even started.

I learned shortly after my diagnosis that regardless of my treatment plan, my reproductive system was going to weather quite a storm from the drugs it would receive. Even if I emerged able to have more biological children, I would need to wait for five years—the full course of the Tamoxifen—before getting pregnant.

Brian and I did the math. If all went well, I would be 38 years old when my treatment wrapped up, which meant if we were lucky, we could have a baby when I was almost 40. Teddy would be 12 and Annabel would be nine. I had faith, or at least thought I could find faith, that my reproductive system would hold up. Regardless, I was terrified to be pregnant again, and that terror wasn't going away. In my mind, pregnancy meant hormones and hormones fueled my cancer, but that was just me playing doctor.

At the appointment, I could barely speak. Nevertheless, we managed to tell Dr. Schmidt that I had been recently diagnosed with cancer. We explained that we were not ready to have a third child, but still wanted the option down the road. We told her that this was really hard for us.

Far too casually, and without so much as an "I'm sorry," Dr. Schmidt explained our best option. Right after my upcoming surgery, I would take hormones so she and her baby-making team could extract my eggs. It was a small surgical procedure and I wasn't scared of the surgery part of it. It was the hormone part that frightened me to my core.

Dr. Schmidt explained that after Brian provided his sperm, they would make embryos in the lab. They'd freeze the embryos, store them, and when we were ready, we could choose a surrogate mother to carry our child. I struggled to breathe during this matter-of-fact explanation. It felt like torture.

As if they knew how awful that appointment would be and how much we would need something good to happen afterwards, our friends—avid Bruce Springsteen fans—gave us tickets to see the Boss in concert that night at Fenway Park. Brian and I held hands in silence for the first few minutes of our walk up Brookline Avenue toward the ballpark. When we walked by a trashcan, Brian threw away the bag with the specimen cup. I didn't blame him.

A few minutes later, we broke the silence and admitted how terrible the appointment had been. We agreed that Dr. Schmidt had been so apathetic and so *cold*. She totally missed the point, or maybe she hadn't even tried to catch it in the first place. We didn't want to make a baby right now. We just didn't want the option to be taken away from us so abruptly. It was as if the doctor had one speech for every patient who sat in her office. Unfortunately, Dr. Schmidt neglected the fact that people arrive there for lots of different reasons.

I explained to Brian what I felt in my gut—a really bad feeling about the process the doctor described, especially the part about injecting me with hormones. I was grateful that the option was available to us and to parents desperate for biological children, but it didn't feel right for me.

I had no idea how Brian would respond. He often talked about having other biological children, so I knew the appointment could have crushed him.

Surprisingly, he didn't sound crushed at all. Instead, Brian assured me that we would never do anything that could hurt me. He agreed that *in vitro* fertilization didn't feel right for him either. He told me he loved me.

* * *

Believe it or not, I had thought about adopting our third child ever since Annabel was born. Every few months, I casually ran the idea by Brian.

Brian's a thinker and a doer, not so much a talker. He never told me what he thought about adoption, although I hoped that he would eventually come around. I completely understood his ambivalence, and didn't feel any need to pressure him. Now, however, cancer had forced the situation straight into our laps.

After we climbed the ramps at Fenway Park to our seat level, we slowed to a stop and looked over at the Boston skyline. With a calm and confident tone that I would never expect from anyone in that situation, Brian told me that he would love to adopt a child when all of this was over. I started to cry, so full of love, relief, and hope that I couldn't respond any other way.

HER2

One week after my diagnosis, I had my legs back under me. By no means was I steady, but I was standing. I was still celebrating that my chest X-ray and my blood work both looked normal, and part of me started to believe that I could beat cancer.

Still, every time the phone rang, my empty stomach jumped into my throat. And every time "Blocked" appeared on the caller ID, a rush of adrenaline raced through my body.

The afternoon exactly one week after my diagnosis, *Blocked* rang. My stomach jumped and the adrenaline rushed. It was Dr. Denver. He had some news.

The HER2 test was back, and it was positive.

The news knocked the wind out of my already flappy sails. It gave me that kicked-in-the-gut, nauseated feeling that makes it impossible to eat or sleep or think straight. Dr. Denver explained to me that this result was "unusual" for a Grade 1 tumor, which is why, I later learned, he began to suspect the tumor was beyond a Grade 1. Due to this unusualness, Dr. Denver wanted to do further testing. He called the additional tests "FISH" testing, which stood for fluorescence in situ hybridization.

In some instances, "unusual" may be a positive thing, but in the cancer world, it's generally not good to be different. For this reason, the word played on repeat in my head. *Unusual...* To my pessimistic side, it meant *uncertainty, unanswered, incurable.* I hated all of those words.

Based on the HER2+ result, Dr. Denver explained that I would in fact receive Herceptin along with chemotherapy. He told me not to worry, but I could tell that other news would have been better. I could also tell that Herceptin was a pretty big deal.

A few days later, the phone rang just as we got the kids settled on the porch for dinner. I looked at the caller ID, moved inside where no one could hear me, and took a deep breath.

As I expected, it was Dr. Denver. He had the results of the FISH testing. I dreaded this call because I had concocted in my head the devastating idea that perhaps, once armed with a clearer understanding of the type of cancer I had, Dr. Denver would tell me that for my type, they have no cure or answers or hope. Thank goodness, that was not how the conversation went.

The FISH testing confirmed that my cancer was, for sure, HER2+. Dr. Denver explained, "If you had to get this type of cancer, you got it at the right time." I knew what he meant—prior to Herceptin, my chances wouldn't have been good.

Then Dr. Denver started to get into some biology, explaining what my cells were supposed to do and how the HER2 protein screwed that up. I could tell that this wasn't going to be good for my imagination so I interrupted Dr. Denver and told him that I didn't want to hear any more. I explained a bit about myself, some of which I had only just discovered.

I told him that I didn't want to understand what was happening in my body, what was failing, and what we were trying to reverse. I didn't want to know that Herceptin works for a certain percentage of women, because I would live in fear of being on the wrong side of that statistic. All I wanted to know was that I could beat this.

"You can beat this," Dr. Denver replied. "The overwhelming odds are that you will beat this. If I was a betting man, I'd go to Vegas and bet on you. And I don't bet money I think I'll lose." Despite his confidence, my legs still trembled and I felt desperately weak. I didn't want anyone to be gambling with my life. But I knew over time I'd been dealt countless good cards, so now I'd dutifully accept the bad ones too.

Later in my treatment, I would come to appreciate the true watershed in breast cancer treatment that was Herceptin. Even now, I'm not ready to research any statistics, but I do know this. At the 2005 annual meeting of the American Society of Clinical Oncology, the large crowd of oncologists and cancer researchers from across the nation erupted in exultation after the presentations by several research groups that described the results of clinical trials with Herceptin. According to several sources, meeting attendees stood up, cheered, whooped, clapped, and even cried. They knew then what I would learn eight years later—that women with HER2+ breast cancers had a far better chance at life now that Herceptin was their ally.

Second Guessing

Prior to Dr. Denver's call revealing the HER2+ news, I tentatively decided on reconstruction following my double mastectomy. I wasn't confident about it and it sure as hell wasn't anything I was looking forward to, but I was headed in that direction.

The HER2+ news, however, changed things. It made me wonder if I should skip reconstruction altogether, and focus solely on beating cancer. Once again, I wanted to beg for my life; offer up almost any of my body parts in exchange for my future.

So I started to wonder, *Should I preserve all my strength for something life-saving rather than something cosmetic? Could the reconstruction complicate something, give me an infection that would divert my body from the more-important task at hand? Could it delay the chemo and the Herceptin? Could it make cancer harder to beat?*

Despite my doctors' assurance that reconstruction would not interfere with my cancer battle, I felt lost on this issue. I was so uncomfortably unsure of whether or not I wanted my doctors to rebuild me after they took me apart.

A Haircut

I never cared much about my hair. At any point in my life, were someone to have stolen my hairbrush, it would probably have taken me weeks to notice it was gone. Air-drying and ponytails were my thing—quick, easy, and out of my face. Nevertheless, the realization that I was going to lose my hair was significant, mainly because I had two young children who were going to ask why.

Teddy was (and still is) a sensitive kid. He is typically cautious of other people's feelings and from a young age, he would get upset to see someone else hurt. My poor mom learned this the hard way when she babysat Teddy one night when he was two. A *Sesame Street* episode came on that included a storyline with an injured Big Bird in an arm sling. Teddy screamed for at least an hour after seeing the sling, terribly distraught that Big Bird was hurt. I had this sensitivity in mind when I decided, just a few weeks after my diagnosis, to get my hair cut.

At the time, my hair was thin, brown, and shoulder-length. I scheduled an appointment at the hairdresser that I've been going to since childhood. I explained that I wanted to ease my young kids into my baldness. A little cut then, a little more before chemo, and hopefully a shaved head would not be so shocking. The hairdresser cut a few inches off so my hair fell above my chin. This approach worked well, because by the time my hair fell out, my kids were somewhat used to my changing hair styles.

September 5, 2012 – One week before surgery
(and yes, Teddy's shirt is on backwards)

Two Boobs or Not Two Boobs

I have a history of making significant life decisions based almost entirely on my instincts. I don't do a lot of research, ask a lot of questions, or thoughtfully eliminate all of my options. For better or worse, I usually just go with my gut.

Thus far, my instincts haven't lead me astray (although ignoring them has). For example, when a blond girl from the city moved to town before my freshman year of high school, I knew she would be my best friend, and 20 years later, Brianne is just that. When I stepped foot on the Bowdoin campus, I had no doubt I wanted to move to Brunswick despite not knowing a single statistic about the school. And the night before I married my college sweetheart, I struggled for what to say about him when I spoke at our rehearsal dinner. I couldn't find the words because I just knew in my gut that we were supposed to be together.

Brian's the opposite, and I'm glad that I at least had the instinct to marry a man who got estimates from eight different companies before he chose one to pave our driveway.

I've since learned that in times of crisis, both due diligence *and* instincts are key. While my mom did the diligence, the instinct part was up to me.

The moment I learned I had breast cancer, I wanted both of my breasts removed. *Immediately.* My gut all but screamed it to me. I knew it then, and still know now, that I won't look back on that decision.

For some reason, however, when it came to reconstruction, my gut was empty. That emptiness left me in an unfamiliar place. *How did people make big decisions when their instincts didn't tell them what to do?* I had no idea.

On one hand, something my mother said rang in my head. "One day, you will be glad you did it," she told me, sympathetic to the shitty-ness of needing to have this conversation. At the time she said that, I could barely fathom that I still had the chance at "one day," and I couldn't imagine that that "one day" could be free from the terror of cancer. But I trusted my mom, even if I honestly couldn't comprehend what she had said to me.

On the other hand, I thought it may have been wrong to focus on anything but beating cancer. Boobs were just boobs—little mounds of flesh, or in my case, little flaps of post-breastfeeding skin. *Did I really even need a replacement pair?*

So I just waited, hoping I would find some clarity.

Gradually, I did.

I became convinced that reconstruction wouldn't interfere with my cancer treatment. I knew that if I ended up needing radiation, it could distort the implants and additional surgery would be necessary, but given the double mastectomy and the location of my tumor, radiation sounded like a remote possibility. More importantly, I knew that once I was cancer-free, I would be happy I had boobs, and if I didn't get them then, I would dread going back for them later.

Teddy gave me another perspective too. We were at the supermarket soon after my first haircut, and we walked down the shampoo aisle. I joked with him that I was sick of buying shampoo and having hair. I explained how I was thinking of shaving my head and being a "carefree bald lady." I made a silly motion of flicking my hair back over my shoulder, even though it was already far too short for that.

Teddy chuckled cautiously and asked, "But if you have no hair, how will people know you're a girl?" I was stumped, so I turned the question back on him.

"Great point, buddy, how do you think people would still know I'm a girl?"

No pause—"Because you wear dresses."

"Exactly!" I replied as I looked down at my mesh athletic shorts, sports bra, and tattered t-shirt. *I better get myself some more dresses*, I thought.

But Teddy got me thinking. Maybe I really did want to keep, or rather, reconstruct, this part of my femininity.

The next day, I spoke with a woman who had gone through reconstruction over 20 years prior. Rebecca gave me the gift of a positive outlook on the process. She told me that reconstruction could be something I look forward to and feel good about, a badge of honor for which I'm proud. After talking with Rebecca, my mind was made up, and at peace. But still, my gut felt empty.

Then I met Amy.

Amy was diagnosed with breast cancer over 20 years prior, when she was exactly my age, with two young girls who I knew from my high school days. "There is so much life after breast cancer," Amy told me over the phone one night. I cried at the hope that thought gave me.

One afternoon a few weeks after my diagnosis, Amy and her daughter, Lauren (via speakerphone from New York), sat down with Brian and me in Amy's sunlit living room. We talked about all sorts of things, some that made us laugh and some that made me cry.

At age 25, Lauren learned that she carried the BRCA2 gene from her mother. Lauren immediately opted for a prophylactic double mastectomy with reconstruction. I thought it was such a brave decision, and I found comfort in talking to women who were so open about their experiences. I hoped I would have the strength to do the same for someone else one day.

When we hung up with Lauren, Amy asked me if I wanted to see her fake boob. Brian immediately "had a phone call to make." He knew from the look in my eye that as frightened as I was to say so, I really did want to see her implant.

I had no idea what a woman's chest looked like after reconstruction, but I had had several nightmares about it. I knew my dreams were ridiculous, but I still worried that I would look like a botched science experiment. I was expecting to see something of the sort as Amy started to unbutton her work blouse. She was confident, calm, and caring, and I pretended not to be nervous.

Before I even had to tell myself to take a deep breath, there it was—a regular, in fact, a *better than regular* breast. Sure, there was a horizontal scar across the middle and a nipple so faint I could barely see it, but otherwise the reconstructed breast was nothing but wonderfully *normal*.

I started to cry. Poor Amy must have thought, *Holy shit, what have I done?*

I collected myself enough to reassure her that I was crying out of appreciation and relief. Relief that I wouldn't look like a botched experiment. Relief that there would be life after cancer. Relief that in a few months, except for my bald head, I would just look like me, or maybe even a better version of me. Most of all, I cried because that emptiness I had in my gut was gone.

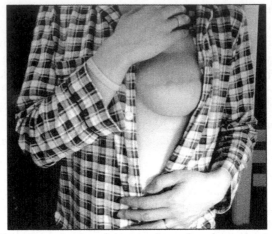

For anyone who doesn't have an Amy when she needs one:
a borderline-awkward, in-my-pajamas, impromptu selfie of
one tissue expander prior to implant insertion – February 2013

Breast Shopping

Once I made the decision to undergo breast reconstruction, I had to make a few more decisions regarding exactly *how*.

My plastic surgeon, Dr. Lee, was the fabulously brilliant and kind woman who led me through this process. Ultimately, she was the one who built my boobs.

Brian, my mom, and I met with Dr. Lee a few weeks after my diagnosis to discuss the reconstructive process that would take place after Dr. Nadia removed all of my breast tissue.

Dr. Lee explained that there were three options. The first one involved implants. Dr. Lee explained that with this option, after my double mastectomy, she would insert a "tissue expander" on either side of my chest between my pectoral muscle and my skin. She would sew in four "drains," or tubes that would protrude from my sides and allow blood and fluid to flow off while everything healed. The idea of liquids draining out of my chest for two weeks post-surgery was less than pleasant. In fact, I really dreaded it.

Dr. Lee explained I would return every few weeks after the surgery so she could inject more saline into the tissue expanders. Apparently my body needed to be eased into the size of an implant, even a smallish one, and the tissue expanders would allow for that gradual process. After my chemotherapy was complete, I would undergo another surgery to exchange the tissue expanders for implants.

I had two choices for implants: silicone or saline. Dr. Lee explained a bit about each. If the saline one popped, she explained that it would just deflate. Eek. If the silicone popped, I wouldn't know until an annual scan to check on it. Yikes. I wondered if that meant every time I got kicked in the boob by my children who playfully tackled me in bed on Saturday and Sunday mornings, I was going to worry that my boob just popped or that it was leaking gel. I thought maybe the saline sounded like the better idea.

Dr. Lee explained that saline is obviously more "watery" and more women choose silicone. I didn't really want watery boobs and once I held a silicone implant and poked it as hard as I could without it popping, I decided that silicone would be my boob of choice.

I already felt pretty good about the silicone implants, but Dr. Lee nevertheless presented a second approach, which turned out not to be an option for me. This approach involved building boobs out of other parts of my body. Mostly because I had barely eaten in weeks, Dr. Lee eventually decided that I didn't have enough fat elsewhere on my body to build two breasts. I pointed out my C-section pouch, but she just smiled and shook her head. I told her I could gain 15 pounds in two to three weeks if she wanted me to. She said that wouldn't be good for my health.

Truthfully, I didn't mind losing this option because it sounded pretty difficult to me—cutting parts of my back or abdomen to sew them onto my front. Dr. Lee described rearranging muscles, at one point detailing some process that included wrapping a muscle from my back around to my front. I was confused and in the end, I decided I would rather look down and see something fake than something that was previously on my back. Dr. Lee agreed this option wasn't for me.

When Dr. Lee began to describe the third approach that was, in her words, even more complicated than the second, I stopped her. I've always liked to keep things simple and I didn't think this option would prove fruitful. She agreed and was happy to continue forward.

Next came my favorite part of the appointment. Dr. Lee explained that she was participating in a clinical trial of a new device that would fill the tissue expander with air instead of saline. The advantages were that the patient would not have to come into the doctor's office to build up the expander—a simple remote control at home could do the trick. Brian and I let out a brief laugh almost simultaneously, and declined this option.

We later confirmed in the parking lot that we had the same thought— Annabel loved remote controls. I envisioned a morning when Brian let me sleep late. He and our toddler would be downstairs and Annabel would find the grow-the-boob remote wherever I hid it. She'd try to turn on the ceiling fan as my right boob grew into a DDD. No thanks. I decided to leave the clinical trial to women without kids who have remote-control obsessions.

My Mom

Since my diagnosis, I have maintained that being the loved one of a cancer patient is often more difficult than being the patient. I would bet that most loved ones, including my own, would give anything to trade places—to be the one undergoing surgery or sitting in the infusion chair, the one whose hair falls out, the "sick one."

For me, cancer has always been so much more about the mental challenges than the physical ones, which may help explain why I think that caregivers have it just as hard much of the time. They may be spared the physical anguish, but they experience all of the mental turmoil, including the additional pain that comes with not being able to cure their loved one's disease.

While I knew it was a crazy way to think, when I wound up in a dark place, I often found myself thinking, *At least it's me and not one of my kids.* I had seen the children at The Jimmy Fund clinic at Dana-Farber and it broke my heart that they were forced to endure so much so young.

The sharp side of that double-edged sword was the realization that I was someone else's child. Granted I was 32, but still, I knew that one of my worst nightmares had become my parents' reality.

* * *

One of the most important lessons that my mother taught me early on was to have high standards for myself and for the people who could affect my life. She never sat me down and told me this explicitly, but I figured it out by watching and listening.

When I was younger, my mom's high standards sometimes made me want to hide in embarrassment. For instance, if I had a teacher who wasn't challenging me or was just flat-out bad at his or her job, my mother didn't sit by passively. She called the teacher and requested a meeting. The day after they met I would learn more than ever before. I loved that, even though I was horrified that my mother didn't keep quiet like most other mothers seemed to.

To this day, my mother never shies away from confrontation, yet she has a knack for making the situation not feel like one. She is honest and straightforward, strong-willed, yet so very kind. She does the right thing, even if there are personal consequences.

My mom always had a healthy perspective, too. She never yelled obnoxiously on the sidelines of my games or meets. She clapped and cheered for me, then went back to reading her book when I was on the sideline. I loved sports and my mom got that, but she knew that school would get me much further in life.

When it came to my cancer battle, all of my mom's many strengths and skills became more relevant than ever before. While I barely had the strength to arrange my first appointment, her actions made it clear—we wouldn't find just *any* hospital for treatment; we would visit one of the best cancer hospitals in the world (which happened to be in our backyard). We would not find *any* team of doctors; we would find a group of the best and the brightest. And she would not sit and pray that things worked out. Instead, she worked for countless hours to ensure that we did everything we needed to do to beat cancer. For her child, my mother would accept nothing less.

* * *

I was only 12 when a British track star by the name of Derek Redmond ran the semifinal 400-meter race in the Summer Olympic Games in Barcelona. I remember seeing the footage back then, as my parents were avid fans of the Olympics.

It was 1992 and the whole world was watching a race that would determine who would run for gold in the 400-meter finals. When the gun sounded, one of the world's finest athletes blasted out of the blocks in Lane 5. His name was Derek Redmond and he was flying—the epitome of grace and ease.

Derek's father and family members stood in the stands, cheering him on and waving the British flag.

For the first part of the race, Derek cruised, his form a thing of true beauty. But then, something happened, and Derrick grabbed his right hamstring.

Derek slowed down, almost to a stop, wincing in excruciating pain. He fell to the ground, as if he were praying on one knee. He gasped for air while the crowd froze, stunned. Derek dropped his head into his perfect bicep. From the video I've seen several times since, it seemed like time stood still.

Then, Derek got up. He started to run. He couldn't put weight on his right leg but somehow, his run was still graceful and strong.

The famous footage of the race shows that soon after Derek started to run again, an older man bolted from the stands. The man was clearly not an Olympic athlete, but he was running with the passion of one. The event staff tried to stop the man, but he refused them and pushed on toward Derek. This man was Derek's father. He wrapped his right arm around his son. At first, Derek kept running, stubbornly, as if he didn't need any help. His father held Derek upright and as they came to the straightaway, Derek succumbed to the reality of what just happened and buried his head into his father's shoulder. Derek was crying hysterical tears while his father was stern-faced and determined.

They ran the last part of that race together. And together, they crossed the finish line.

I'm no Olympian and neither is my mom, but the story of this race reminds me so much of her.

Prior to my diagnosis, my life was moving along like the first half of Derek Redmond's race. I worked hard and I was cruising, blessed with everything I could ever ask for. My mom was in the stands, so to speak, cheering me on.

Then out of no where came the hamstring tear, or in my case, the cancer. I broke, or more accurately, it was revealed that I could be breaking. Like Derek Redmond, I fell to my knees and limped along for a bit. Then my mom rushed out, and while the tears streamed down my face, she stayed strong and determined.

I'm sure that Derek Redmond's father wanted to curl up and cry the moment that he saw his son's dreams crushed in Barcelona, and my mom probably wanted to do the same when I told her that I had cancer. But my mom ran out to me, uncaring about rules or recognition. She carried me. She answered the phone call that confirmed the biopsy results we already knew, because I didn't want to have those words in my memory. She lined up my doctors when I was too devastated to admit I needed them. She babysat our kids so I could nap, figured out the virtual healthcare portal to send questions to my doctors electronically, and made a calendar with all of my upcoming appointments. She came with Brian and me to all of those appointments, and comforted him when I couldn't. She listened to what I felt and wanted, and when I was too upset to know what I wanted, she guided me.

Most importantly, my mom let me cry. She didn't try to convince me not to feel what I was feeling, just like Derek Redmond's father never made any motion for his son to hold back his tears. Instead, my mom let me cry on her shoulder. She told me that I deserved that time to be upset, angry, and scared.

After my diagnosis, I knew that my mom and I had a tough race ahead of us. Our lives had taken an unexpected turn, and we sure weren't going to win any medals. But I believed, even back then, that we would finish that race together. Even if she had to carry me part of the way.

Noisy Genes

Peace. It does not mean to be in a place where there is
no noise, trouble, or hard work. It means to be in the
midst of those things and still be calm in your heart.

I have that quote hanging on the wall in my office. I hadn't thought about the quote in a while, but I remembered it on a warm August vacation day when the Dana-Farber genetics counselor called with the results to the genetic test that determined whether I carried one of the two main breast cancer genes known as BRCA1 and BRCA2.

For some background, one of the several meetings we had on my first day at Dana-Farber was with a genetics counselor, Sally. Sally asked me what felt like 200 questions about my family history and she drew a family tree in which males were squares and females were circles. (Since my dad is not my biological father, it was a futile effort and thankfully, she gave up.) Nevertheless, Sally gave us lots of information about genetic tests, their costs, and their implications. The meeting with Sally was one of our last appointments of the day and I was so exhausted by then that I wasn't following much of what she said. I just wanted to go home.

One thing I did understand from that meeting was I needed to have a blood sample taken so that a lab in Utah could test for BRCA1 and BRCA2. A positive result for either one of genes meant that I was at increased risk for cancer in my "good" breast, as well as for other types of cancer down the road. Even worse, it would mean women related to me could also carry the gene, and that was a can of foul worms I didn't want to open.

"Negative, negative," Sally told me as I stood on the front lawn with my phone on speaker so that Brian and my mom could hear. I didn't carry either gene. It was good news, but cancer taught me early on nothing is ever that simple.

The test my insurance company covered told us with 95% certainty that I didn't carry either one of the genes. To be 100% sure though, the lab would need to run additional tests and those would cost $700. My insurance company already explained it would not cover the additional testing.

I would have debated over whether we could afford the $700, but my mom needed to have that 100% certainty so she gave a few important women in her life an early Christmas gift—$700 to the Utah lab to be sure that the bad genes were not lurking somewhere in that remaining 5%. A few weeks later, we would learn that the additional tests confirmed the negative-negative test result.

Still, the case wasn't closed. As if I didn't know, Sally reminded me when she called with the second round of results that I was "only 32 with breast cancer and no family history." She told me about other tests that we could run to see if I carried any other gene that could have led to my condition. That kicked-in-the-gut, nauseated feeling returned when Sally repeated what she said in our last meeting, which I think I chose to block from my memory. She said that if I carry certain genes, it could mean that our children are at increased risks of cancer, even childhood cancers. That was a thought Brian and I honestly couldn't bear at the time so we decided that I would get well first, then we would discuss further genetics testing for me and the kids. Noise, trouble, hard work, and absolutely no calm in my heart.

After the first call with Sally, we went inside to prepare lunch. Brian's parents traveled to Cape Cod for the day and we all gathered outside on the porch on one of the most beautiful days of the summer.

I calmed down outside with our families that afternoon. I came closer to accepting that in the next year, or two, or 20, cancer could bring us lots of noise, trouble, and hard work. I also started to believe that in the midst of all of that, I would still be able to feel some peace in my heart.

Fear to Fuel

My maternal grandmother grew up during the Great Depression, and she never let anyone forget it. Her hero was Franklin Delano Roosevelt, and she credited FDR with all good in the world, even until her death at age 95. Grandma was a staunch Democrat, she marched on Washington with Dr. Martin Luther King, Jr., and in her 80s, she picketed at Martha Stewart's house when Martha began to sell her products at K-Mart because that superstore also sold guns.

From my childhood through college years, I spent a few weeks if not most of the summer at my grandma and grandpa's house on Long Island. As kids, our troop of cousins would head to Atlantic Beach where we bodysurfed, boogey-boarded, and ate popsicles from the beach hut. At night, we played "Aliens" in the basement, a game we invented that was a combination of hide-and-seek and tag. It always ended with a bloody, stubbed toe or the kids admitting to the adults that we broke something.

When I was old enough to work, I waitressed at a family restaurant near the beach. I could wear shorts and sneakers, hand out fried food in a matter of minutes, and turn tables quickly. It was a great gig for a college student, and I still remember serving Brian his fried-clam roll when he came to visit.

In my spare time during those summers, I kayaked in the ocean by the cliff on which my grandparents' house is perched. And I read. Sometimes I wrote poems, but mostly I read everything I could find, which was a lot, because my grandparents were avid readers and their bookshelves were stacked with everything from the classics to current bestsellers to the economics book authored by my grandpa.

My grandma named their house on the cliff "Cardinal Point." Although I typically scoff at people who name their property, this was different. My grandma loved birds, especially her cardinals. Teddy is already trained to know this; when he sees a cardinal he always reminds me, "Your gwanma wuved vose."

It's probably too early to teach Teddy or Annabel about FDR, but I know my grandma would be trying to if they had the pleasure of spending time with her today. And if my grandma were alive when I was diagnosed with cancer, I know exactly what she would have told me.

First, she'd swear. She always liked a good swear word when she was angry. Then, she'd try to blame my cancer on a Republican—probably Richard Nixon or George W. Bush—but even she would find that a stretch. Finally, she'd get serious and she would tell me, "There is nothing to fear but fear itself."

I heard this quote a hundred times prior to cancer, and I never really understood it. I would think to myself, *No, really, there* are *worse things to be afraid of than just fear.* How about not having enough food to feed your family? Being killed by a drunk driver? Getting cancer? Those actual occurrences all sounded worse to me than just fearing them.

Two weeks after my diagnosis, I wrote about how I'd be a fool to think I had become a stronger person, improved in some way by cancer. I hadn't. So much of the time, I still felt totally shocked, sad, confused, and sometimes even angry. Most of all, I felt scared. I kept replaying the prior few weeks in my head—the words the doctors said to me and the look on their faces when they said them.

Then I thought of weeks that followed—the surgery (or surgeries), the news on how far the cancer spread, the game plan on how we would fight it. I tried to isolate what scared me most.

I realized that my biggest fear at that time was that the treatment wouldn't work. After the HER2 results, Dr. Denver said he expected the surgery would reveal a Grade 2 tumor and while I tried to digest that, FDR's words hit me square in the face.

I was scared out of my mind at the indescribably awful feeling of being scared out of my mind.

I wasn't so afraid of the number of lymph nodes Dr. Nadia would tell me she had to remove, but what my mind would think of that number. I wasn't so afraid of the ultimate stage of my cancer, but that if it was a "3" or a "4," I wouldn't be able to handle the news. I wasn't afraid of being under anesthesia for several hours, but I was terrified of the fear my family would have to endure in the meantime.

Soon after my diagnosis, Brianne gave me a t-shirt that said in big bold font, "Battle Mode." There was something about that slogan that helped me. I know, it's random, and proof that every individual's fight with cancer is a unique one. But those two words took some of my fear away. They made me think that I had power, strength, and spirit that the cancer would have to face now that it had been discovered. Somehow, that confidence turned a bit of my fear into fuel. And since I had a shitload of fear, I figured that meant that I had a shitload of would-be fuel, too.

Part Two

Preparation for Surgery

Courage does not always roar.
Sometimes it is a quiet voice
at the end of the day, saying
I will try again tomorrow.

Julia Anne Radmacher
(artist and author)

Holding Pattern

I could never rightfully describe how difficult the weeks leading up to my surgery were—how terrifying it felt to know that aggressive cancer cells were multiplying inside me, without knowing exactly where they lurked or how much time I had left. Several mornings, I woke up wanting to shout from my rooftop, "How am I ever going to do this?!" because I honestly didn't know. Then again, I didn't have the energy to climb to the rooftop.

The most accurate way to describe the awful period of waiting is to compare it to a scenario I have heard about on the local news—passengers stuck on the runway for hours because their plane can't take off but can't taxi back to the gate either.

I hate to fly and confined spaces make my blood pressure immediately rise, so the stuck-on-the-runway situation feels tortuous to me—much like I felt in the weeks leading up to my double mastectomy, as I waited for a more complete diagnosis, and for the chance to fight the deadly intruder.

I felt trapped and defenseless—I couldn't move forward and couldn't go back. I was stuck in a holding pattern, forced to wait and sit through a process I would never understand. Those around me seemed calm, though I wondered if inside they were freaking out like I was. The captains appeared to have control, and while I trusted them, I didn't know them and they had my life in their hands. I wanted to scream, to flail around like a total fool, swear, punch things, try with all my might to pry the door open and run across the tarmac back to safety. But I couldn't, partly because there was no safety back there.

For five weeks, as everyone around me transitioned from summer to a new school year, I had to sit still and pretend to be composed. I had to act brave, for the sake of everyone around me, and truthfully, for the sake of myself.

* * *

About two weeks prior to my surgery, I had a minor, mostly internal meltdown during a post-doctor-appointment shopping trip to my favorite store—The Container Store. The weight of the holding pattern hit me hard that afternoon and I was a mess as I filled my cart with boxes I didn't need. At the risk of sounding like a screaming brat, I didn't *want* to wait two more weeks while a killer lurked inside me. I wanted to fight back, and I wanted to fight *now!*

On our ride home from the store, my mom and brother talked me away from the cabin door, so to speak. They stopped me from hyperventilating by repeating things like, "We will get through this." I didn't see how that could be, but the fact that they believed it, or at least, that they were strong enough to *pretend* to believe it, helped me loosen my grasp on the door handles.

When I got home and dropped my bags of organizational items in the hallway, The Container Store's slogan caught my eye. *Contain Yourself.* They had to be kidding me—betrayed by the store I love most! Contain myself? How about, *Let yourself throw the biggest fucking fit of your life?*

Half chuckling, half angry at the apparent betrayal, I tried to take some deep breaths. A minute or so later, I realized that my favorite store was right. Just like it knew what I needed to properly organize my shoes and socks and DVDs (among many other things), it knew what I had to do as I waited for my surgery. *Contain myself.* Contain myself while remembering that I was blessed with a trip ahead of me that far too many others wouldn't have—miraculous treatment to fight the disease and an opportunity to beat cancer. Contain myself while remembering that my plane was full of the best-of-the-best co-passengers and the most-skilled pilots. Contain myself while believing that if I sat tight, I would get there safely.

After the mental debacle at the Container Store, Brian and I vowed to take the kids on a vacation once I finished my treatment. When we introduced the idea to Teddy, he announced that we should go to Disney World. Brian and I looked at each other and instantaneously agreed with our four-year-old. I smiled and pretended that I had contained myself. And like every other parent who has fought cancer, or any hardship, I deserved an Oscar.

I Am Here Now

The holding-pattern analogy helped me through some tough times during the weeks prior to my surgery. Still, I feel it's important to share the true depth of how difficult those weeks proved to be.

The worst moments usually came when I twisted information I was given into something even darker than it already was. For example, there was an afternoon in early September when I tried to take a nap.

Brian had taken the kids out and I was dozing on the sofa thanks to the Ativan which always made me tired. I crept closer to the verge of sleep when I found myself replaying my last conversation with Dr. Denver, as I had thousands of times before. I thought back to Dr. Denver's use of the word "unusual" to describe my first set of HER2 test results. I remembered his follow-up call a few days later to report that yes, my cancer was HER2+. Then, in the most evil of ways, my mind twisted my oncologist's words and sent me into a complete tailspin.

I thought about how my unusual cancer could be one for which they had no treatment. I wondered if Dr. Denver perhaps was hiding the harsh reality from me. Sure, they had Herceptin, but that was for women with a "normal" kind of cancer. My kind of cancer, well, it was just deadly.

All of a sudden, I was wide awake and in total panic mode. Despite my pledge a few days earlier to fasten my seat belt and sit tight, I lost control of my own mind. I started to cry, *hysterically*. I could barely catch my breath. I even think I may have wailed, which really must have been a pathetic sight. There I was, alone, shivering under a big blanket, dwelling in the darkest of dark caves—all because I tried to take a nap. It was awful. Maybe not as awful as the first night after my diagnosis, but pretty damn close.

Later that night, I thought to myself that maybe I just needed to get those tears out. *Tomorrow will be better*, I asserted.

But the next day, it happened again. On the way home from a trip to Boston, I crumbled once more. I couldn't stop crying, couldn't even hear any logic that was being presented to me. I could only feel my mom's hand holding onto my leg as I sat shaking in the back seat.

It was around then that I found my own mantra that helped in those darkest of moments. It wasn't anything I read in a book and it sure wasn't anything fancy. I don't even know when I first consciously put the words together, but once I did, my toughest times became somewhat easier.

I am here now.

That was it. Nothing special. Nothing quote-worthy. But those four words got me through many torturous times leading up to my surgery, and in the months afterward. Those four words brought me peace when I couldn't seem to find it anywhere else. *I am here now.* I must have repeated it a hundred thousand times. And each time, I knew that "now" had so much more to offer than I ever before had realized.

The Weight of Weight

As soon as I found out I had cancer, I started to lose weight. In a way, it had nothing to do with the cancer, because it wasn't the cancer cells that were causing me to shed pounds. But the truth is that cancer had everything to do with it as the word alone made me so nauseated with worry that it became almost impossible to eat.

For some context, I am an adult female and I live in the United States of America, which means that I think about my weight. I have a general rule against sharing personal stories about weight, diets, or workout regimens, but like any good rule there are exceptions, and I'm hoping this chapter is one of them.

So let's start with numbers since those are easy and they quell some natural curiosity. When this book went to print, I weighed 150 pounds. When I began chemotherapy, I weighed 20 pounds less than that and when I delivered Teddy, I weighed 51 pounds more. Now for the real stuff…

As a senior in high school, I was deeply loyal to my schoolwork and the sports that I played. I had a family, a best friend, a boyfriend, and a life that I loved. I ate frosting out of the container when I made cake, I devoured plates of mozzarella sticks whenever I found them on a menu, and I consumed countless slices of pizza at team dinners. Best of all, I didn't feel guilty about any of it. I knew who I was in my small New England suburb and I was proud of that person. When I left for college, I felt excited, eager, and blessed.

When I arrived at Bowdoin College—a small liberal-arts school in southern Maine—I felt the same way I had before. I missed my family but I wasn't homesick. At the same time, something unexpected happened.

When the honeymoon of orientation was over, I started to feel lost; not lost in terms of what to do, but lost in terms of how I valued myself while I was doing it.

In my hometown, I had been an above-average basketball player, swimmer, and gymnast. At Bowdoin, I was below average at the first two, and gymnastics didn't even exist. In my hometown, I wandered from class to class with the smartest kids in the school. At Bowdoin, I was surrounded by students (like Brian) who were the valedictorian of their high school class, and totally *brilliant*. All of a sudden, I felt average, *really* average. Despite that after cancer, average sounded wonderful, at the time, it felt tragic—boring and empty, snobby and insecure, complex and yet so very simple.

An ironic thing added to my pain. Before I left for college, I got my hair cut short, basically to the hairdo that I (unintentionally) sported several months after chemo ended.

In August 1998, when I sat down in my hairdresser's chair, I wanted something new and different. As soon as I got to Bowdoin and realized that I was new, and my haircut was different, I regretted that decision. I didn't regret it in any conscious way; I never stared in the mirror and thought to myself, *I wish my hair were long again.* I just didn't feel right with short hair and deep down, I hoped that when it grew back, I'd be confident and happy again.

In search of the confidence and happiness I had somehow lost, I started to exercise. A lot. No matter the time of day, the weather, or how much my knees hurt, I ran, swam, cross-country skied, or stepped up and down on the stair machine at the gym. Today, that all sounds fun (except maybe the stair-machine part) but it wasn't fun at the time. It was absolutely exhausting—both for my body and my mind. I had no idea how to get either of them to rest. My mind became a calculator for calories consumed and calories burned while my body tried to keep up with the math.

In all honesty, my obsession with my weight wasn't about what other people thought. In fact, it wasn't about the number on a scale either (I rarely, if ever, weighed myself). My anxiety was about what *I* thought about my appearance, how I felt in a new place, and most of all, what I could and could not control.

Over time, I grew out of obsessing about my weight. It wasn't that I solved the problem directly, but rather that other priorities took precedence over it—Brian, my teaching job, law school, my kids. Over the years, I found peace with something that previously tortured me, and I was proud of that.

* * *

If someone asked me on August 7, 2012 about my feelings on my weight, I would have said that I was satisfied with it. Deep down, I would have been pleased to lose 10 or 15 pounds—a few from those handles above my hips, a few more from my C-section pouch, and a bit from my inner thighs—but I didn't dwell on those fatty parts.

It turns out that there *is* a very quick way for me to lose 10 pounds, or even 20—a cancer diagnosis. Despite that I'm the rare person who can eat meals through a bout of the flu, on August 8, 2012, I lost my appetite and I lost it bad.

I was so crazy with worry that the thought of most foods made me want to vomit. It didn't help that my doctors typically called with news on my diagnosis around dinnertime. After those conversations, sitting up straight felt like a chore, and scooping food into my mouth felt damn near impossible.

I didn't notice the weight loss at first; it was the least of my worries. But soon I became concerned. I weighed myself and saw that I had lost 10 pounds. In my darkest moments, I thought the cancer had started to kill me.

In my lighter times, however, I started to think that I could control my cancer by what I ate. Looking back, I doubt I had that power, but it felt good to believe I did. While the deadly tumor was still in me, I decided to eat only the healthiest foods and pray that they would do everything possible to stop a single cancer cell from escaping my breast. My life became mustard instead of mayo, cauliflower instead of ice cream. It wasn't painful (although all pain is relative). It was just something I could control amid a storm of things that I couldn't.

Prior to the double mastectomy I was generally frightened to exercise, so I didn't. With absolutely zero supporting science, I thought that exercise could propel a cancer cell from the invasive tumor and nothing was worth that.

It turns out that even without exercise, eating healthy foods really does cause weight loss because I continued to drop—five, seven, 10 more pounds. Despite how much I appreciated the ounce of control I established, I worried that I was withering away.

Sadly, the eating habits of Hollywood helped me, as I distinctly remember telling myself, *Angelina Jolie is alive and she's* way *thinner than I am.* Still, I knew that I wasn't built to look like Angelina Jolie. I was supposed to be bigger than that...healthier than that.

At one point just before my chemotherapy began, I met with a nutritionist at Dana-Farber. She was lovely and gave me some useful information, including a weight range to aim for. One hundred thirty pounds was the lowest point of the range and since I was just that, I felt better.

The most important point I took away from the meeting was the nutritionist would help me if eating continued to be such a challenge. "There are ways we can get you to gain weight even if you're having trouble eating," she told me. I cried tears of relief when I heard that.

* * *

That old saying, "Be careful what you wish for," often comes to mind when I think about my cancer-related weight loss. Sure, my C-section pouch almost melted away and I dropped from a size 8 to a size 4. But after two C-sections, I should have a pouch, and I'm made to wear a size 8. Once I realized that, I felt liberated. The weight of weight eased some more, and life became more about being healthy, and less about being thin.

My Sister Rachel

The end of 2009 through the end of 2010 was a rough time for our family, and for families close to us. One after another, Brian and I attended wakes and funerals of beautiful individuals who left this life far too early.

Perhaps fittingly, fall 2010 had been a rainy one and when our sump pump decided to quit, our basement flooded into a shin-deep icky mess. In dealing with the damage, I didn't sweat the small stuff. Our home insurance didn't cover flooding, but after the tragedies we had seen, money was the least of our worries.

There was, however, one box destroyed by the flood that was different than the rest. When I first saw that the brown cardboard box had been completely drowned in the dirty water, I tried to find perspective; tried to think of all of the reasons why I shouldn't be upset by the loss of these material things. But even weeks later, I couldn't seem to find that peace about this one box.

I had been a Social Studies teacher at a public high school for five years after college. When I resigned in May 2007 to enter the legal profession, I left almost everything behind for my replacement; everything except one box of 10 binders.

I taught World History and Economics, and the binders contained a collection of my favorite parts of learning and teaching those subjects. The binders were full of quotes, teaching ideas, lesson plans, personal reflections, worksheets, song lyrics, PowerPoint slides, newspaper articles, cartoons, magazines, exceptional student essays, and more. These binders were the tangible reminder of a precious period of my life and more importantly, of my first real contribution to the world.

When I couldn't contain it in any longer, I found myself hunched over on my basement stairs bawling my eyes out, trying to explain to my tired, confused, and drenched husband about the box and the binders.

I know it wasn't just the binders I was crying about. It was a culmination of all of the sadness, the wakes and funerals, and a serious lack of sleep due to a demanding work schedule. I also missed teaching, although I didn't let myself admit that just yet.

I knew the binders couldn't be saved and I was crushed. There were hundreds of pieces of paper, many of them in sheet protectors that were literally full of water. The ink dripped and smudged and the newspaper articles couldn't even be unfolded without tearing.

Worst of all, I hated myself for caring so much, especially when I knew what other families around me were dealing with. So we dried up the basement and moved on. But I still couldn't part with the soggy box of binders, and every time I saw them curling up as they tried to dry, I wanted to cry.

At the time of our basement flood, Rachel was living in Boston, working a temporary job until her law-firm position began in the new year. She spent Christmas with us, then moved back down to Virginia. That holiday season was bittersweet, with my sister living at home and all the while knowing she would leave again soon.

Christmas is a big deal in my family. We are religious in our own way—not in the church-going sense, but in the we-are-so-lucky-to-have-each-other way. All of us are giddy around this time, even as we get older. We try to find the right gifts for each other, and we can't wait to watch each other open them up.

When all of the craziness of gift-opening was over, Rachel and Matt emerged with a big waterproof box and placed it at my feet. It was filled with 10 binders.

As I sat there shaking in joyous disbelief, Rachel handed me binder after binder. I touched each page as if it were gold. Then my whole family, who was bursting to explain Rachel's secret project, started to tell me what my sister had done.

Over the previous months, she took one binder at a time out of our basement. Wet page by wet page, she photocopied each one for a dry version. Through internet searches, she found and replaced each damaged magazine and she retyped pages of my own notes that were smudged and barely legible. She found archived newspaper articles and printed them onto crisp, clean paper. She bought durable new binders, made tab dividers just like I had, and found a box that would survive a flood. Rachel recreated something that I never in my wildest dreams thought could be fixed.

I doubt I will ever use those binders again, and I'd bet Rachel knew that as she stood at the copy machine for hours. But that box in my basement was and is something so much more to me. It's proof that my sister will do anything to make me feel better, even if she doesn't fully understand it. It's proof that page by page, day by day, and month by month, some things that were once destroyed can be put back together again.

Dr. Funt

I could have used a therapist long before my cancer diagnosis, but for many reasons, I didn't seek one out. In fact, back in 2010, my primary care physician (Dr. Thomas) had given me an oft-Xeroxed piece of paper with names and phone numbers for nearby therapy offices. It was during that terrible time I wrote about in the previous chapter—when we had experienced so much loss around us. I had gone to see Dr. Thomas because

I had had a headache for weeks, and I was convinced it was a brain tumor. Dr. Thomas said that my headache looked to be the result of excessive teeth grinding—something she labeled "TMJ"—and for that I was very relieved. Nevertheless, I burst out crying on the exam table, which had to have been a hint that something else was wrong.

Unfortunately, Dr. Thomas didn't have much to say. She just gave me the list of therapists and suggested that I call one. I left thinking that I would never call any of those numbers, and that I would have to figure out my problems alone. I was too busy, too proud, too distracted, and too cheap to seek help. Most of all, I was too disrespectful of my own well-being.

When I was diagnosed with cancer, however, all of that changed. I was no longer busy, proud, or distracted, and when I heard that my insurance covered it, I was ready to find someone to help me sort out the madness in my brain. Most of all, cancer gave me the confidence to admit I needed help, and that I was worthy of it.

When I was offered an appointment with Dr. Funt, a mental-health professional at Dana-Farber, I took it. Call me crazy, but I thought I would sit down with this man and he would comfort me, at least, a little bit. I figured I would cry a little and he would repeat lines that he had delivered a million times to people like me who had been shocked by a cancer diagnosis. I would feel relief when the hour was up and I would have a strategy or two to help me cope. At the end of the appointment, he would tell me everything would be okay. It was a lovely vision, as so many visions are.

Sometimes I get a real kick out of the difference between my visions and my reality. I could provide countless examples including buying a car, registering for wedding gifts, and getting my one (and only) pedicure. Add kids to the mix, and the examples are endless. For a slight detour, I must describe one of my favorite examples of how my visions can so drastically diverge from reality.

After the last day of school every year, my mom would take my sister and brother and me to the bookstore to buy a stack of books to read over the summer. I loved that trip not only because I love bookstores, but because it meant the start of camp, trips to my grandparents' house, time with cousins, ice cream trucks, and countless other summer joys.

A few months before my diagnosis, I decided to re-create the tradition in our house on one of the few nights that Brian was late getting home. So Teddy, Annabel, and I marched off to a local bookstore. When we got there, I realized I forgot the diaper bag. *No big deal; we'll be quick*, I thought.

"Come on guys, let's find some great books for the summer," I announced as we held hands in the parking lot.

"I want to pway wif va twains," Teddy responded. *Oh yes, the friggin' trains.* They were a welcome distraction when Teddy was too young to care about books, but now that he was older, I was frustrated that the bookstore had become "va stow wif va twains."

I'm a real militant mother, so of course we stopped to play with the trains.

About five minutes later, Teddy told me he had to poop. We found the bathroom and he went, as I tried to stop Annabel from crawling into the next stall.

Now, back to the family tradition, I thought. Teddy faked a minute or two of caring about which books we chose then he headed back to the trains. *Oh, what the hell, that's fine,* I thought. I took a seat to watch my kids box out other kids in order to protect "their" trains.

Then I smelled something. *Please don't be coming from my child.* But it was. In fact, Annabel, who always seemed to know when I forgot the diaper bag, had a large and rancid gift for me.

Back to the bathroom we went, Teddy now with trains in hand. I don't typically consider myself a dumb person, but sometimes, I really wonder what was going through my head. I actually know what I was thinking the moment I lifted Annabel onto the changing table—*if I put her in her car seat with that diaper full of poop, it will come out all ends and I'll have to clean out the whole car seat.*

So I decided I would take off her diaper, dump the package into the toilet, use toilet paper to wipe her butt and the diaper, and put the somewhat clean diaper back on her. That was the vision.

The reality, however, involved Annabel screaming on the changing table as I tried to fling poop from her diaper into the toilet. When I missed, we had a serious mess on our hands (it wasn't really poop you could fling).

Poor Teddy tried to help. But there was no salvaging this diaper. *Not a problem,* I thought, *she's empty now, she can just go without a diaper.*

We cleaned up the bathroom so that aside from the smell, there was no evidence of the desperate parenting that had taken place there. We washed our hands, and proceeded to the register to buy our stupid books.

Annabel peed on the way home, and I ended up having to wash the car-seat cover anyways.

That night, we read one of our new books and the summer began, family tradition restored. Kind of.

Now back to that appointment with the therapist, Dr. Funt. Let's just say the disparity between the vision and the reality was about as big as the disparity I found at the bookstore with my pooping children.

It didn't start off well when Dr. Funt couldn't find me despite that I checked in at the front desk and was seated in the waiting room. When he finally called me in, he led by asking me if a "palliative care fellow" could sit in on our session.

"Sure," I replied as the PhD, MD, who was about my age, took a seat in the room. But inside my blood pressure rose, and it was already high according to the vitals I just had taken. I thought to myself, *Isn't "palliative care" for people who are about to die?*

I sat down, sick to my stomach.

"What brings you here today?" Dr. Funt began. I laughed and cried at the same time.

"Um, cancer. I was just diagnosed with cancer and I'm scared out of my mind."

Pause. Blank stare in my direction.

"What are you scared of?" *Was this guy serious?*

"Maybe what everyone's scared of when they hear they have cancer— that I'm going to die," I replied, crying because it was so hard to admit this fear and laughing because my own internal voice was jokingly asking: This *is therapy?*

"I see," the doctor answered. *Pause.* I wondered if I was supposed to talk more. In the movies, the therapist asked the questions.

"Do you have family in the area?" he continued, still looking down at his clipboard.

"Yes."

"How's your husband dealing with this?"

"He's upset."

"Do you have brothers or sisters?"

"Yes. A sister and a brother."

"Where did you go to school?"

"Bowdoin College."

I was stumped. Was I in the wrong appointment? We continued this superficial back-and-forth for a while longer. Finally he asked me what was helping me cope. I told him that what helped most was hearing the stories of people who have had serious battles with cancer and won. He nodded.

More silence.

I told him that my most imaginative mind had created swollen glands, underarm tumors, and, as embarrassed as I was to admit it, multiple sclerosis.

"So is your Ativan working?" he responded.

"Well, I started the Ativan when I found out I had cancer, so we've got a big variable to account for, don't we?" I couldn't keep my feisty side at bay any longer.

Blank stare. Silence.

Finally I asked Dr. Funt, "So what is your job exactly?" Maybe I really was in the wrong appointment. He told me that he meets with people and helps them find what will work for them. Okay, so maybe this was a big miscommunication. I thought he was actually going to provide me some counseling, so I took some responsibility for how badly the appointment went. That was the only reason I didn't get up and leave.

But it was bad. *Really* bad. Dr. Funt was so disconnected that in an entire hour, I didn't feel a single ounce of empathy or understanding from him.

At the end of the appointment, the palliative-care fellow spoke up. "Has anyone told you what an amazing job you're doing?" he asked.

I started to cry again—a different kind of cry.

"There are many people who are told what you've been told and can't get out of bed or take care of their kids. But you're doing all that and you're doing a great job. And you're the type of person who will continue to do a great job through your treatment."

I can't remember if he said that I would be cured, but it didn't matter. What the seasoned expert could not achieve in an hour, this novice achieved in one minute. He turned a bit of my fear into a feeling of pride and accomplishment, and a bit of my doubt into confidence. He acknowledged my pain, and looked at me as if he wanted to make it better.

When my mom and I walked out of the appointment, I told her that I thought we had just been taped for an episode of "Cancer Candid Camera." Dr. Funt was a perfect character for such a skit. Then my mom and I enjoyed some good laughs about that appointment, and laughter is always a great medicine.

In the end, I give Dr. Funt credit. He called me the night after and helped me set up an appointment with Dr. Grace, a psychologist out of the breast care center. Ever the optimist, I clung to a positive vision of my appointment with Dr. Grace.

When I met Dr. Grace a week or so later, she didn't just meet my expectations; she far exceeded them. She became a key leader in my cancer treatment, and I visited her on almost every infusion day. My appointments with her were often teary and exhausting, as I said things out loud to her that I wouldn't have said to anyone else for fear that I would upset them. But that honesty, that purging of thoughts that had swirled in my head, helped more than I could ever explain.

If there's one thing I learned from the Dr. Funt debacle, it's the realization that vulnerable people, including myself, often need to turn to strangers for help. Every day, men, women, and children walk through the doors of hospitals, schools, nursing homes, gyms, and lawyers' and therapists' offices desperate for compassion and guidance.

The professionals that receive us have a challenging, and indescribably important responsibility. They have to choose their words wisely, because each and every one matters. They need to be careful of their facial expressions and their tone, because we read into every one. Somehow, with the volume of their clientele, the busyness of their days, and their own personal priorities, those professionals need to treat each of us as unique, and at the same time connected by a similar hope—that even though we are afraid and weak and maybe even downright ornery, we have arrived at their doorstep to try to get better.

Fresh Air

Prior to my bilateral mastectomy, I thought that having my breasts removed sounded like one of the most painful and most complicated procedures imaginable. It was a complete mystery to me—how my body would be able to heal after my surgeon removed so much of what naturally was *me*. Then again, countless mysteries surround me every day; things that seem to work even though I have no idea how—airplanes, skyscrapers, my touchscreen phone, and my taste buds, just to name a few.

I didn't realize until months later that so much of my surgery-related fear existed because the whole process was so mysterious—done in a place I had never been by people I didn't know (and all while I slept). Granted, I didn't want any explanation of surgical techniques or how the anesthesia would knock me out but not kill me. I just wanted proof that in the hospital, this process was somewhat routine. I wanted proof that the procedure would work and that I would not have a mental breakdown in the meantime.

That proof came about a week before my surgery. I was invited to the hospital for two pre-op appointments—the first, to collect my complete medical history (again) and show me around, and the second to explain what to expect from the surgery itself.

The first appointment was nothing more than me answering in the negative to a hundred questions.

"Do you smoke?"

"No."

"Do you drink?"

"Barely."

"Do you have any allergies?"

"Vicodin makes me throw up."

"Have you ever had an issue with anesthesia?"

"No, except that it makes me really sick afterward."

I especially liked one of the last questions. "Do you have any other health issues?"

"You mean besides cancer?"

"Um, yes."

"Not that I know of. But then again, I only just found out about the cancer."

After the Q&A, the nurse showed my mom and I around the hospital. We saw where I would check in on surgery day, where my family could sit (or pace) while waiting, and the inpatient floor on which I would recover. As we walked around, I even had an opportunity to tell the nurse what I anticipated to be the worst moment of that day—being wheeled away from my family and into the operating room. The nurse explained to me that the anesthesiologists could pump me with enough sedatives that I wouldn't even know we had gone wheels-up on the gurney. "Yes, let's do that," I told her, watching to see if she wrote anything down on her clipboard.

*　*　*

I don't believe in signs, like something or someone that God puts in a person's path to tell him or her to think a certain thought or act a certain way. But I do believe that if we look closely, often we can find exactly what we're looking for.

I came to the hospital a week before my surgery in search of fresh air. For weeks I had been stuck in that metaphoric airplane cabin, suffocating in a holding pattern. The pre-op appointments helped me breathe a little deeper, mostly because I was able to better envision how the big day would unfold.

I learned what I needed to do before surgery (not eat after midnight, and wash myself with a special antiseptic body wash). I learned how long the procedure would take (approximately two to three hours to remove the breast tissue, the cancer, and the sentinel lymph node, and another two to three hours to insert the tissue expanders). And I learned what I could expect following the procedure (how I would have to care for the scars, how the doctors would manage my pain, that my pee would be blue as a result of the dye they would inject into my body to test which lymph nodes may contain cancer cells). Thank goodness for the blue-pee warning. Forget cancer—I would have been dead of a heart attack without that heads-up.

The real breaths of fresh air, however, came when I least expected them, and in the form of three remarkable women.

As we waited for my first appointment, I happened to glance through the window and into the hallway. At just that moment, Dr. Nadia, my breast surgeon, walked by in her scrubs and surgical cap. She happened to glance into the waiting room, and much to my surprise, she saw me. The look on her face in that instant meant everything to me; it was a simple look—one of recognition. Dr. Nadia *knew* me. Me, one of her thousands of patients. Me, who she met only once before. Dr. Nadia didn't hesitate for a moment; she just strolled into the waiting room to say hello.

Without hesitation, Dr. Nadia hugged me and smiled. She looked me in the eye. She remarked on the great news that my BRCA test came back negative. She said she was excited to see me next week and that she would take great care of me. I told her I decided on the double mastectomy and she nodded, "That's great, I completely understand."

In the end, maybe that was all I needed to hear—that she understood, that she was prepared, that she would take care of me. In response, I just said "Thank you" over and over, trying to fight back my tears of appreciation.

That day in the hospital, my mom and I also happened to cross paths with two women, both nurses, who I knew from my hometown. Kathy and Carole both addressed a key issue that no one had yet thought to mention—that my medical team would make sure my family was alright during my surgery. With so much focus on me and on the medical procedure, so little focus had been on my family—how they would receive the news about whether my cancer had spread, and how the surgery team would take care of them after that. I knew I would be asleep when the results of the lymph node testing were revealed, so my family would have to face that news before I did. This worried me terribly. Kathy and Carole must have known that because they repeated several times that my family would be well cared for while I was in surgery. Nothing meant more to me than that.

That day, these exceptional women—my pilots, my flight crew—pushed open the windows of my stalled plane. They peeled my fingers from the armrests, steadied my steps, and led me to the cockpit for a quick peek into the future. From that window at the front of the plane, I saw the flight path and blue sky. I felt a breeze from Orlando, Maine, and all of the other destinations that I would reach one day. And I took a deep breath of fresh, cool air that never felt so good.

Coping

Despite the fresh air that I discovered after that day at the hospital, I still had a few moments before my surgery when I completely freaked out. For instance, a few nights before surgery day, I fell asleep sobbing in Brian's arms. I actually don't even remember falling asleep. I just remember the crying—uncontrollable tears and gasps for breath, as the rain pounded on the air conditioner outside of our bedroom window.

As I sobbed, Brian held me. He let me cry, and told me that I should let it out—that I had every right to feel the way that I did, that he loved me. I just kept telling him that I loved him. And although I couldn't adequately explain it at the time, I had come to realize a huge irony—it was love that made cancer so horrifically scary, and love that fueled a fire in me to survive.

*　*　*

Over a year after my surgery, I gave an interview at the Dana-Farber Cancer Institute as part of a program titled, "How to cope with a breast cancer diagnosis." Not surprisingly, the interviewer asked me how I coped with my diagnosis. I was an amateur on camera and I explained something about how coping isn't always a conscious thing and that most of the time, when I was in a really bad place, I just grasped on to anything that could get me out of it, even if it was just letting myself cry, or counting to 10, or repeating over and over, *I am here now.*

A few weeks after that interview, I sat at my computer working on this book. I was rereading a blog I had written about my husband just days before my surgery when I realized that I had totally botched the *how do you cope* question. Unknowingly, I had arrived at a far better answer—the best coping advice I could ever give:

Choose a really great person with whom to spend your life.

Yes, that was precisely how I coped most of the time. I had a man who held my hand and told me he loved me; who, long before cancer, could run the house if I had a really busy week at work. I married someone who surrounded our family with good people and good times, who cooked us dinner every night, who took such pride in our yard and our home, and who talked to our kids about all of the most important things in life—like working hard and being nice. I found a guy who could not only raise our kids without me if he had to, but who could raise them the way that I wanted them to be raised.

My best coping strategy was simple, but not easy, and it all stemmed from a decision I made six years prior—to marry a person who would do anything to make my life happier, better, longer. And who let me cry and slobber all over his t-shirt in the meantime, if that's what I needed to do.

Go Time

For the few weeks leading up to my surgery, every time I saw my dad, he would ask me, "So are you mad yet?" He meant mad at the cancer. He would clench his teeth when he said the word, *mad.* But there was so much love there, too.

In response to my dad's question, I would just shrug and supply some vague response like, "Not quite, dad," or, "I'm trying."

"You need to get mad," he would respond.

I knew where he was coming from. My dad had overcome seemingly insurmountable obstacles since childhood—growing up poor (with severe dyslexia) in a tough area of Boston, and working (even as a young teenager) to provide for his mother and four sisters when his father drank too much. My dad successfully overcame the strong urban tide that had carried many of his childhood friends to jail, or worse, to their graves.

In the weeks prior to my surgery, I felt like I was disappointing my father when I admitted that I felt a number of things, but anger wasn't one of them. Every now and then I would feel something close to anger when I thought about how unjust it all seemed. But I had seen too many examples of bad things happening to good people to think that I had any right to feel angry about my own injustice. It wasn't the fighter's attitude my dad was hoping for.

Nevertheless, the afternoon before my surgery—September 11, 2012—something clicked.

Before I had to pick up the kids from school, I decided to take a walk around a small, familiar loop in my hometown. As I walked, I soaked in the crisp air, in awe of one of the most beautiful days I had ever seen. I blared my music through my earphones and I remembered the night before. It was then, for the first time since my diagnosis, that Brian had broken down.

While the kids slept, my husband bawled his eyes out. He's a big guy, and I was shrinking, so my hugs weren't as comforting as his were, but I tried. I repeated back all the things he said to me a few nights prior when I had lost it. That I loved him. That we would get through this. Once again, we cried ourselves to sleep.

I recalled that dark night as I walked under the gorgeous sun. I was overcome with emotion—appreciation for all of the love and support I had received, excitement that it was finally time for takeoff, an uneasy certainty of the time ahead of me. And all of a sudden, mixed in with all of that emotion, surfaced a bubbling anger. A feels-so-good-to-finally-feel-it *anger*.

It didn't take long to figure out where it had come from, either—I was angry that the cancer made my husband cry. I was angry that it had become my mother's full-time job, that it had interrupted so many good things, and that it was threatening to take my life. I was angry, so fucking *angry* at the disease. And I was ready to kick its ass.

Ready

We live just beside the public high school in my hometown; the high school from which I had graduated 14 years prior and where I taught after college. At the end of my walk on the day prior to my surgery, I passed the school with 20 minutes to spare before I needed to leave to get the kids. Unknowingly, I found myself drawn in. I hadn't visited the school in years. But something came over me, and I needed to find Mr. Badoian.

At the time this book went to print, Mr. Badoian was 87 years old and had taught math for 61 years. He was my math teacher for three out of my four years of high school.

I will never forget our homework assignment on the first day of freshman-year algebra. It is probably the same assignment this year's class had to complete—we were to memorize our perfect squares from one to 50. I can't remember if Mr. Badoian quizzed us on those squares the day after, but it didn't matter. Because after only one class, Mr. Badoian already established such respect that most of us, even as puny freshmen, would rather answer his question correctly than get an "A" on any quiz.

Mr. Badoian's testing techniques were unique. For instance, he never announced tests. His philosophy was that we should prepare every night as if a test awaited us—why would we postpone real understanding until the night before an announced exam? We knew there was a test when we walked into his room and white papers, blank-side-up, lay on our desks. (It was a favorite before-class joke—when Mr. Badoian was not yet in the room, of course—to put a blank piece of paper on the first desk at the entrance of the room. I fell for it every time.)

Mr. Badoian also had a unique grading system. A zero was a perfect score—that meant no points had been taken off. It took me years to earn my first zero, and I sometimes wonder if by that point, Mr. Badoian just felt like he needed to humor me. Then again, he was far too honorable for that, but surely the test on which I received a zero was a relatively easy one. I was always the slowest one in the class but I worked hard enough to stay there.

Less than a year before my diagnosis, when I decided to leave my job at a big corporate law firm, I found myself reflecting. I wrote Mr. Badoian a letter thanking him for all he had taught me. I told him that he taught me the real meaning of attacking a problem and working through it—the true meaning of hard work and preparation.

* * *

On the afternoon before my surgery, I was oddly drawn to Mr. Badoian's classroom. It was 3 PM, over an hour after school ended, and I found only one teacher in the building. Of course, that was Mr. Badoian.

When I walked in, he was seated at his desk, behind his thick glasses, reviewing the work of an eager (and appropriately terrified) student who stood at his shoulder.

I had no idea why I was there, and neither did Mr. Badoian. I told him that I just wanted to say hello, but then I started to cry. I knew that seemed odd, so I told him (voice shaking) about my cancer and my impending surgery.

He hugged me. His hearing aid buzzed in my ear.

Then Mr. Badoian told me, "I'll pray for you, because that's what I do." I had no idea that Mr. Badoian was a praying man but the news comforted me because every mortal listened to and followed the orders of Mr. Badoian. So I hoped that his God did, too.

Later I wondered why, on the day before my surgery, I needed to see my old math teacher, of all people. After much pondering, I finally figured it out.

I think there are a lot of people who like a good fight, a challenge, a chance to prove they can do something that seems improbable. Those people accomplish all sorts of things—they practice law, sports, and medicine. They climb mountains, scuba dive, take a yoga class, or walk for charity. They start their own businesses, do crossword puzzles, or learn to play an instrument. They teach, they coach, they write, and they do math problems. They take up running when they are born with no legs, and they learn to play baseball when they have no arms. Some of the funniest stand on stage and make us laugh. Some of the brightest try to find lifesaving cures. And some of the bravest and most selfless join the military.

Of course no one chooses misfortune, just as I didn't choose to get cancer. Nonetheless, those fights are placed in our laps and we're forced to react. We have no choice but to take the problem, dissect it, and find our own answer.

I think this is why I wanted to see Mr. Badoian that day. I think it's why on my walk, I thought about my dad and his quest to get me to feel anger about my cancer. Even though this wasn't the fight I wanted, it was the fight I was given. And while solving math problems in high school may not be as difficult as beating cancer, those math problems had helped shape the fighter in me.

When I saw my dad later on the eve of my surgery, I told him that it finally happened—that I was angry. He gave me a high-five and a hug, and he told me, "You're ready then." Really, I was.

Part Three
Bilateral Mastectomy

Through the centuries,
we faced down death
by daring to hope.

Maya Angelou
(poet and author)

Off to Sleep

Thanks to Ativan, writing, my family, more Ativan, and weeks of mental preparation, I was surprisingly composed when I arrived at the hospital to have my breasts removed and reconstructed. Surgery was scheduled for 1 PM, so Brian and I dropped the kids off at school together before we headed into the city.

The drop-off was less painful than I had imagined it would be, probably because: (1) the kids' principal Michelle gave me a heartfelt hug and heartfelt hugs really help, and (2) I didn't let myself dwell on the thought of not seeing Teddy and Annabel for the next few days. But as Brian and I pulled away from the school, it was like we stripped off our happy masks and slapped on our game faces. Because *finally*, it was game time.

I checked in to the hospital while my family attempted to hide their nerves in the waiting area. As the woman behind the glass clicked away at her computer to "find me in the system," the rest of the day started to feel like a monster lurking in my closet. I fought to stay composed. After a series of my usual answers ("Tara Shuman, 3-10-1980"), we had our marching orders and our mini-parade made its way to the surgery area.

The hours before I went under anesthesia are stored in my brain as snapshots. I remember some moments so vividly that I could paint every detail of them within a four-cornered frame. Then there are chunks of time between the snapshots for which I have absolutely no recollection.

Soon after we arrived in the surgery wing, a nurse handed me a johnny and directed me to a large bathroom to change. I shut the heavy door and found myself in a rare moment. *Alone.*

I took off my t-shirt, folded it, and put it in the plastic bag with my name on it. I unclipped my bra, and looked at my boobs in the mirror. Still, there was no part of me that was sad to see them go. Despite their droopy and innocent appearance, they felt like time bombs ticking inside me.

I stood there for a few seconds—half-naked in hospital socks with sticky bottoms.

I wondered, *Should I pray? Should I ask God to help me through this?* But talking to God didn't feel like the right thing to do at that moment, so I said a different kind of prayer—ironically, feeling somewhat guided by a higher being to do so. I stopped and felt the energy of the many good people who sent me messages in the days prior.

I will be thinking of you. I will be praying for you. I will send good thoughts your way. You can do this.

I swear, those thoughts and prayers and encouragement were almost tangible for a few moments under the florescent lights of that sterile hospital bathroom.

The next snapshot in my memory happened between two curtains in the surgery preparation area. It was a bustling scene of activity as several nurses attended to me for a variety of reasons, from confirming the type of surgery I sought (*bilateral mastectomy with reconstruction, please*) to instructing me to take off my wedding ring. I hated not wearing that ring, even just for the day, but I felt better when Brian put it on his neck chain, next to the cross that his grandma gave him, and tucked them both safely under his t-shirt.

Over the next hour or so, the nurses weighed me, asked me more questions, inserted IVs, and started some medications. When my plastic surgeon, Dr. Lee, came in, she pulled the last of the curtains shut so we could be alone. Then, with a blue marker and dotted lines, she mapped out her plan on my chest. She was so precise about it, and while I am a total control freak about most things, ceding control to her to rebuild my boobs didn't bother me one bit. Reconstruction wasn't related to the cancer, and at the time, cancer had my full attention. Still, I wanted all parts of the surgery to go smoothly and I trusted Dr. Lee that it would, mostly because she cared, and because this looked like something she did every day. Then again, it was.

Once the nurses worked through their pre-op task lists, my family came back in pairs to wish me luck. I don't remember much about those conversations. I know they weren't easy, but they weren't excruciatingly painful either.

Finally it was Brian's turn to say his goodbyes, and he came back by himself. I looked up at him for a few minutes, whispering over and over, "Everything is going to be fine." I would like to think that I was saying that to make him feel better, but it may have been largely for myself.

Those last few minutes with Brian before I left for surgery were so intensely personal. Nothing interesting happened and besides "Everything will be fine" and "I love you," I don't even remember anything else we said to each other. Nevertheless, those few minutes proved to me a lesson I will never forget—that when it came down to it, love was more powerful than fear.

I don't remember being rolled down the hallway into the operating room. I just remember that once we got there, I couldn't see a thing. My eyesight is horrendous and I always wear contact lens or eyeglasses because if I didn't, I would be seriously injured within a matter of minutes. But contacts weren't allowed in surgery and before the nurses rolled me away, they took my glasses and added them to my plastic bag.

After they lifted me onto the operating table, I saw bright lights and several blobs of blue scrubs shuffling around me. *That* part—the complete lack of control—was terrifying, although I could tell that something was already pumping through my veins to counteract the fear. It was as if my brain knew it wanted to be scared but couldn't connect the wires to actually feel that way.

Then I heard Kathy's voice.

Kathy was one of the women who gave me the precious fresh air the week before. I knew she worked in the operating room, but I didn't know she would be with me when I fell asleep.

"Kathy, is that you?" I asked her, even though I knew that it was.

There's a Maya Angelou quote that I love, and that reminds me of what Kathy did for me in those minutes when I could barely see her.

People will forget what you said,
people will forget what you did,
but people will never forget how you made them feel.

I don't remember what Kathy said to me in those last few moments before Dr. Nadia got to work. I just know that she was there, next to me, and I know exactly how she made me feel. She made me feel like it was okay to go to sleep. And she made me feel as though the four words Brian and I had repeated to each other for weeks—*everything will be fine*—were actually true.

Waking Up

I never knew what a sentinel lymph node was until a few weeks prior to my surgery when Dr. Nadia explained that it was the first node that would receive the cancer if any diseased cells had exited the breast. During the surgery, Dr. Nadia would remove the sentinel node first. If it contained cancer cells—something a pathologist in the operating room could determine with help from the blue-pee dye—then Dr. Nadia would remove the next node, then the next, until hopefully, she found a node that the cancer had not reached.

Some of the most inspiring stories I heard prior to my surgery were of women who had had several lymph nodes removed and, years later, were healthy and strong. I prepared myself for the possibility that cells from my tumor had been given the chance to meander elsewhere. By surgery time, I had accepted that Dr. Nadia may need to dissect me like a lab rat before she was able to remove all of my cancer. I actually found peace with that. I just wanted the chance to fight.

* * *

The first thing I remember after my surgery was waking up and thinking that I literally had just fallen asleep. Anesthesia, like my snooze button, amazes me that way.

In the blink of an eye, my real boobs had vanished and hard tissue expanders had been sewn in their place. My sentinel lymph node had been extracted and tested for cancer, and my family already had heard the news.

"The sentinel node was clean," Brian explained when my eyes opened, or maybe even before. He was beaming and crying and looking at me as if I had just accomplished the most fantastic feat there ever was to accomplish. It was like a scene from a cheesy movie. Only it was very real, and we didn't look like movie stars.

I smiled.

"Good news?" was all I could muster up.

"Good news," Brian repeated back to me, smiling through his tears.

No doubt, it *was* good news. We wouldn't know the lymph node results with certainty until a week later when the final pathology report came back. But the fact that the pathology tests performed during the surgery revealed no evidence of the cancer in my sentinel node, or even the vessels leading to it, meant that Dr. Nadia didn't need to remove any additional lymph nodes. That made her portion of the surgery relatively short—less than two hours. More importantly, because the cancer hadn't metastasized, it would be considered *curable*, not just *treatable*. I was eternally grateful to exist anywhere near the word "cure." Of course, there was still the pesky HER2 protein, but I savored this victory anyway.

Since cancer was always more of a mental struggle than a physical one for me, news that the cancer hadn't metastasized made the physical pain a lot easier to bear. Of course my chest hurt. In fact, it felt like a ton of bricks was resting on it. It was terribly painful to cough or sneeze or even laugh, but with medication, the pain was generally in check.

After the anesthesia wore off in the recovery room, they admitted me to an inpatient floor and rolled me up to a room at the end of the hallway. I remember very little of that evening—the saltines, the ice-chips, a lovely visit from a high school friend who worked as a nurse on the floor. I also remember the much-appreciated surprise that the scopolamine patch behind my ear had kept the post-anesthesia nausea at bay.

Then there was the itching. The absolutely *relentless* itching. The doctors assured me that the itching was a relatively normal reaction to the anesthesia. *But no one told me about that*, I thought to myself.

The night after the surgery, once my family had gone home to try to sleep, Brian sat in the recliner at the foot of my bed and typed an update to my blog. He called it "Checkmate Day," which I loved, as initially I had titled my blog, "Total recovery. Full stop. Checkmate. I win." Actually, I had stolen those words from an email my cousin sent me after my diagnosis, and Brian stole his blog title from the sign that the kids' principal had put up in the school parking lot that morning to wish me good luck.

When Brian finished writing, I asked him to read it back to me. I'm not sure if he read me the whole thing, or if I was awake for all of it if he did, but I know that what I heard made me smile. Too tired for any edits, I had just one addition. I wanted Brian to be sure we acknowledged people who hadn't received good news that we had. I wanted those people to know that there was still hope. Because there was.

Despite feeling like the luckiest person in the world, I knew that had I found the lump just a few months later, my situation may have been very different. That's why, prior to my surgery, I never let myself think that my sentinel node would be clean. I wasn't being pessimistic, rather, optimistic on a longer timeframe. *Beating cancer is possible*, I told myself, *but don't expect it to be easy*.

Brian followed my instructions and added a paragraph to the blog as I dozed in and out of a sleep, repeating, over and over, how much I loved him.

Recovery

The itching continued all night, so much so that Brian, curled up on a recliner half his size, got more sleep than I did. Even into the wee hours of the morning I wasn't worried about sleep, nor was I worried about the terrible gas pains in my stomach or the discomfort in my throat from the breathing tube. I was just so relieved that this gigantic step was in the past. That the cancer and I no longer had to co-exist, at least, not physically.

I woke up abruptly the next morning to a team of medical interns hovering over my bed. There were at least six of them and their teacher, a surgeon whose name I never caught, wanted to show them the results of my surgery.

As you can imagine, it was awkward and disconcerting to wake up to a crowd of students eager for me to take off my johnny so they could examine my boobs. Brian was none too pleased that we hadn't even been given a warning. I, however, was so grateful, relieved, and high on pain meds that I didn't think it was so bad to be studied like a guinea pig. Lord knows I wanted to encourage anyone's interest in becoming a breast surgeon since the world (and the surgery calendar) could certainly use more of those. So I opened my gown and let them unwrap the gauze around my chest while I gritted my teeth in pain.

* * *

Later that morning, after everyone but me had peeked underneath the gauze, I made some big strides. First, a nurse removed my catheter, then I got out of bed and walked down the hallway, and after that, I even changed out of my johnny and into the nifty shirt the hospital had given me the week before. I tucked the drains into the interior pockets of the sexy gray top that Velcro-ed in the front. (The nurses religiously emptied the drains to measure the fluid that collected from my insides. It was far less disgusting than I thought it was going to be, which was another reason for relief.)

Of course I felt pain, but it was bearable. Plus, I wasn't shy about using the red-button at the end of a little baton attached to the IV bag of painkillers. On the first day after my surgery, I pushed that button like I was a contestant on Jeopardy. I didn't have to worry about overdosing because the machine wouldn't allow it. Since I was in no mood to be heroic, I welcomed the medication with open veins.

As I emerged from the mental fuzziness of a major surgery, I was pleased to hear Dr. Lee's report that her portion of the procedure had gone smoothly. Not only was she able to insert the two tissue expanders into the hollow spots where my breasts had been, but Dr. Lee was even able to "inflate" them a bit. While I expected to be completely flat following my surgery, instead, I had a very small set of hard and numb artificial boobs! Dr. Lee would gradually inflate the pockets with saline over the next few months, but for the time being, I was quite content.

* * *

About 30 hours after my surgery, I was ready to go home. It was fast, but I felt ready.

After the physical therapist attempted to teach me exercises for home (I fell asleep while she was talking), a nurse rolled my wheelchair to the front of the building and slowly (*very* slowly) I ducked into the car. The nurse positioned a pillow under the seat belt and strapped it over my raw chest, although even the softest of pillows wasn't going to ease the pain that accompanied every bump and turn.

For the next four days, I lived in a big, comfy recliner that my best friend Brianne and her family had bought for me. I called that recliner my "healing chair."

My Healing Chair

One afternoon a few weeks prior to my surgery, Brianne was visiting when a nurse from my health insurance company called to "offer resources" to me (*translation*: control my medical costs, however possible). The nurse asked me a whole bunch of questions, including whether I had a recliner for after my surgery.

"No. Why? Do I need one?" I responded while Brianne sat patiently nearby.

The nurse responded that it would help a great deal. Even though Brianne couldn't hear the nurse's response, she obviously figured it out because a few weeks later, Brianne gave me an envelope full of money that she had collected from her family. She instructed me to go and pick out a recliner. I cried at their generosity.

My family and I set out a few days later in search of the perfect chair. We found it almost immediately. When we went to pay for it, the woman behind the counter explained the warranty as one that "lasts 25 years or through the end of your life, whichever is shorter." Well, *shit*.

Obviously the lady had no idea that for all I knew, I had advanced-stage cancer, but, *seriously?!?* I wanted to burst into laughter and tears at the same time. I chose the former and cracked a joke to my mom, although I really felt like puking all over the showroom floor.

On the way out, I said a little prayer that I would live to see the end of my chair's warranty.

My healing chair found its first home in the corner of my parents' bedroom. I lived in that chair, in my childhood home, for four days post-surgery so that I could build up my strength before my playful one-year-old and tireless four-year-old started to tackle me again. Those days passed like most do when recovering from a major surgery—very slowly at the time, yet in retrospect, so very fast.

During those four days, Brian came to visit every chance he got. He helped me strip my drains twice a day although let me assure you, "stripping" could never be less sexy. While I held my shirt out of the way, my loyal husband pulled the fluid and pieces of tissue through the plastic tube while being sure not to pull on the stitches that kept the tubes sewn into my body. Then he emptied the contents of the drain into a plastic measuring cup. I can still remember the sounds of those little bulbs squirting out my insides. It wasn't cute, but then again, cute was not a priority.

The Sunday after my surgery, while the New England Patriots kicked off on mute on my parents' TV, I got sick. I had removed the scopolamine patch from behind my ear that morning, and I still wonder if that was the cause of the violent nausea.

Luckily for Brian, I waited for him to arrive that afternoon before I threw up in the bucket he was holding. Then I fell asleep while he lay beside me and watched our home team lose.

In those first few days after my surgery, I was like a newborn baby—eating, sleeping, and pooping were my greatest accomplishments. Since I couldn't even keep track of what day it was, I relied on my family to give me the medications I needed at the times that I needed them. They never missed a beat.

Gradually, from my place in the chair that my best friend gave me, I was lucky enough to receive one of God's greatest gifts—my body healed.

The Pathology Report

Despite that the real-time pathology results from the operating room are typically accurate, the final results needed a week to process. This meant that an important appointment lurked on my calendar—one week after my surgery—when I would put the pillow back under my seat belt and drive into Dana-Farber to meet with Dr. Denver. At this crucial meeting, we would begin to plot my next steps.

The night before that appointment was an eerie one. It was unseasonably warm and the skies darkened early. The wind howled and the windows creaked. It was unnerving, and my nerves were already in a fragile state.

To calm ourselves, Brian and I went back to basics—pizza with the kids, a movie, some ice cream. It's remarkable how the basics can provide comfort, even when a storm rages outside.

When Dr. Denver entered the exam room the next morning, all I cared about was my pathology report. I needed a final answer on my lymph nodes and I needed it desperately.

It was clear from the start of our conversation, however, that my oncologist was not focused on my lymph nodes. Rather, he was focused on my chemotherapy options. Looking back, this was a great lesson in communication because it's difficult to have a conversation click when two parties are starting from completely different vantage points.

Gradually, our paths converged. Dr. Denver confirmed that my cancer had not spread to my lymph nodes, and even better there was no evidence of it in the vessels surrounding my lymph nodes. *Translation*: I got a solid start off the blocks in the marathon that is beating cancer. I hadn't anticipated such a great start, and had survived for weeks on stories of those who had lived many years after a diagnosis despite having been tripped up in their first few steps.

After we discussed my lymph nodes, it was back to discussing the pesky protein.

To describe HER2, Dr. Denver drew a rough circle on a piece of blank paper.

"Here's a healthy cell," he explained. Then he drew a little line through part of the circle and added small circles to both end points of the line. "This little barbell on the cell—that's the HER2 protein."

I felt sick to my stomach, and kept listening only because I was too disoriented not to.

Dr. Denver explained that HER2 "is expressed" on healthy cells and (*insert more biology than I want to remember*) helps them grow as cancer cells. Well that sure didn't sound good. (*Severe nausea. Room spinning.*)

"Herceptin, however, is drawn to the protein," Dr. Denver explained, with a more upbeat tone. Then he pointed to the deadly barbell. He explained that Herceptin stops the barbell from giving the cancer cells the growth signal.

I learned later that Herceptin is a biotherapy—an antibody—and it gave HER2+ breast cancer patients like me a chance by working to stop the HER2 protein from doing what it's programmed to do. It all sounded like a pretty miraculous checkmate to me.

Dr. Denver went on to repeat what I heard him say several times before (not that it *ever* got old to hear it)—that Herceptin changed the course of breast cancer treatment. I always felt like Dr. Denver wanted to come clean and admit, "You wouldn't have made it without Herceptin." I appreciated that he was never that explicit about it.

Dr. Denver went on to explain that my tumor was a Grade 2 of 4 and that it measured 1.2 centimeters in diameter. I have since marveled at how something so small could be so deadly.

With the tumor and the sentinel lymph node extracted, I understood the next step—to make sure that no cancer cells had slipped through undetected. That would be chemotherapy's mission.

And so my mom, Brian, Dr. Denver, and I discussed my chemotherapy options. Truthfully, I didn't think I would have options. I thought the doctor would tell me exactly what I had to do next, and in two respects, he did.

"You will get one year of Herceptin infusions," Dr. Denver announced with conviction. "And you'll take Tamoxifen for five years," he continued. Tamoxifen is a pill-form hormonal therapy for patients like me whose cancer is estrogen and progesterone receptor-positive.

While the Herceptin and Tamoxifen were automatic, the chemotherapy regimen required some careful consideration. Given my type of breast cancer (triple-positive) and the grade of the tumor, Dr. Denver presented three chemo protocols. Option one was the least aggressive, option three the most aggressive, and option two a middle ground. For over an hour, we talked about the different drugs involved in these protocols as well as related clinical trials, past studies, and side effects.

My initial reaction was that I wanted option three—as aggressive as possible—take no prisoners, or all prisoners…you know what I mean. This would consist of 12 weeks of Adriamycin (drug name doxorubicin) and Cytoxan (cyclophosphamide), followed by 12 weeks of Taxol (paclitaxel) and Herceptin.

Dr. Denver wasn't surprised by my instinct to attack the cancer with the most powerful weapons, likely drawing on his memory of my please-remove-these-boobs-*now* attitude. But Dr. Denver explained that it wasn't that simple.

In earlier years at Dana-Farber, and in places with less-sophisticated cancer care, the norm was (or *is*) to unleash the most powerful medications on the cancer. Dr. Denver explained that recent studies had shown, however, that for certain types of cancers, less-aggressive treatments were equally as effective as the "kitchen-sink" approach. My doctor was also weary of a relatively small percentage of patients who experienced congestive heart failure as a result of Adriamycin. At just 32 years old, a failing heart sounded especially bad. Plus, option three would involve a regimen twice as long as the others. Dr. Denver summarized that it would take the heaviest toll on my body. I didn't have to drive up to Maine to remember that I really don't like tolls.

So we moved on to option two. Option two involved 12 weeks of chemotherapy—Cytoxan and Taxotere (drug name docetaxel)—combined immediately with Herceptin. Without the Adriamycin, there was less risk of heart damage and the side effects were those which I always had assumed came with chemo—fatigue, nausea, and hair loss. There were also a few more-serious potential side effects—for example, blood clots—but their possibility was remote (I repeated, "remote, remote, remote…" in my head whenever those possibilities haunted me).

Finally, there was option one. This choice was based on a relatively recent clinical trial. It involved 12 weeks of Taxol, which was a medication in the same family as Taxotere, along with Herceptin. Dr. Denver explained that this less-aggressive protocol had shown excellent results, with far less strain on the body.

After all three of the protocols were laid out on the exam table so to speak, I had an idea. "If we go with option one and the cancer comes back, can we then use option three?"

Unfortunately, it didn't work that way, and Dr. Denver's answer to this question is, to this day, one of the hardest realities for me.

"If the cancer comes back, it's not curable," he explained with a sympathetic scrunch of his lips. "We can treat it, and prolong your life, but our shot at a cure is now."

"Oh. I see," I responded, looking away. I had a twinge of embarrassment at how dumb my question probably sounded to someone in the field. Then I felt that awful nausea again.

I later understood that because I had no more breast tissue, if the breast cancer were to return, it would mean that it had traveled and done that thing that many cancer patients dread most—*metastasized.*

* * *

Making a decision regarding my chemotherapy regimen was as much about my mind's needs as it was about my body's. I trusted the clinical evidence that the Taxol-Herceptin combination could be all that was necessary for my body to defeat cancer. Regardless, I knew that this wasn't enough for my mind. I knew that I could only be at peace if I took a more aggressive route.

We delayed the ultimate decision until the "tumor board" at Dana-Farber weighed in on my case. Over a week later, after half of the board of cancer experts agreed that they would advise for option two, I made up my mind for good. And with the exception of one night, I never looked back on that decision.

Stages of Comparison

I am usually confident enough to compare myself to others and not get bent out of shape when I don't measure up. I feel okay about myself even if I'm the weakest one in an exercise class, I don't feel stupid asking a question that may actually *be* stupid, and I don't feel like a bad mother for screwing up birthday cake from a box. Generally I believe that healthy competition is a good thing. I don't believe in eliminating class rank and I like it when youth sports award first, second, and third places.

In the Kingdom of the Ill, however, it's different. Drawing comparisons between myself and other cancer patients has been, and still is, particularly complicated.

* * *

On one hand, it brought me great comfort in the worst of times to know that I was not alone—that many women trudged ahead of me and emerged from treatment in one piece.

I wasn't the only one who felt this type of comfort—Teddy felt it too, and I discovered that one Saturday morning when I least expected it.

Teddy had joined me on a trip to Dana-Farber to attend a short portion of a conference for young-adult cancer patients. I had never been to any meeting like that, mainly because I knew I couldn't handle being in a room with so many people with whom I could compare myself. However, my therapy lady was running the conference and after she invited me, I figured I would give it a shot. I brought Teddy because he wanted to "dwive into Boston" with me, and because some things were easier when he was around.

A few miles away from the hospital, Teddy asked me from his car seat, "Will Keegan's mommy be at va meeting?"

Keegan is Kristin's son, and Kristin is the first person Teddy ever knew with cancer.

To answer Teddy's question, I explained, "No, Keegan's mommy won't be there." When Teddy looked subtly disappointed, I continued.

"Kristin gets her medicine there, in the same place that I do. It's just that she won't be there *today*." Teddy looked more content, and I knew why.

Despite that he was only three years old, Keegan was a key part of Teddy's comfort with my cancer. Consciously or subconsciously, I believe that Teddy thought something like—*If my mom isn't the only mom who has breast cancer, then breast cancer must be okay.*

That Saturday morning, Teddy helped show me that when it came to cancer, I was a lot like him…which brings me to the one and only night that I ever doubted choosing option two.

* * *

It was just before October—National Breast Cancer Awareness Month—when everything from socks to newspapers goes pink. With October on her mind, Kristin posted a Facebook status about her breast cancer story. Selfishly, I remember very little of what she wrote in that post. But I remember one thing as clear as day. Kristin wrote that she had Stage 1 breast cancer.

When I read that word—*Stage*—and that number—*1*—I burst into quiet, uncontrollable tears. Without any intention to do so, or any self-warning that it was a terrible idea, I drew a comparison between myself and one of only two other young women I knew at the time with breast cancer.

I probably need to give a bit more context for my tears to make any sense. After my surgery, I figured that Dr. Denver would tell me the stage of my cancer as if it were the most important thing that had ever been revealed to me. Obviously he wouldn't hold up a cardboard scorecard over his head or anything; nevertheless, I imagined the announcement would be dramatic.

But it wasn't. In fact, Dr. Denver never even told me the stage of my cancer. Obviously I wasn't going to look at my pathology report or, heaven forbid, *ask*. The answer would just fuel future nightmares and I didn't need any more of those. So I played doctor with the information I had gathered.

While crying over Kristin's post, I considered my Grade 2 tumor. Given my medical training (I took a liberal-artsy biology class my freshman year of college), I figured that meant that I had Stage 2 breast cancer.

Here is where my acting like a five-year-old comes in. When I thought that Kristin had a lesser-stage cancer than I did, I completely freaked out. Like, *completely*.

Of course, I didn't want Kristin's cancer to be Stage 2 like mine was, but I had never thought through what it would feel like to have it worse than the person whose path I felt like I was following. *Did this mean that our paths would diverge? Did this mean that she would be fine and I wouldn't? That her kids would have a mother and mine wouldn't?*

I couldn't control anything, including my tears.

My mom happened to call as I sat at my computer bawling my eyes out and trying to be quiet so as to not disturb Brian. I whisper-wailed to my mother in incomplete sentences. "She's getting Adriamycin (*gasp, gasp*). And I'm not. But (*blow nose*) Stage 2…and I…and I should get what she has (*cry*)." Despite that I made no sense, my mother (and Brian who had joined me by that point) understood.

Once I collected myself enough to speak coherently, I explained that maybe I should go with option three after all. "If Kristin's cancer is Stage 1 and mine is Stage 2, I should at least get what she had. Maybe Dr. Denver didn't tell me the stage because he knew I wouldn't be able to handle it." I don't remember anything else I said that night as my boogers and tears fell all over the phone and my keyboard. I just remember being so confused and so, *so* scared.

* * *

A few months after that awful night, I worked up the courage to ask Dr. Denver's physician's assistant, Sydney, about the stage of my cancer. I prefaced the question by telling her that I did *not* want her to tell me the actual stage, but that I just wanted her to explain why they never made it a point to give me that information.

Sydney explained that speaking about the stages of breast cancer is simply not very useful anymore. She explained that they know so much more about the different types of the disease that the old-fashioned stage identifiers were barely relevant. I found comfort in the fact that the experts' knowledge had outpaced the language used by the general public.

At the time this book went to print, I still had not verified the stage of my cancer. Maybe one day I will want to know. But for now I'm fine without it, thank you very much.

In the end, I've learned that vulnerable people need to be very careful when making comparisons. On one hand, survivor stories still give me my most-powerful doses of hope and inspiration. But there is another very sharp edge to that sword.

Alone Time

Two weeks after my surgery, I felt good. My drains were out and I had taken a shower. After 10 days, that first shower was unsurprisingly refreshing. But it was also somewhat of a disappointment.

What I had anticipated to be a physically and emotionally cleansing experience was instead an odd realization that I couldn't feel anything when the water hit my chest. The numbness on the outside and the lingering pain on the inside created a strange contrast that made the expected simplicity of my "first shower" quite unnerving (no pun intended). Luckily, I didn't have time to freak out because it was a Saturday and we were late for Teddy's soccer practice. So I just shampooed, soaped up, and reminded myself that I would get used to the feeling of not feeling.

Another unexpected issue surfaced the Monday after that first shower—everyone who had kept me company for the two weeks after my surgery went back to work. Except me, of course.

* * *

I held a full-time job my whole adult life, and even in college I worked around 30 hours a week. For three of the five years that I taught high-school social studies, I attended law school in the evenings and the combination often amounted to 16-hour work days. When I graduated from law school, my job at "the Firm" cost me at least 50 hours a week plus another 10 commuting. To say that I kept myself busy with work is an understatement, and for the most part, that wasn't a bad thing.

Then it came time for me to be alone without any tasks at hand. At that point, I felt lost.

Of course, there also were logistics that concerned me about everyone going back to work, but I knew that day by day, we would figure those out. Annabel was only 20 months old and she still slept in a crib. Dr. Lee gave me strict instructions not to lift anything over 10 pounds for six weeks after my surgery, and Annabel weighed at least double that. Since Brian left for work before the kids woke up, I had always been in charge of making breakfast, packing lunches, getting the kids dressed, buckling them into the car, and dropping them off at school—all of which had to be accomplished before my commuter train pulled into the station.

That routine sounds far too simple when I summarize it in one sentence, but anyone who has been there knows that it's a flat-out miracle when it's accomplished each morning. My favorite part was tackling my kids to the carpet, a move I had perfected in an effort to put on (or put *back* on) some article of clothing. Ten days after surgery, however, I couldn't lift Annabel out of her crib, into her high-chair, or into her car seat—and I most certainly couldn't tackle anyone.

So we did what most people would do—we called on our village to help us (literally) raise our children. Friends and family members came over in the morning to get Annabel out of her crib and into her car seat so that I could drive the kids to school. Teddy even helped give his little sister a boost when she needed it, and admittedly, I cheated a bit here and there. Somehow, we made it work.

Logistics are one thing; they can be figured out, like a puzzle. However, the emotions that swelled inside about moving from *surgery phase* to *prepping-for-chemo phase* were a lot more intense, and far too complex to be treated like a puzzle.

I realized early on that my fear about this transition had a lot to do with my fear of being alone. Sure, I still had appointments a few times a week, but they were not part of my daily routine like they had been for the few months before. This meant I was going to be by myself. Not a lot, but definitely more than I ever had been before. No work, no kids, no noise, no duties, and nothing to distract my overactive brain. For me, that reality felt so awfully overwhelming.

It was the very thought of solitude that prompted me to begin taking the anti-anxiety medication that my doctor had given me weeks prior. Despite her assurance that many people take this type of medication while in cancer treatment, I had refused. I hated pills. I didn't want to allow a foreign substance to toy with my emotions, even if it was in an effort to straighten them out. I wanted to be me, and if that meant being all screwy in the head, then so be it.

Gradually, however, I changed. Maybe it was the realization that I was going to need some serious drugs simply to survive, so I might as well also take the milder ones to calm my nerves. Regardless, a few days before my first week alone, I took the first half-pill.

Mr. Badoian had a quote in his room that I will never forgot:

You are who you are when no one is watching.

A few weeks after my double mastectomy, I knew who I was when people were watching. But when no one was watching, then how did I feel? When my job didn't need me, was I still useful? When nothing had to be done, what would I do? I knew one thing, for sure. I would write.

Inflation

I will never forget the first time that I looked in a mirror at my reconstructed chest. I was alone in the bedroom, about 10 days after my surgery. It was dark outside and I was rebandaging myself for the night when suddenly, I was curious enough to take off my shirt, surgical bra, and gauze and face the mirror from across the room.

Given the distance between me and my pale reflection, I couldn't see the long, raw scars that sat atop the ridge of stitched-together skin. I could, however, see the shape of my new breasts. And that shape was remarkable. Terrifying, shocking, unbelievable, and wonderfully *remarkable*.

In a crazy way, I never felt so proud of my own body. That pride had nothing to do with the shape of my fake boobs, because those were just little pockets full of saline. Rather, that pride had everything to do with my realization that I had come so far since my left boob was squished into the mammogram machine. I had come so far since the radiologist handed me the phone number for the new cancer-patient line. I had done many things that I had been so afraid to do.

After my diagnosis, I hated the saying, "What doesn't kill you makes you stronger." I worried that cancer would kill me before I had the chance to become stronger. But as terribly clichéd as it sounds, facing my reconstructed chest in the mirror really did make me feel stronger.

A few days after I first saw my new chest in the mirror, I visited Dr. Lee so she could inflate the tissue expanders with more saline. Driving into the hospital with my mom, I wondered how they would get the additional saline into the thick pockets that had been sewn into my chest.

I found the following items on the countertop when I entered the exam room:

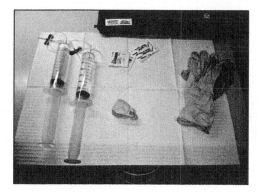

Hmm, I thought. *This should be interesting.*

After examining the incisions and telling me that the left one wasn't healing as nicely as she would have liked, Dr. Lee took a blue tool from the counter (the middle object in the above photo) and began to run it across the top of my right breast. A magnet in the middle of the tool swung back and forth. When my surgeon reached a particular point, almost in the center, the magnet hung perfectly straight. Dr. Lee had found the "port" of the tissue expander. This was the entry point.

Next Dr. Lee took the oversized syringe and stuck the thick needle into the port. That was it—eerily similar to a hand-held pump used to inflate a basketball. The large needle didn't hurt since it entered where my nerves no longer existed, but it certainly felt strange—kind of like a distant pain that my brain thought it would (or should) feel, but couldn't.

Dr. Lee pushed on the syringe as saline filled the pocket underneath my skin. I watched my breast slowly grow. It was by no means drastic, but before my very eyes it happened. After the same process on the left side, we were done. It was unbelievable.

Dr. Lee would inflate me a few more times over the next several months before I reached the C-cup that I was before pregnancy, breastfeeding, and cancer sucked the life out of my boobs. Each time, I found the process crude yet remarkable. And each time, I came to realize more and more that the human body is a truly extraordinary thing, even when it needs a little tweaking. Or better yet, *especially* when it needs a little tweaking.

My Allies

As Brian, my mom, and I sat in the exam room waiting for Dr. Denver on the morning we would make the final chemotherapy decision, I burst into tears. It was one of those holy-shit-I-can't-believe-I'm-here cries—heartfelt and ugly. But also fleeting, because when Dr. Denver entered the room, we got down to business.

I have already written about the fact that when the tumor board at Dana-Farber heard my case, they split between the least-aggressive and mildly-aggressive options. Only one oncologist favored the most-aggressive option three. With these results, and with what he knew about my personality, Dr. Denver felt very confident about option two.

Option two was an aggressive approach to meet and beat my type of cancer, but it didn't carry with it the cardiac risk of option one. Clinical data apparently showed that the most-aggressive drugs would not provide me any added benefit, and Dr. Denver didn't want to create any unnecessary risk.

* * *

A few days prior to my appointment with Dr. Denver, a friend forwarded me the script of a speech that literary critic and author William Deresiewicz had delivered to the first-year class at West Point in 2009. In his speech, Mr. Deresiewicz explained:

> I find for myself that my first thought is never my best thought. My first thought is always someone else's; it's always what I've already heard about the subject. … It's only by concentrating, sticking to the question, being patient, letting all the parts of my mind come into play, that I arrive at an original idea. … I need time…to make mistakes and recognize them, to make false starts and correct them, to outlast my impulses, to defeat my desire to declare the job done and move on to the next thing.

As I pondered my chemo options one last time, I thought back to this part of the speech. *Had I been patient? Had I stuck to the question without prematurely moving on?* Despite my terrible habit of not taking the time to think in the way that Mr. Deresiewicz had encouraged the plebes to think, when it came to my chemo options, I believed that I had put in the necessary thought. Even if the protocol we chose ultimately didn't destroy the cancer, I would never look back with regret that I didn't take the time to think about it. I outlasted my initial impulse to choose the most aggressive option, and mulled over the advice of some of the best doctors in the world.

Option two it would be, and I had faith that it was the best one for me.

For the rest of the appointment, Dr. Denver mapped out the next few months. In one week, Dana-Farber would administer the first chemotherapy dose in a three-and-a-half-hour infusion—one hour of Taxotere, one hour of Cytoxan, and a loading dose of Herceptin for 90 minutes. Dr. Denver explained that the infusion nurses would monitor everything carefully on the first infusion, as most allergic reactions tend to happen immediately. Three weeks after that, I would receive my next infusion, and so on, for four rounds, although the Herceptin infusions would continue for one full year. It sounded like a solid plan, and I have always found comfort in plans.

The week that we decided on option two, I made a joke to my mom about chemo being poison. My mom stopped me and said that I couldn't ever think or speak of it that way.

"It's not poison, it's lifesaving chemicals," she said.

But I was someone who cured a headache by drinking water rather than taking aspirin. Admittedly, I *did* think of chemo as poison. In fact, there were indescribably awful nights when I lay awake thinking of the drugs that would soon destroy parts of me. I shook at the thought of toxic chemicals killing my hair, dulling my skin, and stealing my energy and my ability to fight even the weakest of germs.

My mom, however, gave me a new perspective: the reality that I needed a new perspective.

So I renamed the chemo drugs. They became my "Allies"—my little army that would enter my bloodstream and go to work on the enemy.

Detour: Some Thoughts on Truth

Teddy was four and Annabel was one when I was diagnosed with cancer. Since that time, the concept of *truth* had occupied my mind, particularly as Brian and I talked to Teddy, and less so to Annabel, about my cancer.

Teddy has always been impressively observant, and I knew that he recognized something was wrong on the day of my mammogram. After all, I had left for my train into Boston yet I was home just a few hours later. Teddy immediately asked why I wasn't at work. I told him I had been at a doctor's appointment and that I was so tired afterward that I decided to come home. It wasn't a lie.

Honestly, I don't even remember what else we first told Teddy about my cancer or when. I do remember, however, that a day or two after my diagnosis, the phone rang.

"Mommy, it's pwob-ab-wy the doc-tow," Teddy announced nonchalantly.

He was right—it was.

I answered the phone, numb with fear and yet utterly amazed that Teddy's world was still safe and secure—interrupted only by several phone calls from his mother's doctor.

When I think back to that unbearable time prior to my surgery, I realize that it was so difficult largely because there was so much unknown to us. We knew that I had cancer, we knew that my major organs were still functioning, and we knew that my chest X-ray "looked good." But we didn't know much else.

And so my reality became what my mind invented. Headaches were brain tumors. Nausea and weight loss were my body failing me.

When we noticed that Teddy was onto us, we started talking to him about it. I told him that I had a "weird thing" inside of me that the doctors had to take out.

"I'm not sick," I explained, "and the doctors are going to make sure that I don't get sick."

We explained that lots of people get surgery to fix parts of their bodies. We told him that some of the people he loved most—his grandfathers and grandmothers—all had surgeries at some point in their lives. Papa and Granddad had surgeries to make their knees better, and Teddy's friend's dad just had hip surgery. When I told Teddy that he and Annabel were both born from a surgery to my stomach, he wanted proof. I showed him my C-section scar and told him how amazing it was when the doctors took him out of my belly then sewed me back up. He didn't share in my enthusiasm for the C-section story, and I loved him for that. Because even at four, he could tell that my enthusiasm was fake (no Oscar for that performance).

Gradually, Brian and I were more honest with Teddy about what was going on. We admitted that I was no longer going to work while he was at school; instead, I was going to doctor appointments. There wasn't any use lying to him, as he already had asked me why I wasn't wearing my work clothes in the morning. Once again, he was surprisingly fine with the truth.

With all that we *did* tell Teddy in the first few weeks, we never used the word *cancer*. We knew too well his amazing ability to make associations. We could see it all play out—on the TV or on the playground, he would overhear that someone died of cancer. He would remember that I had cancer, and he would begin to wonder if I was going to die. It wouldn't be good, for him or for us, so we hid that part of the truth from him.

When Brian and I met with Dr. Grace a week or so before my surgery, she told us that in her psychology practice, she was particularly interested in helping parents speak with their children about illness. After she listened to us describe Teddy, she told us it would probably be best to gently introduce him to the word *cancer*.

A few days later, on the way to school, the topic of my surgery came up and I repeated to Teddy what I told him before. "The doctors are going to take this little cancer out of my boob," I explained, terrified to say the word out loud to him. I was surprised when he didn't ask any more questions, and relieved that he didn't seem worried. We moved on.

* * *

Even at one year old, Annabel often asked me if I was going to the "doc-tah" that day.

"Yes, baby girl, I am. So that I can stay healthy just for you," I told her many times. (I told her a similar thing when she was two, and, after I swallowed my Tamoxifen pill, she asked if she could have some of my bwest can-sew medicine when she got owd-o.)

I'm proud that *cancer*, *doctors*, and *medicine* are not sad or scary words in our house. They're simply reality—nothing more and nothing less.

One day Teddy and Annabel will know the truth about my breast cancer. They will know that at 32 years old, Brian and I were scared out of our minds; that we cried behind closed doors, mostly because of how much we loved them and each other. They will know that we struggled with how much truth was too much, and how much wasn't enough. And they will know that even though we could never find the perfect dosage of truth that they (or we) could handle, we most certainly loved them enough to think a hell of a lot about it.

Part Four

Chemotherapy

You gain strength, courage, and confidence
by every experience in which you really stop
to look fear in the face. You must do the
thing you think you cannot do.

Eleanor Roosevelt
(activist)

Allied Victory

Dr. Denver prescribed me steroids for the day before, the day of, and the day after each chemotherapy infusion. On the day before my first treatment, I took the Dexamethasone as instructed and started to drink water by the gallon. My medical team had told me that water would help wash the toxins out of my body, and it would also make it easier to find a vein for my IV. (I could have had a "port" implanted and connected to a large vein in my chest but I preferred to receive the chemo through an IV in my hand or arm.)

Before I could start the chemo, I needed sign-off from my plastic surgeon. When Dr. Lee examined the scar on my left breast, however, she half-smiled and half-winced. I knew that wasn't a good thing. I was well aware that the scar didn't look good—it was raw, red, and not even close to being healed yet. Dr. Lee asked when I was scheduled to begin chemo.

"Tomorrow morning," I answered cautiously.

She reexamined the scar, as if trying to find a hidden piece of evidence that could convince her I was ready.

Dr. Lee found no such thing. And so she explained that we had to delay the chemo at least one week.

I was crushed. *How could we possibly delay the day that I had been anticipating for weeks? What would I do in the meantime? Sit around and wait? I hated* waiting. I wanted to take action...*immediate* action.

Dr. Lee explained that she saw necrosis on my left breast. Essentially, it was dead tissue and that wasn't a good thing. Necrosis wasn't particularly dangerous either, but the chemotherapy would make it difficult, if not impossible, for a wound like mine to heal. We had to give my body some time to do what it needed to do. If we didn't, we risked infection and that could have made things very complicated.

On the way home, I spoke with my oncology team. Sydney explained that this sort of a delay was normal and it was nothing to worry about. She instructed me to stop taking the steroids. I did, and out of useless protest, I stopped drinking water too.

Patience does not come naturally to me, but I looked around for perspective and soon found peace with the week-long delay. Even with this minor setback, I knew how lucky I was. I had faith that in a week's time, Dr. Lee would clear me to begin my chemotherapy.

For the next week, I tried to be careful. With a four-year-old and a one-year-old, however, that wasn't easy.

When the weekend rolled around, we took the kids to Edaville Railroad, a small but locally legendary amusement park that Brian and I both enjoyed as children.

At the park, I tried not to lift the kids or do anything that could aggravate my scar. But when Annabel and Teddy both wanted to go on the two-seater flying-elephant ride, there was no way I was going to force either one of them to sit it out. So I boosted Annabel up onto Dumbo and climbed in myself. As we circled and adjusted our height, Annabel smiled gleefully. I thought about how adorable she was, and about how I may have just opened the scar.

I was disappointed in myself when I arrived at Dr. Lee's office two days later. I knew the scar still didn't look good. In fact, the night prior when I saw blood on the gauze, my heart sank and I regretted the flying elephants.

Much to my surprise, however, the bloody scar was actually a good thing. Dr. Lee explained that she saw live tissue, and that was precisely what I needed for the green light. When she cleared me to begin chemo the next day, I cried through my smile. I was so relieved that it was finally time.

On the way home, I swallowed the Dexamethasone pills. The steroid kicked in almost immediately, and that stuff is *strong*. No joke—at three in the morning prior to my first infusion, I felt like I could have run a marathon. Eventually I caved, followed Sydney's suggestion, and took an Ativan so that I could catch at least a few hours of sleep.

* * *

Driving into Dana-Farber the next morning, I wasn't scared. Okay, maybe deep down I was a little bit scared, but I convinced myself that it would be better for everyone if I held it together. Plus, I was still so relieved to have been given the green light to begin treatment and I was so pumped up on steroids that I felt ready to conquer the world.

Brian held my left hand as the nurse inserted the intravenous needle into my right arm. The nurse explained that she couldn't numb the area, despite the size of the needle, because pain at the IV site would be the first indication that my body was responding badly to the drugs.

Now fitted with the entry gate for my Allies, we moved upstairs to the breast oncology floor. As we waited in line to check in, I noticed two young women behind us. For some reason, I had a gut instinct that one of those two women was Maggie, a fellow Bowdoin graduate that a mutual friend had introduced me to over email a few months prior.

Despite the fact that Sara had exchanged our contact information, Maggie and I had never connected, probably because I was too frightened to speak to anyone with a story so similar to mine. I had never seen Maggie's face—not even in a photograph—but still, I had a feeling that she was standing behind me.

My family and I sat down to wait for our appointment with Dr. Denver. After the young women behind us checked in for their appointment, they sat nearby. Once they left for the infusion suite, I told my mom that I thought one of the girls was the woman Sara had told me about months before—Maggie.

My mom looked surprised, and told me she heard the name *Maggie* while they were sitting there.

"No way," I responded as chills ran down my spine. "It couldn't be."

I texted Sara and asked her what Maggie looked like.

Yes, this woman looked like that.

Sara texted Maggie to ask if she was at Dana-Farber that day. She was.

Through our triangle of text messages, Sara told me the number of the infusion space where Maggie had gone for her treatment. Sara also told me that Maggie wanted me to come visit.

I didn't want to wander back to that space just yet, so I waited. When it was time for me to go back to the infusion suite to be weighed and prepped, the nurse told me that Maggie had asked for me to swing by her room.

"You'll be taking her chair when she's done," the nurse told me.

Unreal, I thought, and may have even whispered it out loud.

It turned out that Maggie and I faced the same aggressive type of breast cancer. We had similar chemo regimens, but not identical. And even though Maggie was four years younger than I was, she was about eight months ahead of me in her treatment. That meant that when I met Maggie in October 2012, she was in the Herceptin-only phase of her treatment—a 30-minute infusion every three weeks of the antibody that disables the deadly HER2 protein.

In the first few minutes of our meeting, I felt like I had known Maggie for years. We talked about our cancer and our treatment, but we didn't dwell on either one. We also talked about the nurse practitioner exam she would take the following week (she passed!). We talked about my kids, we joked about the craziness we had been through, and Maggie told me she would bring me all of the headscarves she used to wear when she was bald. When we realized that we were on the same three-week infusion cycle, we were elated. This wouldn't be the only time Maggie and I would bump into each other on Yawkey 9, and we made a date to get together on our next two treatment days—Halloween and the day before Thanksgiving.

When Maggie's infusion was complete, I watched the nurse unhook her Allies. Like I thought years ago about Sara, I thought to myself, *I need to become friends with this girl.*

After the nurses cleaned the room, I took Maggie's chair to receive my first dose of chemotherapy.

I don't think that Maggie could ever know what seeing her in that infusion chair did for me that day. She is so modest that she would say she did nothing. But that could not be further from the truth. Maggie was my guiding light that day, and she continued to be as I moved through my treatment.

I have seen firsthand that strength and positivity are contagious. Maggie had put so much good karma into her infusion chair that anyone who occupied it next would have benefitted. I was blessed to have been that person, and I can only hope that I left the same good karma for whomever came after me.

* * *

Nine hours after we had arrived at Dana-Farber, my family and I left Boston feeling pride and relief at the huge step we had taken.

Round one. Complete.

I arrived home to normalcy—splashy baths and naked children giggling down the hallway, snack requests, and reluctant bedtimes. Exhausted, yet simultaneously wired (those pesky steroids again), I realized that not only had I survived the day, but I had lived it too.

Goin' Bald

The day after my first treatment, I felt fine and spent my steroid-induced spurts of excessive energy on good, simple things—a walk with a friend I had known since we were seven, some eating, cleaning, and writing. It was an uneventful day, and when it comes to cancer treatment, that was a very good thing.

The next day I felt fine too. My aunt Helen and cousin Kirsten came to visit from New Jersey. We shopped and had lunch together, something that none of us are ever able to do during a typical work week. But this wasn't a typical work week, and I knew that Helen and Kirsten hadn't come to Boston just to shop and have lunch. They had come to be with me when

I got my head shaved, an appointment I had scheduled for the day after.

* * *

It had come as news to me that not all chemotherapy medications cause hair loss. When I learned that, I wondered if the Taxotere or Cytoxan would make me bald. As soon as Dr. Denver told me that they would, I knew that I wanted to take matters into my own hands, or at least, pretend to. It was a control thing (obviously), but it was also practical—I didn't want clumps of my hair to shed all over the place.

Over the 25 years of growing up in my hometown, I passed the building next to the public library countless times without taking notice of it. I don't remember when the salon opened on the first floor of that building, probably because I never quite fancied myself posh enough for a salon. Nevertheless, when my friend told me about the owner, Monique, and what she did for people like me, I knew I had found just what I needed.

Above the salon, Monique had created a special space for people who would shave their heads or be fitted for a wig. The space was modest, private, clean, and full of natural light. The high ceilings and large rooms made it comfortable, despite the six of us who had arrived there together that October day. And the space felt safe, if not the reason we had gathered there.

My Cousin Kirsten

Without talking about it directly, my parents taught me at a young age that jealousy is a complete waste of time. For the most part, I have lived by their subtle advice. Since I was a little girl, however, there was always one exception—I was painfully jealous of my friends who had an older sister.

I'm the oldest child in my family, and for so many reasons, I love that role. But often, especially when I was young and awkward, I longed for an older sister. Not just any older sister, either. I had the one I wanted all picked out. She happened to be my cousin, Kirsten.

As a kid, I felt like I was in the presence of a celebrity when I was around Kirsten. At first I would get nervous because I was so excited to see her and I didn't want my excitement to be too obvious. The nervousness would quickly give way to awe and enjoyment as I spent time with my only older female cousin on my mom's side.

Kirsten lives in New Jersey, so growing up we would see each other about three or four times a year, with longer stretches in the summer and around holidays. During those times, my maternal aunts, uncles, and cousins would gather at my grandparents' house in Long Island or at my aunt and uncle's house in New Jersey. Though I would be excited to see everyone there, when I walked through the door, my first question was always, "Where's Kirsten?"

Kirsten and I differ in many ways, but we also have a lot in common. The most obvious similarity is our precious connection to our mothers. Our fathers and husbands could describe it best, but the truth is we both admire, adore, and respect our moms in a very similar I-would-never-live-more-than-a-few-miles-away-from-her type of way.

* * *

Growing up, I was a tom boy (or whatever the politically correct term is now). In middle school, I fell in love with the sport of basketball and for a few years I ate, slept, and dreamt about little else. I collected basketball trading cards and played in my driveway any chance I got. On the most exciting days of the year, my dad took me to the sacred Bawston Gahden to watch the best players in the world play. I loved our pre-game dinners at the Four's—turkey clubs and onion rings gobbled up in anticipation of the fun ahead.

The only thing I enjoyed more than watching basketball was playing it. I played in any pick-up game I could find, which usually included all boys. When I got to high school, the JV boys coach even let me practice with his team once my girls varsity practice was over because he knew I wasn't ready to leave the gym.

When basketball led me to my best friend, I knew I loved the sport even more, and Brianne and I enjoyed four years of playing high-school basketball together. I never gave up on gymnastics, and perhaps that sport counterbalanced my tomboy-ness, but only slightly, because with my black sneakers and long mesh shorts, even a tiara couldn't have negated it.

I experienced a dreadfully awkward preteen phase during my middle-school years, and despite that others did too, I felt like I was the only one. I often thought I was ugly, but I had no desire to do much to change that. I loved school and sports and my family, and I found comfort and confidence in those things.

Meanwhile, I *loved* being around Kirsten. When I visited her house, I would sit on her bed, surrounded by all of her wonderfully foreign *girl* stuff. She had countless scrunchies and headbands, every color of Champion sweatshirt manufactured (with socks to match), dangly jewelry, and lotions that smelled nice. She had boxes of make-up and while she knew just the right shades for different complexions, I didn't even know which part of my face to apply it to.

At Christmas time I loved seeing all of my cousins, but nothing felt complete until Kirsten arrived. She was the funny, popular, beautiful, and artistic one who took care of all of us. Although we were semicomfortable in our nerdy skin, we all felt cooler when Kirsten was around.

As we got older and our holiday traditions changed, we saw less of each other, and I missed my cousin terribly. Even when we were both busy shaping our early-adult lives, Kirsten would send an email or a card reminding me of how much she loved me. Every time I received one of those notes or packages, I would attempt to rein in my wish that we lived closer because that could only happen if our moms lived within a few miles of each other—and they didn't.

When life's grand events started appearing on the family calendar—graduations, bridal showers, bachelorette parties, weddings—it didn't matter to Kirsten that she had to travel long distances to attend them. I still hung on her every word and marveled at every fashion choice she made as I looked down in disappointment at my own.

Luckily, I have matured a bit. I'm no longer jealous of my friends with older sisters. I have been blessed with my own sister and brother and I wouldn't trade them for the world. Plus, I have an older cousin who made me feel beautiful and strong and confident, and who dropped everything to join me at my head-shave appointment the morning before my first chemo symptoms set in.

My Head Shave

The morning of my head shave, Paul, my father-in-law, drove the kids to school. I still wasn't supposed to lift either of them, although when I had to, I did.

After Paul boosted Teddy and Annabel into their car seats, I visited both sides of the back seat to give them each a kiss.

"Who's going to be balder than Da-ddy tonight?!" I joked to try to ease them into the reality of how I would look the next time they saw me.

"Mommyyyy!" Teddy and Annabel replied gleefully. With that, I knew I was ready.

We were ready.

* * *

When my small entourage and I arrived at the salon a few hours later, I became more nervous than I had anticipated. It wasn't so much the head-shave part that had me shaky, but the fact that this had turned into a bit of an event. I love events; I just don't like to be at the center of them.

When we entered the salon, a young woman wearing all black directed us up a big wooden staircase. Not a minute later, Kirsten started to unpack her bags.

For some context, Kirsten is slightly obsessed with Halloween. While I would rather purge my house of everything Halloween-related and buy it again the next year, Kirsten keeps *everything*. I doubt that she anticipated that those costumes, wigs, and boas would come in handy when her little cousin got cancer, but low and behold, they did.

On that beautiful October day, we tried on bright-colored wigs, posed as rock stars and as Dorothy from the Wizard of Oz, and acted decades younger than our ages. None of it had been planned, but it was just what we needed—a chance to enjoy the light side of life before we faced the heavy part.

When Monique finally invited me to sit down in the chair, we all got quiet. My family hugged me as if it were time for me to head out alone into the wild. I appreciated that they realized in that moment, despite all of the love that surrounded me, that I was alone in a way. We all were.

I sat down, facing the mirror. My family sat nearby in chairs of varying heights. Monique calmly explained what she was doing, then she focused on doing it.

Monique cut my hair shorter, with scissors, as I watched my reflection. *This isn't so bad,* I thought.

Five or 10 minutes later, Monique made the first cut with the buzzer. For the next minute, I struggled to breathe. I felt like I lost all control, like the disease was a villain destroying part of me and there was nothing I could do to stop it. My world spun for a few seconds, and I tried to force down the lump that had crept into my throat.

Then my mom did the most helpful thing she ever could have done at that moment—she burst into tears. I was surprised because it was the one and only time I ever saw my mom crack. She wailed a few times, "It should be me! It should be me!"

I couldn't see clearly through the tears that had welled up in my eyes, but I could make out that my Aunt Helen—my mom's oldest sister—held up my mom and tried to comfort her.

*   *   *

Most caregivers likely assume that they are helpful only if they don't break. I learned in Monique's hair salon that there are some significant exceptions to that rule. My mom crying at the sound of my hair being buzzed off happened to be one of them.

Because when my mother started to cry, I started to reason.

"It's only hair, mom," I assured her. "It will grow back." Tears fell onto my black apron as I repeated it a few more times, "It's only hair. It's okay." I wasn't saying this because I believed it, but because I wanted my mom to.

Lest you think I was strong or brave, let me assure you that I was not. I was just sucking wind from one moment to the next. I was sad, so very sad, that my mom had to see this. I didn't feel bold or beautiful or healthy in any way. I felt like a sick cancer patient who had lost a grip on everything.

Fortunately, those awful feelings passed, and they passed quickly. I caught my breath and repeated in my head, *It's only hair, It will grow back*, and *I was one step closer*. After that painful minute, I believed all of it again. I think my mom did too.

Monique was done about five minutes later. After she brushed the loose hair off of my neck, I leaned back and felt my scalp. At that very moment, my friend Jennifer snapped the photo that I chose for the cover of this book. I need not say anything more because the photo says it all—at that very moment, I felt wildly victorious.

We took some more silly photos after Monique taught me how to position my wig and care for it. When we were done, we packed up Kirsten's bags and walked back down the big wooden staircase.

I hadn't considered whether I would wear my wig when I stepped out into the big wide world as a bald woman but at the last minute, I decided not to. My gut reasoning was simple—I felt more like myself without the wig on.

On the short walk to the car, I felt as if I were strolling through town naked. At the same time however, it was wonderfully refreshing to feel the air on my scalp, and to know that another huge step was behind me.

My family and I went out to lunch after that. When my dad joined us at the table and saw me for the first time without any hair, his eyes got pink and watery. He struggled to look at me.

I knew it would be hard for my dad to see me that way and I had contemplated wearing the wig to lunch so that the obviousness of my illness would be less of a shock to him. I decided against it however, mostly because I knew my dad would adjust when forced to.

I was right. A minute later, my dad's eyes had cleared up and he could look at me without explicit fear or nervousness.

After some pizza and pasta, it was time to head home to see Brian and the kids.

Our arrival home happened too quickly to control, although I'm not sure I could have controlled it even if I had been able to slow down time.

Teddy was playing in the front yard with our neighbors when we pulled into the driveway. I kept my hat on when I got out of the car, but he clearly had anticipated that I would look different. He approached me deliberately—curious and cautious. When I lifted my hat, my four-year-old looked confused but not scared. He let out a hesitant little laugh at my new look. I let him rub my head while I acted out a giggle. I gave him a big hug. After no more than a minute, he went back to playing.

Annabel was a different story. She was just one-and-a-half at the time, and when I entered the house, she had absolutely no idea who I was. She started to cry. I tried to comfort her and she recognized my voice, but for a minute, that only made things worse. I imagined she was thinking something like, *Why do you sound like my mommy but you don't look like her?* I felt like a monster in my own house as she screamed in fright.

My little girl continued to cry, and I continued to talk her through it.

"Baby girl, remember I told you that I was going to get my hair cut? That's all that happened. Look, no hair!" I took her hand and let her pet the tiny stubbles. She immediately stopped crying when it clicked that I was still me.

"Mummy he-ew cut!" she exclaimed.

"Yes, I got a haircut!" And just like that, my littlest one made peace with the simple fact that I was bald.

* * *

For the next month or so, Annabel often would gleefully exclaim,

"Mummy he-ew cut! Mummy he-ew cut!" She would pull me down to her level so she could rub my bald head and I would tickle her in response. We would both laugh and what could have been a series of painful moments was a series of silly ones.

Although Teddy's initial reaction was more measured than Annabel's, his curiosity over my baldness was more lasting. Most of the time he couldn't care less, but a few times it was obvious that he was still processing all of it.

For example, one Saturday morning shortly after my head-shave appointment, Brian, Annabel, and I gathered on the sidelines to watch Teddy's "soccer practice" at the high-school field (with four-year-olds, that term requires quotes). When the session was over, we piled into the car— me in the passenger seat, Annabel in her car seat, and Teddy in his booster seat behind Brian.

Teddy is like Brian—he is not terribly talkative, but he's always thinking.

As we drove away from the soccer field, Teddy said something to me that I will never forget.

"Mommy, put your hat back on."

It wasn't so much a request as a calm, matter-of-fact command. His contemplative tone revealed that he had been thinking about it for a while.

What I felt in that moment brought me back to my elementary-school days when I was teased by an older boy because my cheeks always turned bright red. I felt small and hurt. Yet for my son (not for that fourth-grade bully), I also felt deep sympathy.

I know that I could have had a long talk with Teddy that day about how it's good to be different, about how we should focus on the inside not the outside—*blah blah blah*. But he was four and I was tired. So I just put my hat back on. I figured he was entitled to one soft command, mostly because I knew that he never meant to hurt me—much like I never meant to hurt him.

Symptoms

Prior to my first infusion, Dr. Denver sat down with me, Brian, and my mom to provide us with information about the drug regimen we had chosen for my chemotherapy. Like nervous students, we took turns scribbling down key points into the spiral notebook we brought to all of my appointments.

When it came time to explain the symptoms of Taxotere and Cytoxan, as well as their biotherapy partner, Herceptin, Dr. Denver clicked into information sheets on his computer and started to print them out.

As the paper slid out of the printer, I reminded Dr. Denver of my hypochondriacal tendencies. I told him that if I read those sheets of paper, I would feel each and every ailment listed, probably before the chemotherapy even entered my bloodstream. So Dr. Denver handed the sheets to Brian. Sure, I signed the forms to acknowledge that I understood potential consequences of the medication, but I didn't so much as glance at anything above the signature line.

*　*　*

While some people research endlessly after a cancer diagnosis, others hide from clinical information like it's more dangerous than the disease itself. I fell into the latter category. I have never researched anything about my cancer or chemotherapy, save how to spell medical terms so that they were correctly named in my blog. I did not, and still don't, want to know anything more than that.

At the same time, as I was experiencing symptoms, I found it very helpful to know that others experienced the same things. I didn't wish that sort of pain or discomfort on anyone, but I felt less scared and less alone knowing that others had felt what I did.

In hopes that someone reading this book could feel less scared or less alone by knowing that I experienced what he/she or his/her loved one is experiencing, I will outline my chemotherapy symptoms in this chapter. These are nothing more than my own experience and I don't intend to share them in any clinical context.

Bloating

After my first treatment, I felt like someone had inflated me, because basically, they had. I received six or seven bags of fluids through an IV that day, so it's no wonder I felt terribly bloated.

I did not, however, feel sick.

In fact, I didn't feel any other symptoms of the chemo until the third night after my infusion. That night, I woke up sometime after midnight feeling absolutely awful.

Nausea

Obviously I felt nauseated several times long before cancer, but the chemo nausea felt different. It was *heavier*—like it started deep inside the pit of my stomach and weighed things down from my neck to my hips, making everything in between feel queasy and uncomfortable. I never became nauseated to the point of vomiting, although Brian joked that if I had to puke, at least he wouldn't have to hold back my hair while I kneeled over the toilet.

That first night that the nausea reared its ugly head was a scary one. The fear was largely based on a lack of control, like it so often is. As I experienced foreign sensations, I felt like I had lost a grip on my own mind and body.

On one hand, it was terrifying to realize the strength of the medications I was forced to accept and to be reminded of the seriousness of the situation. On the other hand, there was something reassuring about actually *feeling* the impact of those drugs. Deep in the night when Brian and I were exhausted, shaken, and overwhelmed, I reminded him that all of the symptoms were proof that the medication was working. Because we had to believe that it was.

Fluid in My Feet

Over the next few weeks, I felt several strange symptoms that I had never felt before. When a new one set in, I would mention it to Brian so that he could consult the hidden sheets and confirm that what I was feeling was to be expected.

About one week after my first treatment, I was at a work event when I felt as if pockets of fluid had pooled at the bottom of my feet. It didn't hurt; it was just odd and uncomfortable. Brian claimed that this side effect was printed on the sheets, but I'm still not sure I believe him. Even now, over two years later, I'm still too chicken to check.

Mouth Discomfort

The awful discomfort I felt inside my mouth as a result of the chemo was one of the symptoms I hated most. One week after my first treatment, my mouth felt as if I had chewed metal-flavored gum after burning my tongue and gums on hot soup. Food tasted different, and some foods were particularly bad. Salad dressing was the worst, as anything with vinegar was completely unbearable. I quickly came to realize that the more bland the food, the better, so I stuck to things like bread and pasta. The mouth symptoms arrived about a week after each treatment and lasted seven to 10 days, leaving me a few days of respite before the next round.

Hemor-whats?

Perhaps the most painful of the symptoms I experienced was more of an indirect symptom.

When the nausea set in, I began to take an anti-nausea medication prescribed by my doctor. A lovely side effect of that medication was constipation, and a week or two later, it hurt so much to go to the bathroom, sit, or walk that I would tear up when I did those things. Unfortunately, they are not exactly actions I could avoid.

I'm not one to get embarrassed easily, but I didn't know how to admit that my ass hurt so much it was making me cry. Finally, I asked my P.A. about it. Thank goodness for Sydney, as I would never have gone to Dr. Denver with this problem.

After I decided that I would call Sydney to ask her about the (literal) pain in my ass, I had a long conversation with myself about how to describe the problem. I found myself laughing out loud in the shower one morning as I recalled one of Teddy's doctor appointments when he was two years old. Back then, Teddy was in a phase where he constantly itched himself…down there. When we met with his pediatrician, I told the doctor that Teddy was "always itching his balls." Brian looked at me, horrified. I had no idea why.

When we were walking to the car afterward, Brian told me that he couldn't believe that I used the word "balls" to the pediatrician.

"What else was I supposed to call them?" I asked. Brian gave me some clinical words, and we laughed the whole way home.

In my conversation with Sydney years after that trip to the pediatrician, I awkwardly used clinical terms that I would never use in real life ("rectum"?!). Sydney told me it sounded like I had hemorrhoids. Again, not uncommon.

I had heard of hemorrhoids, but until Sydney explained them (something about constipation and broken vessels), I had no idea what they were or that they hurt so much.

Sydney gave me some tips on how to quell the pain, and I immediately shuffled to the pharmacy to get the over-the-counter remedies. I also upped my water consumption and my stool-softener medication. A week or so later, I was a new person.

Nosebleeds

Although they were not physically painful, the nosebleeds I experienced during chemo were the most frightful of my day-to-day symptoms. I have never been good at dealing with blood and a few times in my life, I fainted at the sight of it. Since the chemo nosebleeds were thick, gushing, and long-lasting, I tried desperately to avoid them. For instance, I never blew my nose since that would initiate an immediate bleed.

By my second round of chemo, I knew that the nosebleeds were going to happen and there was nothing I could do to prevent them. I just had to have faith that they would eventually stop, and (thank goodness) they always did.

Weak Nails

The issues with my fingernails take the superlative as Longest-Lasting Symptom, as even over one year after my last chemo treatment, I still had issues with my nails.

This symptom didn't set in until about halfway through the drug protocol; at first, I didn't even associate it with the treatment. Every time I caught a fingernail on something, it would bend back as if it were close to falling off altogether. I'd screech in pain.

I later learned that nails get weak as the result of some chemotherapy medications. As my fingernails bent and broke, they provided a constant reminder that I was facing an ugly disease.

Hot Flashes and Menopause

I experienced moderate hot flashes throughout my treatment, although I didn't experience early menopause like Dr. Denver mentioned I could. My period disappeared during chemo, but it returned a few months after my last treatment.

Hair Loss

Between two and three weeks after my first chemo treatment, my hair started to fall out in large clumps. I knew the time was coming because for days, with the slightest pull, I could yank my hair straight out of my head and it didn't hurt in the slightest. It was as if the hairs were clinging to my head, just waiting to be pulled.

I was in the shower when the dramatic hair loss first occurred. Since I had had my head shaved, it was only stubble, but I cried anyway.

I yelled for Brian to pause the videogame he was playing with the kids and come upstairs. He saw my hair in my hands, and assured me that it would all be okay.

"I know it will," I told him, and he kissed me. But when he went back downstairs, I cried a few minutes more.

* * *

As I have explained before, it didn't bother me to be bald. Strangers only rarely stared. Mostly they just tried to sneak in as many glances as they could to try and figure out why I looked the way I did. Some people flashed me what Maggie had termed "the cancer smile." It was a mixture of *You poor thing* and *You go, girl!*

I learned early on that kids don't have cancer smiles. Kids just stare. And stare, and stare. The first time it happened, I was in Target by myself and I almost started to cry. I felt like a monster to the little girl who couldn't take her eyes off of me.

It didn't take me long to learn to enjoy the innocent stares of young children. I would smile and wave and if they were really puzzled, I would say something like, "Do you like my silly haircut?" They never answered, and by then their parents were usually horrified, so I would just stroll on.

I wore my wig once, a few months after losing my hair. We were going to a dinner with Brian's hockey team and I felt like mixing it up a bit. Brian and the kids were waiting for me in the car and when I hopped in with my wig on, they were all surprised and confused. Brian asked me why I was wearing it.

"I just felt like it," I answered.

"But it's not you," he said, with a tiny tinge of anger that sometimes creeps into his voice when he's caught off guard.

The kids didn't say anything, perhaps a bit too perplexed for words.

So I slid the wig off and left it on the floor of the front passenger seat while we ate dinner with 25 high-school hockey players who all pretended not to notice that I had no hair.

Shortly after the end of chemo (January 2013)

Two-and-a-half months after the end of chemo (mid-March 2013)

Five months after the end of chemo (June 2013)

One year after the end of chemo,
with a trim along the way (February 2014)

Mary

In August 2011, while my family and I were on vacation in Rhode Island, I got a work email that I fretted about, then decided to ignore. The email was blasted to associates like myself who worked with pro bono clients out of a health care clinic in a tough area of Boston. Our work was part of a program that connected medical and legal professionals in an effort to assist low-income patients.

The email explained that a potential client—a 45-year-old Vietnamese woman (Mary)—was dying of breast cancer and needed legal assistance. Mary's doctors gave her no more than six months to live.

My heart ached when I read the case summary. I felt spoiled—healthy and happy and vacationing by a pool. Several times I drafted an email agreeing to take the case, but I never sent it, mostly because I thought that I could never emotionally handle working with someone who was about to die.

A few days later, another associate, Liz, with whom I had worked on a different case, emailed me to ask if I would join her on Mary's case. Obviously Liz was stronger than I was. I fretted some more.

Then I said yes.

From August 2011 through July 2012, Liz and I worked tirelessly for Mary, her two teenage children, and the children's father. When I switched law firms, I continued to work with Liz and Mary to ensure that when Mary passed away, her children would not be left alone. We were relentless in our effort, ultimately reaching Senator John Kerry's office for some much-appreciated support. After hundreds of hours of work on a strategy that we were told by our mentor attorney would be "impossible," we succeeded.

Our client was overjoyed. Sick and exhausted, but overjoyed.

A few months before I was diagnosed, I had to complete a self-evaluation for my annual review at my law firm. I wrote about our success on Mary's case. I described it as my proudest accomplishment as a lawyer. Truly, it was.

When I was diagnosed, however, everything about my relationship with Mary and her family changed. I didn't want to talk to any of them, despite how much I cared about them. Somehow I got through a conversation just a few days after my diagnosis, but I still don't know how I did it. Because thinking about Mary, never mind speaking with her or her family, brought forth my deepest fears. And at the time, I couldn't begin to tackle those.

Liz, being the hero she is, powered on. She helped the family with some important remaining details. But to them, I fell off the face of the planet...

…Until a few months later, just around the time of my first treatment.

That week, I heard that Mary wasn't doing well. She was continuing her weekly chemo regimen at Dana-Farber. But years ago, her cancer spread to her lungs and her brain. We never talked about clinical details, but I knew the gravity of the situation.

When I heard that Mary was ill, I decided that I wanted to see her. Since I was on medical leave, I arranged to visit her while Teddy and Annabel were at school one October day.

On the morning of my visit, I went for an early walk. I thought about Mary as I sweat out toxins and fought off the nausea from the chemo I received six days earlier. I thought about how scared I was to face this tiny woman, and how sad I was to have to say goodbye.

A few hours later, I packed my car with goodies and headed into Boston.

Mary's house was much like I had imagined it would be—a multi-family that was in need of serious renovations. I smelled gas as I walked up the front steps and made a mental note to ask Mary about that.

The doorbell didn't work, and at first, I was nervous that I mixed up the time or the date of our meeting. Finally, Mary's husband came to the door and welcomed me inside. Two of her cousins who had never been to Boston were there as well.

Mary always wore her wig, but when she saw me wigless, she took hers off and laughed. She didn't put it back on until we left the house. I loved that.

Mary couldn't speak any English, and I couldn't speak any Vietnamese, so we usually communicated with a translator on speakerphone. We also smiled a lot, nodded, and usually once every meeting, cried together. That October day we spoke through Mary's cousins, who spoke excellent English.

From that small, clean apartment in Dorchester, we caught up on the last few months over some water and fresh grapes. We laughed, and like she often did when we sat next to each other, Mary held my hand.

I wasn't nervous or scared or sad as we joked about our matching bald heads and my fake boobs. Despite her nosebleeds, headaches, and extremely frail frame, Mary was so full of life that her energy was contagious.

An hour later, the family asked if I would join them for dim sum. I wasn't sure was dim sum really was, but of course I said "Yes!"

I moved the two car seats to my trunk, and after several group photos in front of my car (it was very important that my Toyota be in the picture), we all loaded in and were off to lunch.

When we arrived at the restaurant a few blocks away, we were immediately served a feast of countless bowls of foods I had never before seen or tasted. I wasn't opposed to trying new things, but my taste buds were already askew and the texture of much of the food made me want to be sick.

I tried to move the food around on my plate, but it was no use pretending. My hosts watched my every move and I could tell how offended they were going to be if I didn't eat. So I ate. And despite the terrible indigestion I experienced afterward, it was a truly lovely meal.

*   *   *

Since Mary didn't drive (or have the money for a car even if she did), she had no convenient way to show her cousins around certain parts of Boston. I had a few hours left before I needed to pick the kids up from school, so I asked if they would like me to drive them down the street to Castle Island so they could see one of my favorite spots in the city.

They accepted with great enthusiasm.

As we drove past the Boston Globe and Boston College High School, the Vietnamese conversation grew louder and more excited. Anything that said "Boston" on it was something special, and we had to stop and take pictures.

One of our stops, at Carson Beach in South Boston, allowed me and Mary a few minutes to talk alone. While her family got out to take photos on the cold and windy beach, Mary and I remained in the warm car together.

Mary tried to speak to me. When she couldn't find any English words, she pulled out a small notebook and wrote. I saved the piece of paper.

With an innocent smile, Mary explained that she was 33 when she learned she had breast cancer. Mary wanted to know my age.

"Thirty-two," I answered, and she wrote it down.

Then she explained on the little piece of paper that her daughter was four years, five months old, and her son was two years, five months old, when she was diagnosed. I nodded to show I understood. Then I crossed out the "2" to explain that Annabel was only one-and-a-half. We smiled and laughed. Not because it was funny, but because we felt a bond.

When Mary's family got back in the car, energized and warmed by tourist fever, Mary asked them something in Vietnamese.

Mary's cousin listened and then turned to me.

"She wants to know if your cancer is on the bone."

I explained that it was not.

"My doctors took out my cancer," I said slowly, with distinction between the words and hand gestures dramatic enough for a game of charades. Mary listened to the Vietnamese translation. Her smile grew and she held my hand tighter.

"Yes, gude!" she exclaimed, in English. Mary's cousins explained to me that Mary's tumor grew on her bone. It quickly moved into other bones, then into her lungs and her brain.

Through that explanation, Mary somehow kept smiling. Then she wanted to see more of Boston, so we drove on. It was even more windy and cold at Castle Island, so our walk was brief and my offer to buy everyone ice cream at a local landmark—Sully's—was kindly rejected. We took more pictures, which I will cherish forever.

Me and Mary at Castle Island – South Boston, October 2012

When I dropped everyone off back at Mary's home, the family spent 15 minutes explaining with great energy and alternating languages the contents of a grocery bag they had prepared for me. It was full of natural remedies for my cancer. I took each gift with both hands, as I have learned to do with my Vietnamese friends (to take with one hand is rude). Then I drove home.

On my ride back, I felt embarrassed that I had prepared for a day of goodbyes. Because the time with Mary hadn't been about that at all. Instead, we ate grapes and dim sum and watched the airplanes land over Boston Harbor. For the first time in all of our meetings, we didn't cry once. There was way too much to be happy about.

Nosebleeds

I will never forget the first time that Mary got a nosebleed at one of our meetings. It wasn't a heavy one and it stopped quickly, but the blood on the white tissue was as red as anything I had ever seen. Mary tried to hide it, but it was no use. She looked so sick to me in those few minutes—so vulnerable, frail, and helpless.

Ten days after my first treatment, I got my own first terrible nosebleed. Thank goodness, Teddy was visiting my parents at the time.

When Annabel saw the blood, she immediately went into the freezer and brought me Bumble Bee, our soft ice pack shaped like a bee that we use when the kids bump themselves.

"Mama boo boo," Annabel repeated over and over.

"I'm okay, baby girl, just a little boo boo on my nose." It was some of the best acting of my life because I was absolutely terrified. The blood gushed out, and then came what I thought for more than a second could have been part of my brain (yes, I'm joking, but what the hell was it?!).

Brian was scared too, and after consulting the trusty symptom sheets, he said we needed to page Dr. Denver if it didn't stop. When it was still gushing several minutes later, we used Dr. Denver's pager number for the first time. Even though it was a Sunday afternoon, I didn't care. I was too frightened to harbor any guilt.

Dr. Denver called back within a few minutes. He spent about 15 minutes on the phone with me, asking me dozens of questions. While we talked, the bleeding stopped.

Dr. Denver told me that everything would be fine. Still, considering the strength of the bleed and my answers to some of his questions ("Yes, my gums bleed too..."), he wanted me to come in the next morning to have my platelets checked. Dr. Denver wanted to be sure that my platelet count was high enough so that my blood would clot properly. He assured me again that it was likely fine, but he wasn't taking any chances.

My mom rearranged her workday and drove me to Dana-Farber first thing the next morning. Brian had to work, having already missed so much time early in the school year, but I knew if the results called for any follow-up, he would be there right away.

On the windy drive into the city, I felt sick with worry. I had something I wanted to tell my mom too, and while I never hesitate to talk to her, I was nervous about this.

Silence.

Deep breath.

"Mom, if I need a blood transfusion, do you think they could give me blood from someone I know?"

She needed a second to process this most random of questions.

"Yes, I'm sure we could figure that out."

"It's not that I think the blood is infected or anything," I explained, by this time crying. "It would just be so weird to have a stranger's blood in my body. I don't want...I can't..." I didn't know how to explain it any more than that.

Soon after the nurse drew my platelets in the lab, I was called into an exam room on the breast oncology floor. Sydney arrived with the results a few minutes later.

Before she even sat down, she told me that my platelet level was fine. I was so relieved. Sydney went on to explain some of the science behind platelets and chemotherapy, and by her tone, I started to think it was a preface to bad news.

I had to interrupt. "So is there a 'but' coming here?"

"No," she laughed, so I encouraged her to continue. But I was too distracted by my utter relief to listen anymore.

* * *

As the weeks went on and the heavy nosebleeds continued, I changed my mind about transfusions. Maybe it was because I started to accept that at some point I likely would need a blood or a platelet transfusion. Maybe it was because I started to appreciate the invaluable generosity of perfect strangers—people who took the time to donate platelets or blood for nothing in return. Or maybe it was because things would soon become so complicated with my chemotherapy that a transfusion seemed relatively simple.

Detour: Some Thoughts on My Yellow Bracelet

A few days after I was diagnosed, Brianne bought me the famous yellow LIVESTRONG™ bracelet. I loved that bracelet, not for its color or its symbolism in the public eye, but for the two words that were etched into it—Live Strong. Those words gave me strength, and I loved that my best friend knew me enough to know that they would.

From my cancer cocoon, I had stopped following the news. Still, I heard bits and pieces of the never-ending saga with Lance Armstrong and doping. A few weeks after my surgery, I heard that Armstrong had stepped down as Chairman of the LIVESTRONG Foundation and that Nike, whose logo appears alongside lots of LIVESTRONG gear, ended its relationship with him.

When I heard about Armstrong's ugly departure from LIVESTRONG, I thought that the yellow bracelet had too much messiness attached to it. Sure, Armstrong's cancer-survival story was still inspiring, but it was tainted and I wanted a bit of distance between myself and my $1 rubber bracelet. So I banished it to my jewelry box.

But right away, I missed it.

The next day, I read a *TIME* magazine article by Bill Saporito, a cancer survivor and journalist. In the October 17, 2012 article, Mr. Saporito wrote:

> Livestrong is about hope. And as anyone who has ever
> been given that terrible diagnosis knows, people who
> have cancer need to have hope. Desperately.

Desperately.

That word resonated with me.

When I put that bracelet on for the first time, it was at a point in my life when I *desperately* needed hope. It was at a time when I knew that my cancer was aggressive, but I didn't know how far it had spread; a time when I thought that I might be too sick to enjoy my kids' next few birthdays, and may not even live to see the ones after that. At the time, *desperately needing hope* was an understatement.

Many moments during those first five weeks, I just tried to breathe, eat, and stand up straight. Somehow, that yellow bracelet helped. Those two words *helped.*

Live.

Strong.

The words lead me to the mantra that I still repeat every day, especially in those moments when I feel completely overwhelmed by fear and uncertainty—*I am here now.*

Live. Strong.

They helped me 10 days after my first chemo treatment when I was hunched over the kitchen sink, praying for my nose to stop bleeding. In those moments, I wasn't thinking about Lance Armstrong. I wasn't thinking about any cycling titles or doping allegations. I was thinking about the fact that at that moment, I was very alive, flexing every hope muscle in my body to try and be strong.

After I read that *TIME* article, I went back upstairs and put the bracelet back on my wrist. Since then, I've thought a lot about it and decided the following...

Many of us wear symbols on our bodies, our clothes, our bags, wherever. We think we know what another person's symbol means but so often, we don't.

Does that pink ribbon mean that she's a survivor? Does it mean that she lost her mother to breast cancer? Does that green number 5 mean that kid thinks about Scott Herr and his family as much as I do? Does that colorful bumper sticker mean her child has autism? Does that yellow bracelet mean he is battling cancer? Most of the time, I have no idea.

As I fight the urge to boil down a symbol or a saying to something simple, I remind myself that in reality, each tells a long and complex story unique to the person who adorns it.

For instance, my yellow bracelet has nothing to do with Lance Armstrong. In fact, it's not even about cancer. For me, that yellow bracelet is about people who stand up in the face of adversity and decide that nothing is going to keep them down. Sometimes those people are athletes. But for me, most of the time, they're not.

For me, the bracelet I wear every day is about regular people who have done extraordinary things—people who may never win a title or an award, but who have made the world a better place.

Two weeks after my first infusion, I put my LIVESTRONG bracelet back on for people like Brendan Burke. I never had the pleasure of meeting Brendan, and Brendan did not have cancer. But years after his tragic death, Brendan continues to inspire me.

I met Brendan's older-sister Katie when we were in high school, and we've remained friends ever since. Katie sat with me for hours one August afternoon shortly after my diagnosis. For most of the time, we caught up about brainless, fun stuff. We also talked about Brendan and cancer and fear and pain.

I dare not even attempt to sum up Brendan's life here as there is no way I could do it justice. I will say, however, that Brendan lived strong, and after his passing, his legacy and remarkable family continue to do the same. Brendan left this world a better place in so many ways, including by being the first person to stand up in the hockey community and say that he was gay. Katie supported Brendan when he came out, just as she had done from the day he was born. Katie and her family continue to support the *You Can Play Project*, an organization dedicated to ensuring equality, respect, and safety for all athletes, without regard to sexual orientation.

I don't know how I would go on if I lost my brother, but Katie does so with grace and kindness. Katie lives strong and I wear my bracelet for her.

I also wear my bracelet for people I will never meet who took simple yet extraordinary actions. These people hid Jews during the Holocaust, dragged their comrades from battlefields, walked into a school in order to racially integrate it, and stood in line for days to vote in a new democracy. As random as these historical individuals may seem in a book by a cancer patient, they are not random to me. These people give me perspective that my struggle is by no means the only struggle in the world. They remind me that the simple things are often the most difficult.

I wear my bracelet for people like Gabby Giffords, who literally fought for her life when news stations had already announced her death and who encouraged her husband to follow his dreams back into space even though she was still recovering from a gunshot wound to the head. I thought about Giffords' story when Brian came to me a few months after my diagnosis and told me that he was not going to coach hockey that season. My husband loves coaching hockey, his players adore him, and even though it wasn't a space mission, I knew it was something he needed to do. So I told him it wasn't an option. He was going to coach. And he did.

It was really easy to get selfish in my cancer cocoon—to think that the universe revolved around my battle. When that happened (or more accurately, when that *happens*), my LIVESTRONG bracelet reminds me that the universe is much bigger than my individual fight. It reminds me of a young man who changed the lives of athletes and fans everywhere by saying that gay people can play too. It reminds me of people in history who brought about great change by standing up for what was right. It reminds me of people who fight for their lives in spite of the odds. These people lived strong and inspire me to try to do the same. They are why I wear my yellow bracelet.

My Second Treatment

My second chemo treatment was scheduled for Halloween. I took the steroids the day prior and by the wee hours of Halloween morning, I was so wired that I wrote a blog of endless blabbering. Those 3,000 words were not fueled by fear, because truthfully I wasn't scared. Those words (upon words upon words) were just a way to exert the excessive amounts of energy that the Dexamethasone churned up in me. Since the day ultimately took a dramatic turn, what I wrote that morning before the sun rose feels particularly poignant. Here is a portion of it:

Happy Halloweens
Excerpts of a blog
published October 31, 2012

The first Halloween I can remember I was probably about five or six, and I decided I wanted to be a ballerina. Thinking back, it was a funny choice of mine because I never did ballet or took to girly stuff. Several embarrassing family photos adorn my parents' house of later Halloweens with me dressed as a football player (I wore my dad's Boston College game shirt) or a washing machine (Rachel was the dryer).

On Halloween, my parents would get home early from work and we would carve pumpkins. Once the pumpkins were lit and the newspaper full of innards had been emptied into the trash, it was time for trick-or-treating.

On that ballerina-Halloween, my parents tried to convince me to put on a warm coat or pants over my leotard, tutu, and tights. Since a jacket would have ruined my costume, I refused. They tried again, but I was more stubborn than they were. Or better yet, my parents had a more effective technique—they let me go out without a jacket to figure it out for myself. So I did, and a few houses later I was begging for anything to keep me warm.

My dad had quietly stashed my coat in a red wagon that he used to wheel us around in, and costume or no costume, I put that thing on and zipped it up tight. Of course I was still cold and I'm sure my dad patiently dealt with my complaining—he was always so good like that.

As I got older though, and Halloween was no longer about my dad pulling us around in that red wagon, I wasn't such a fan. In middle school, I wished I could disappear for the night. I was too old to be a kid but too young not to be.

I started to love Halloween again when Teddy was two. By that time we were settled into our new neighborhood, which was perfect for every holiday. Brian volunteered to stay home and pass out candy while Rachel, Sean, and I took Teddy out for a trick-or-treating adventure.

I remember those nights so clearly, and loved every moment of them. Better yet, I loved *almost* every moment; I could have done without the minutes of physically forcing Teddy to wear his jacket. You would think I would have learned, especially because that kid is so hot-blooded. A few doors down, he was sweating and begging me to hold his coat.

Eventually, we joined a big group of neighbors and their kids. Rachel, Sean, and I laughed as Teddy tried (and failed) to keep up with the group. He was always the last one to the door, typically having tripped at some point along the way. We would help gather the candy that fell from his bag although I'm sure he left a little trail of chocolates and peanut-butter cups that we missed in the dark. Then we would stand back and watch him wait for his turn to fill his bag.

The first few times I watched my son stand there on a neighbor's stoop, I found it to be such a remarkable thing. My little guy had started to become independent, and it kind of melted my heart.

I have dropped my kids off at full-time day care since they were babies, so I'm not really one to get all emotional at the sight of my kids doing their own thing without me. Nevertheless, watching Teddy run ahead on Halloween was powerful. He didn't really want me...he wanted his friends.

At first I tried to make conversation as we walked between houses.

"What kind of candy did you get, buddy?"

But Teddy didn't know or care. He was trying to keep up with kids whose legs moved faster than his did. So I quit trying, and became the person who held the parts of his costume that he shed as he heated up. All the while, I enjoyed my son from a distance. And I loved him so much.

This year, Teddy decided to be a pirate. Since Annabel is going through a phase where she constantly wants to take her clothes off, we thought our best shot at her costume was whatever costume Teddy wore. So she will be a pirate too.

It's a neat thing watching our kids become more independent. Annabel won't even let us help her get dressed or put her shoes on anymore. "I can do it!" she yells, and then she flips on her jacket or puts her "snee-koes" on the wrong feet. I don't dare switch around her shoes or fix her jacket when it's upside down, because if she put them on that way, that's how she wants them. So I let her be. Just like my parents did with my tiny ballerina costume on a frigid Halloween night, I will wait for her to figure it out for herself.

A few days after my first chemo treatment, I spoke with my mom about what she thought of it.

"It went great, huh?"

She agreed that it had. I told her I wasn't scared, but asked her if she had been. She paused. "Well, I did have to watch my kid get chemotherapy." Good point. That couldn't have been easy.

I have said it several times, but I'll say it again for the record. A lot of the time, I think it's easier being the patient than being a loved-one of the patient. I can't imagine watching any family member or friend, or (*gulp and shudder*) one of my children, go through this. In fact, the most oddly comforting thought I have about my chemo is (knock on wood) that I'm not driving Teddy or Annabel into Boston for it. I know what it feels like when they stick me with the IV, when my Allies start to flow into my veins, and when the symptoms set in after that. I know I can bear all that but I don't know how I would handle watching someone I love do it.

Meanwhile, my loved ones need to do just that.

They are forced to sit and watch me keep going. I'm sure they feel like I do when I watch Teddy run full speed down the hill of a neighbor's yard after he collects his Halloween candy. I desperately want to be right by his side to hold his hand so he doesn't fall. Or I want him to be clad in full pads and a helmet. Every year I try to get him to be a hockey player for just this reason, but he chooses to be something that doesn't involve full padding. So I stand by, warn him if I see danger, and help him pick up his candy when he falls. Then I watch him run ahead again without me.

The Battle of Round Two

Having written half a book before the clock struck 5:30 AM on Halloween, I was feeling quite festive about the holiday. I put on an orange-striped sweater, black leggings, and the Halloween necklace Teddy made me. My mom, Brian, and I drove into Boston in good spirits. In all honesty, I was completely at peace with my second round of chemo.

About a week prior, when I told my mom how comfortable I felt with this stage of my treatment, she joked that she didn't want to let her guard down just yet. Good thinking on her part, because on Halloween day, we ended up needing some serious guards—and some guardian angels too.

* * *

After the nurses drew my blood and inserted my IV, we went back to the breast oncology floor of the hospital.

My appointment with Dr. Denver went very well. He told us that my counts looked excellent. He asked about my symptoms and offered advice on how I could deal with them. At the end of the appointment, I reminded Dr. Denver that it was time for him to tell me that he still thinks I will be cured. He smiled through his compulsory "Yes, I think you will be cured." I told him he was welcome to enter a note in the computer about that too.

It wasn't until noon that the Herceptin started to flow into my IV. It went fine, and unlike the first loading dose which lasted an hour and a half, this infusion (and all of the Herceptin infusions for a year after that one) took only 30 minutes.

When the alarm sounded that the Herceptin was done, my infusion nurse Kerry came in to start the Taxotere, the first of the two chemotherapy drugs I was scheduled to receive that day. Following strict safety protocol, after Kerry set up the bags of drugs and programmed the attached machine, another nurse double-checked that everything was prepared correctly.

I had heard that Dana-Farber had implemented these heightened protocols years ago after a terrible tragedy in which a patient received an incorrect and fatal dose of chemotherapy medication. My mom, Brian, and I all knew that tragic story, so we were always quiet while the second nurse checked the drugs.

Oddly enough, that second round was one of the only times we were *not* quiet during the safety check because we had got to talking to Kerry about our hometown. After the second nurse walked out, I thought *Gosh, I hope we didn't distract her.*

We learned that day that Kerry grew up in the same town that I did—Canton, Massachusetts. I could imagine the house she described as her childhood home, and we laughed about mutual friends we had and what a small world it is.

Then, just a few minutes into our lighthearted conversation, something happened.

In a split second I felt my whole chest tighten, like the medicine had lit a flame inside me. Then my throat closed and I tried to yell that I couldn't breathe. But I wasn't able to yell.

I keeled over and Brian rushed over to hold me up so I didn't fall out of the chair. I only remember the next half hour or so in bits and pieces although I know with the utmost clarity that it was the most terrifying half hour of my life.

My first thought was that the dosage had been wrong and that I was being poisoned to death. An allergic reaction never crossed my mind, because I (incorrectly) assumed that any allergic reaction to the medication would have happened on the first dose. I never considered that I had gone into anaphylactic shock, but low and behold, I had.

Much of what I will describe here is based on what Brian and my mom later told me, because at the time, I could do nothing more than simply try to breathe.

Within seconds, a team of about six doctors and nurses rushed to my infusion chair. Each one had a job, and apparently they didn't even need to speak to each other to know precisely what that job was.

I remember a man in blue scrubs and glasses standing above me. He positioned me back in the chair, although I remember that I kept falling forward. The back of my head hurt the next day, so perhaps he held me up by my head through some of the process. The man also insisted that I try to describe my symptoms, and for most of the time, I was able to wail them out.

"I can't breathe."

"My chest is tight."

"My face is going to explode."

"My arm hurts. My feet hurt."

"I can't breathe."

"I can't breathe."

"I think I'm going to die."

Then there were the words I remember saying the most. "Please help me. *Please.*"

And that is just what the team did.

They pumped me with massive doses of steroids, Benadryl, and who-knows-what-else.

When I was able to lift my head off my lap for the first time, I vaguely remember Brian and my mom's horrified gasps.

"Oh my God," they said in unison. My face had swelled like I never imagined it could. My eyes were almost swollen shut and my nose was as wide as my mouth on a regular day. Inside of me the same swelling had occurred, which is what caused my blood pressure to fall so low that Kerry wouldn't even tell me afterward what it had been. My airways also began to close, which was why I felt like I could barely breathe.

I remember Dr. Denver arriving a few minutes later. He asked questions of the team that was stabilizing me.

Still, I was just trying to breathe through the fire in my chest.

Kerry knelt down and looked me in the swollen eyes. "Do you know where you are?" she asked.

"Dana-Farber," I answered.

"What year is it?"

"Nineteen...No. Two thousand two. No, two thousand twelve," I answered. Sometimes I really do get confused about the year, so I didn't worry too much about that.

They told me afterward that I received plenty of oxygen through the entire episode, which meant no permanent damage was done. To my body and brain, anyway. My spirit still had a bit of healing to do.

As I started to come around, I remember asking Dr. Denver if this meant that I couldn't receive the drugs I needed to save me. Actually I think I may have asked him this several times, since the chaos of the reaction as well as the massive doses of drugs confused me terribly. Dr. Denver assured me that it did not mean any such thing.

"I've got lots of plans," he said.

Still somewhat delirious, I joked back, "Well, I've got lots of plans, too, so you better make sure your plans work." Nervous laughter followed from everyone else in the room.

I also asked Dr. Denver why this happened today, and not in my first treatment. He said that the first dose can act as a "primer" and the second round essentially reacts with the first. I didn't understand but clearly he did so that was enough for me.

* * *

In the few months prior to my allergic reaction, I dealt with a lot of fear, but it was all fear about dying in months or years. The fear I felt in the infusion suite on Halloween was a whole different fear—a fear that death was actually upon me. I never experienced anything like that, and I pray that I never have to again.

After I was stable and the oxygen was flowing peacefully into my nose, Kerry covered me with blankets and told me to try to rest. She explained that I would feel strange because the Benadryl would make me drowsy while the steroids made me restless. She was right. My mind and body couldn't decide if I was ready to sleep or to sprint.

Dr. Denver explained that he needed to make some calls to craft a new plan and that he would be back to talk. Brian left for a few minutes to make sure the kids were doing okay, and once we were alone, my mom and I sat in silence, trying to recover. We joked a bit too, but I think we were both still shaking even as we chuckled about the shock of the situation (no pun intended).

When Dr. Denver returned, he explained our next steps. He did not want to change my course of treatment because that would be too complicated. He explained that Dana-Farber had a department dedicated to allergies and that my next step was to meet with an allergist. He explained that it's very difficult to get a quick appointment with an allergist, but he also said that people in my situation are bumped to the top of the list.

Ultimately, Dr. Denver planned to have the allergy team "desensitize" me to the Taxotere and get that pesky Ally into me for my last three rounds of chemo. As part of the desensitization process, they would premedicate me with massive doses of steroids and antihistamines, then infuse me at a very slow pace. What should have been a one-hour Taxotere infusion would become a five- or six-hour infusion. Dr. Denver explained that these will be long days at Dana-Farber—around 12 hours. But I didn't care if it took weeks, so long as it worked.

I felt a strange sense of failure when I left Dana-Farber that day. Loaded up with lots of drugs—none of which were for the chemotherapy I had come for—I had never been so deeply disappointed.

I also couldn't help but notice the coincidence from earlier that day, when I wrote about how sometimes it's harder to be the loved one of the patient than to be the patient. I cannot even begin to imagine what that whole scene had been like for Brian and my mom.

Later that night, as the swelling in my face continued to subside, I joined my family at our neighborhood Halloween party and then for trick-or-treating. It was a beautiful night, and I cherished the fresh air like I never had before.

Teddy ran around with his friends, still at the back of the pack, but he tripped a lot less that year. Annabel gathered candy at the first few houses we visited, then spent the rest of the time walking on the side of the street gobbling it up. When we all returned home, Brianne, Seamus, Brian, and I helped Teddy organize his candy. Then Teddy and Annabel enjoyed hundreds of grams of sugar and went to bed.

After the kids fell asleep and we turned off the front lights, the day's events started to hit me. The plan we had to defeat my cancer seemed derailed. I felt lost.

I tried to convince myself that it was only a bump in the road; that a team of the world's-most-skilled professionals would find a way to get me the drugs that I needed. But it wasn't easy to process that I was deathly allergic to medications that were supposed to save my life.

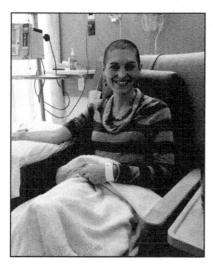

Beginning Herceptin at my second infusion

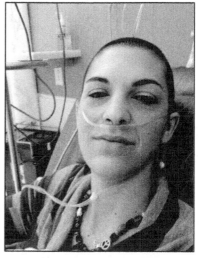

Stable after an anaphylactic reaction to Taxotere

Part Five

Bumps in the Road

I have always believed that hope is that stubborn thing inside us that insists, despite all the evidence to the contrary, that something better awaits us so long as we have the courage to keep reaching, to keep working, to keep fighting.

Barack Obama
(United States President)

Everyday Courage

I didn't know much about cancer treatment when I started chemo, but I knew enough to expect the road to be a bumpy one. I heard stories about delayed treatment because patients' bodies were too weak to receive the next round of drugs. After my nosebleed scare I learned that chemo could necessitate a blood or platelet transfusion. But I never anticipated a bump as big as an anaphylactic reaction to my medication. In fact, it felt less like a bump and more like a 50-foot brick wall.

Home alone the morning after my reaction, I forced myself to write about what had happened in the infusion suite. I hoped that writing about it would make me feel better. Unfortunately, it didn't.

My body was exhausted and sore—the exhaustion due to the powerful intravenous steroids wearing off, and the soreness a result of the massive swelling that occurred. As usual, however, the physical issues were negligible compared to those of the mental variety.

The night prior I had been in auto-drive. Anyone with two young kids on Halloween would have been. But in the days that followed, after I dropped the kids at school, reality started to set in; the reality that I was allergic to my chemotherapy—allergic to the very drugs that were supposed to save my life.

Initially, I was numb with frustration. I didn't want to cry or scream or eat. I didn't even want to write. What was the point? I had nothing to say.

Then I got mad. I wanted to scream from my rooftop, "What the fuuuuuck?" Then I got numb. And tired again.

Two days later, I had a follow-up appointment with my breast surgeon. My mom and I grabbed a quick lunch before the appointment. But we didn't chat like we usually do, and eating was hard.

We were deflated.

During our lunch, my friend Sara emailed me about the desensitization process. Sara is a nurse, and once I replied to her email, she called me. She told me that she often cares for patients in "desens" and she explained how successful the protocols can be in getting drugs into people who are allergic to them. For the first time in days I felt hope, and my mom did, too. Nurses and friends hold that great power, I guess.

Weeks later I learned that the process of desensitization to chemotherapy was developed by a physician named Dr. Maria Castells. Dr. Castells designed a protocol that slowly administers increasing doses of the drug in a way that allows patients' bodies to accept what they had previously rejected. It's risky, but it has proven to be successful.

As we sat in Dr. Nadia's waiting room that Friday, my cell phone rang and the much-anticipated *Blocked* appeared on the caller ID. I knew it was Dana-Farber. As I slid my finger over the screen to answer the call, I prayed that whoever was on the other end had an appointment with the allergist all lined up for me. I prayed there was a new plan.

No such luck.

Dr. Denver's nurse practitioner was calling to tell me they were still scheduling the appointments, and if I hadn't heard from the allergist by noon on Monday, I should call Dr. Denver. The nurse was kind and sympathetic about my situation, but I barely managed a friendly tone in return. I tried desperately to hide my disappointment at the idea of the weekend beginning without a plan of attack.

On Sunday morning, I woke up prepared to turn a corner. I had a relatively good night's rest, so I decided we were all going to church.

Excuse my French, but getting ready for church is always a complete shitshow. The proof of how much I enjoy that one hour of peace lies in how much frustration I endure to get us there.

After several temper tantrums, empty threats, and a few swear words, we were off to the "Church with the Yellow Door," as it's known to many people in my town. To us, it is the Unitarian Universalist church we joined a few years ago.

My Grandma was a dedicated UU, and I always loved joining her on random Sunday mornings during the summers that I lived with her. At first, the little things impressed me—the relaxed atmosphere, the rainbow flag hanging outside the front door, the members' charitable efforts. As I learned more, and especially when I became a parent, I grew increasingly fond of the church's message. I think it's best explained by the congregation's covenant that emphasizes things like love, truth, service, respect, freedom, and harmony. You know, all those things that Brian and I were screaming about as we threatened Teddy to get his ass in the car so we wouldn't be late.

That morning, I sat in the pew and read the cover of the week's Order of Service. I noticed the title of the day's sermon: "Cultivating Virtue #2: Courage." *How fitting. I sure could use a dose of courage this week.*

I read the quote in large print on the front of the pamphlet. It was by

Maya Angelou, one of my Grandma's (and my) most favorite authors and poets:

> Courage is the most important virtue, because without
> courage, you can't practice any other virtue consistently.
> You can practice any virtue erratically, but nothing
> consistently without courage.

I read it again and again. I liked the quote, but it didn't resonate with me like some quotes do, partly because I didn't understand it at first. *I could be patient without courage, couldn't I? I could be fearful but still kind, no?* I tried to sort out the quote in my head as the service began.

Many UU services include a time for joys and sorrows. During that time, people stand up and share personal news with the congregation. That day, I wasn't the only one for whom cancer weighed heavy on the heart. It seemed as if almost every person stood up to share a sorrow about the illness of a loved one. And almost every illness mentioned was cancer.

As I listened, I felt my chest tighten. I wondered if it was fear, anxiety, or the week's dose of Herceptin damaging my heart. Since learning I was in the small percentage of people who were allergic to chemotherapy, I started to think maybe I was also part of the group for whom Herceptin was toxic to the heart. I didn't like being so pessimistic, but statistics had not been all that kind to me in the past few months.

I felt for every person who stood up to share a sorrow, and for their loved ones who were suffering. Selfishly, as I tried to convince myself that my heart was okay, I also felt sorry for myself.

Frozen in the pew, I realized how much the week ahead absolutely terrified me. I didn't know when I would be back on track for treatment, and worse, I feared that what happened before could happen again. It was like I had written about before—the idea of fearing fear. I was overwhelmed by the thought of how scared I would be as I watched the Taxotere drip into my veins, waiting to discover if my body would reject it so violently again.

During the service, I also thought about a children's book that my mom recently had given to the kids (or maybe she had given it to me). Either way, the book was by Bernard Waber and it was titled "Courage." I read the book several times to the kids before my allergic reaction and already had several lines and illustrations that I loved. For instance, on page 22: "Courage is deciding to have your hair cut."

Mr. Waber wrote that there are "awesome kinds" of courage and "everyday kinds." In the upcoming week, I hoped to muster up the everyday kind of courage—the kind that would help me get out of bed in the morning before my next treatment, kiss my kids goodbye while they slept, and journey into Boston for a long and possibly complicated infusion. I hoped to find faith that, drip by drip into my IV, everything would be okay.

You can practice any virtue erratically, but nothing consistently without courage. It is so true. Because in the few days after my allergic reaction, when I felt no courage at all, it was hard to practice anything else. It was hard to have faith or hope. It was a struggle to be generous. And it was impossible to write.

Three days later, after we tucked the kids into bed, I found myself back at my computer, writing about courage in a blog that became the backbone of this chapter. As I wrote, I felt that somehow, in the next few days, I would find courage for Round 2-B of my chemo. If only because I had no other option.

I had not consistently shown courage in those days after Halloween. What I *had* done was realize that sometimes Plan A explodes into a heap of dark, scary shit. And that it takes an everyday kind of courage to develop and accept Plan B.

What I had learned is that sometimes, the everyday kind of courage is also the awesome kind. In fact, maybe they are the same thing after all.

Freaking Out

It took longer than expected to get an appointment with the allergist, and since no amount of Ativan was going to calm me, I didn't bother taking it. Once we finally scheduled the appointment, I had over one week to wait for it. That wait was not easy to accept. I worried that every day we delayed treatment was another day for the cancer to regroup. (I have since learned that is not necessarily true.)

While waiting, I tried to work, but it was nearly impossible to focus on anything long enough to be useful at my lawyer job. Work assignments that I used to complete in a few hours, I couldn't even accomplish in a few days. Eventually, I decided to accept the generous medical leave my employer had offered me, and stop working for my health care clients until my treatment was back on track.

In the meantime, my stomach burned with fiery anger and frustration; mere minutes later, I would then feel deflated and numb. Despite all that I told myself about courage, I often felt less courageous in one minute than I had felt the minute before. I was indescribably terrified and the only thing that could *really* help was a plan.

I started writing again, but most of it remained unfinished and unpublished. I figured readers would grow tired of repeated stories about my freakouts and analogies about how hard it was to wait.

Fortunately, my homemade mantra—*I am here now*—got me through many tough moments. I also found myself thinking more about hope and about optimism; not just about their importance, but about how complex the concepts now seemed.

As much as I tried to take it one day at a time, I couldn't help but think about the final verdict from the allergist—his or her decision as to whether or not I could continue with my chemotherapy protocol.

A part of me felt a deep sense of hope that the allergist would determine that I would be able to carry on, and that they could safely administer the drugs after that. But a bigger part of me knew that it may not be all that simple.

I have always considered myself an optimist, but cancer definitely put my optimism to the test. Cancer showed me how scary it can be to hope for something that is so deeply *wanted*. To take such a big risk. To be so vulnerable.

Before my surgery, I hadn't let myself take that risk—didn't even allow my brain to fully process the feeling of desperate hope that my cancer had not spread. I didn't allow myself pure optimism, at least not in the short run. I assumed that the cancer spread and I focused my optimism on the bigger picture—that no matter where the disease had gone, I could still beat it.

Before my allergist appointment, I found myself in a similar situation—I was cautious with my hope and my optimism. Balancing on a fine line at a time when I felt so terribly unbalanced.

The Allergy Verdict

My allergy appointment finally arrived. I (obviously) took anxiety medication that morning and thank goodness I did, because early in my string of meetings, a young physician explained the desensitization process to us as "one that seems to work even though we aren't really sure why."

Was this lady serious?

I smiled a fake smile, and suppressed my desire to shake her and scream, "Listen lady, just pretend that you know why it works because I'm scared shitless right now!"

This doctor and I weren't exactly clicking and I failed to comprehend several of the foreign clinical terms she was attempting to communicate. So I cut to the chase. I told her that I needed to receive Taxotere 10 days ago and I asked her what needed to happen during this appointment to get me back on track.

The doctor slightly improved her bored and apathetic state to explain that they would put a few drops of Taxol (Taxotere's cousin) under my skin to see if it caused my body to react. If it did, I could go forward with desensitization. I was a bit confused as I had assumed *not* having a reaction at this appointment would get me where I needed to be. Apparently however, a mild red rash under my skin would prove that I was allergic to the Taxol in a way that will allow a medical team to try it again. Finally, almost two weeks after my failed treatment, I had a clear goal.

A short time later, a nurse made three pricks on my arm and labeled each one with a pen—one histamine (H), one control (C), and one Taxol (T). Then we went to the waiting room to (obviously) wait.

Almost immediately, the H dot itched like hell. I didn't care. It was the T dot that I cared about. But nothing was happening there, and my heart sank as I watched it fail to change. *Damn it.*

I tried to stay positive. To flex my hope muscles.

Fifteen minutes later, the nurse called us back, and when the doctor looked at the T dot, he instructed the nurse to move up the arm to try for a reaction there. Same process. Same waiting. Same heartbreaking disappointment that the T dot did not turn red.

I dragged my broken heart back to the exam room, expecting the bad news that I could not continue with the Taxotere. This would require a shift in chemo protocol. I recalled Dr. Denver saying after my reaction that his definite preference was to keep me on the protocol we originally had chosen, although there were other options if necessary.

To my utter surprise, the allergist said he thought he saw enough of a reaction to warrant a positive result. I didn't see anything, and at first, I couldn't even celebrate because I didn't believe that what we needed to happen had in fact happened.

It was very anticlimactic.

I asked the doctor if he was sure, *really sure*, and he said he was.

Okay then.

Cleared to receive the chemo through the desensitization process, I next needed to secure an inpatient bed. Since I required one-on-one care, they would admit me to the ICU for the treatment.

I was awfully ambivalent about the ICU. On one hand, it sounded like a dreadfully scary place—a place where the sickest people went. For that very same reason, I figured it would be the safest place for me to receive the drugs that clearly had the power to kill me.

My family and I waited anxiously for the hospital to call and tell us that an ICU bed was available. A few hours later, my phone rang and my adrenaline pumped when I saw that *Blocked* was calling.

A bed was available. I should arrive at the hospital at 6 PM.

I never thought I would feel relief with the news that I could occupy a bed in the ICU but that night I did. Because finally, we had our plan.

Detour: Some Thoughts on Life Insurance

After Teddy was born, I told Brian that I wanted to buy life insurance. He didn't really respond, and I took that as a green light to pursue the idea. An insurance salesman named Gus had been hounding me for months and as a first step, I answered one of Gus's calls. Then I scheduled an appointment for him to come to the house to speak with us.

When Gus arrived, Brian wasn't in the mood to talk. It was the end of a long workday and we were trying to get Teddy to bed, so I admit, the circumstances were not ideal.

Brian answered the questions that were asked of him, but he wasn't happy about it. I forged ahead anyway, driven by the simple reality that my salary mattered a lot to our finances and if anything ever happened to me, my family would be financially screwed.

Brian and I got into a fight after Gus left. Eventually, I ended up feeling like a jerk. I thought Brian was irresponsible by not being as enthusiastic as I was about buying life insurance. I came to realize, however, that Brian was really struggling with the thought that comes with any conversation about life insurance—that it kicks in after life kicks out.

Of course, once I understood the real source of my husband's hesitation, I thought it was sweet. And I took it as another green light to keep going with the paperwork.

I never knew how much one's health and other demographic factors affect the cost of life insurance. The fact that I am a female made my rates lower than Brian's. Being nonsmokers did wonders for us too.

A few days after Gus's visit, a nurse came to the house to take our blood and urine samples, and ask lots of questions about our medical history. The insurance company even contacted our doctors. Ultimately I was placed in the healthiest possible bracket, and since then, money has been debited automatically from our account for our life-insurance policies.

* * *

In the weeks between my allergic reaction and my next attempt at chemotherapy, I had some dark thoughts, particularly about the reality that I would be at least two weeks behind my medication regimen.

The dark moments would appear at the most random of times. For example, once it hit me when I was cutting Annabel's toenails. (Her little nails curl under almost immediately after they grow out so I cut them every week to make sure that they don't become ingrown.)

One night as I was clipping her ticklish little toes, I couldn't help but think to myself: *If anything ever happened to me, would Brian know to cut her nails every week? Would there come a day when I would need to make a list for him of things like this, things I do that he may not know to do?* I thought the same thing as I put out the big plastic water bottles for the delivery guy to pick up and replace with full ones. Despite my compulsive organizational skills, I still forget to put those bottles out sometimes. I wondered to myself, *How many would stack up in the garage if I weren't around?*

Lest I mislead, let me be clear—my husband is amazing. On a regular day, he works his full-time job, picks Teddy and Annabel up from school, plays with them, makes them dinner, makes *me* dinner, and has the kids' bath going before I even get home from work. Whenever I try to do what he does, it's an embarrassing disaster. I know how blessed I am that I have to cite toenails and water bottles as the things that may not be accomplished in my absence. It's that very thought that sometimes brought me unparalleled peace.

Another source of peace was the life insurance that Gus sold us on that frustrating night two years before Annabel was born. Even after cancer, I didn't expect to use it. But I was so grateful that it was there.

Similarly, in the thick of my treatment, I found peace in the blog that I continued to write. Although I had started the blog more as a way to just keep breathing, it slowly evolved into so much more. It had become a way to communicate with my children. I wrote things about myself and about my memories that I wanted them to know when they grew up.

The blog was to me then what this book is to me now: a priceless source of comfort, a reluctant deference to the unanticipated, and a virtual life-insurance policy for the people I love.

Round Two, Take-Two

I was relieved, not only about getting the green light to receive Taxotere through desensitization, but also about securing a bed in the ICU. In fact, I was so relieved that when I arrived at the hospital that night, I hadn't even considered what I would find there or what it would feel like to walk past some of the hospital's sickest patients to the room I would occupy for a night or two.

When I climbed into my lumpy bed, I felt so sick and so healthy at the same time. There I was sleeping in the ICU at one of the best academic medical centers in the world while I was healthy enough to exercise earlier that day. The juxtaposition made me think that the procedure ahead of me was riskier than everyone was letting on.

Soon after, it was the usual business—vital signs, pills in little cups, heart tests, doctor and nurse visits to discuss protocols and procedures, and the insertion of my IVs (there would be two—one for the drugs and one for lifesaving liquids if anaphylaxis were to occur again).

The infusion would start early the next morning, so Brian slept in a recliner that they rolled in for him. My mom slept in a hotel room across the street.

I barely slept at all, mostly because the pre-chemo steroids (with dosages even higher than before) felt insanely powerful. I was ravenously hungry and full of an uneasy energy that I couldn't seem to quell. Since I couldn't cope with seeing my ICU neighbors, I knew that leaving my room wasn't an option. So I escaped in the only way I knew how—I wrote.

That night, I wrote a long and circuitous blog about how my diagnosis had evoked a strong anger in me toward a particular group of people— people who smoked. At the time, it seemed like a very reasonable reaction—I took care of myself, never smoked, and still got cancer (okay, I tried to take a puff once as a teenager and roundly failed). Others neglected their health, smoked by the carton, and still evaded the awful disease. I conveyed my anger amid several random diversions, and perhaps because I was stuck in the ICU, I felt entitled to do that. In retrospect, nothing is as simple as I made it out to be, and I realized later that my anger was displaced.

By the time I finished my writing rant, it was almost 2 AM and I still wasn't even the slightest bit tired. The rounding nurse recommended that I take Ativan to get some sleep. That sounded like a good idea, mostly because it was after midnight—which meant I couldn't eat anymore and I could no longer stand being so hungry.

Thankfully, Ativan beat out Dexamethasone, and I caught a few hours of drug-induced sleep while my bed inflated and deflated beneath me.

The next morning, my team got to work. The tasks they assigned to me were simple: (1) Keep calm. (2) Don't eat. Unfortunately, I have a history of being awful at both of those things.

Given the significant (and I mean *significant*) amounts of Benadryl, antihistamines, steroids, and Ativan they pumped me with, I remember little about the 12-hour infusion that finally began mid-morning. I remember the countless bags of clear liquids hanging next to me, each one with slightly more Taxotere than the one before it. I remember being so sick of Jell-O and chicken broth that by the end of the day, the thought of either one induced nausea. I remember how badly my arm started to ache by the end of the night. And I remember the scariest part...

* * *

I did well through the first six or seven big bags of drugs and had no reaction. There was lots of worry, watching, and waiting, but no reaction.

When the last bag arrived, I knew that my dosage would begin at 20 something-per-something, then increase to 40 for another interval, then jump to 80 for another three hours. Eighty something-per-something was the dosage that had caused me to react two weeks prior. No doubt, I was nervous to approach that speed again.

I did fine at 20 and the relief in the room was tangible.

When my nurse turned the speed up to 40, however, my family and I immediately noticed the number on the heart monitor start to climb.

And climb.

I didn't feel well. My insides felt hot. My infusion nurse was right there to turn off the machine and insert some more Benadryl into my IV. *Shit.*

We waited.

It sucked.

Somehow, my body leveled out and we decided to forge ahead.

My nurse started the Taxotere once more. I carried on at a speed of 40 for 15 more minutes, even relaxing myself enough to flip through pages of a book called "Hope" that I had recently purchased in the hospital gift shop.

Then came the acceleration to 80. That, my body couldn't handle. In much slower motion and with far lesser intensity, I felt symptoms similar to those that instantaneously overcame me on Halloween—heat in my chest, throat closing, chest tightening, more heat, flushing, more heat, shortness of breath.

All eyes were glued to the heart monitor.

My heart rate was rapidly accelerating.

"It's starting to happen," I told those gathered by my bed. But everyone already knew. And everyone already had started to act.

My nurse stopped the Taxotere and immediately administered other drugs through my IV. My body gradually returned to safety and once we all regrouped (again), we returned to the Taxotere at a reduced speed of 40. We stayed at 40 for the rest of the infusion. Somewhere around midnight, the infusion was complete.

I felt victory—a crossing-the-marathon-finish-line type—full of pain, relief, glory, and utter exhaustion.

When I wrote about this episode in my blog a few days later, I described how I had found some magical inner strength that had powered me through the impending anaphylaxis. It would be so neat if that is what actually happened. Upon further reflection, however, I'm not quite sure that was the case.

*   *   *

I never understood the true power of the mind until I had my first real panic attack several weeks after the ICU stay. It was awful, as I detail in a later chapter. After that attack, I started to wonder if it were anxiety that made my heart race and my chest tighten during my ICU treatment weeks earlier.

Of course I will never know with certainty what happened in the ICU that night—whether my mind was able to garner a strength powerful enough to overcome a significant allergic reaction, or whether it was simply panic that heated up my chest. Either way, I guess it doesn't really matter. Because two weeks to the day after leaving Dana-Farber, swollen and deflated, I fell asleep full of the lifesaving drugs that I had so desperately missed.

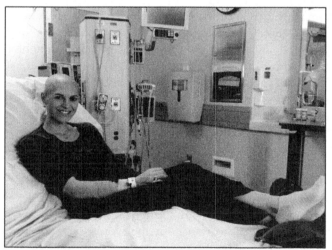

November 2012 – Brigham and Women's Hospital ICU

Neutropenia

I had a few relatively small issues after my second successful infusion, including some unanticipated hives and severe pain in my infused arm. Thankfully, the hives subsided with some Benadryl. The pain in my arm, however, persisted for several months. My doctors said it was phlebitis, which is a hardening of the vein, and the vein in my IV arm was, indeed, hard as a rock. The top of my forearm also felt as if someone had beaten it with a baseball bat, so I received my last chemo infusions through my left arm despite having had the lymph node removed from that side. The numbness on the surface of my right forearm never subsided, but it turns out that feeling in the forearm is kind of like a gallbladder—we don't really need it for anything.

Thanksgiving came and went a few weeks later. Thanksgiving had always been one of my favorite holidays. But with cancer, it was complicated. I was ambivalent about the holiday in ways I could never have anticipated. I was so thankful, as I had always been. But I was also constantly scared of my own body. Scared of what it could do when it was unhappy. Upset that there were so many questions with no answer.

The day after Thanksgiving, I woke up feeling awful. I figured it was due to overeating combined with regular chemo nausea. I had no idea that inside, my body had become completely defenseless.

* * *

Chemotherapy attacks rapidly dividing cells—those that help make hair, nails, and of course, tumors. Since white blood cells also divide rapidly, chemo drugs find and destroy them too. And because white blood cells are the cells that we need to fight off infection, an unintended consequence of chemotherapy is it can destroy the body's ability to protect and heal itself.

Prior to my first treatment, Dr. Denver explained that chemotherapy would cause my white blood cell count to plummet. About seven to 10 days after each infusion, my white blood cells would hit their lowest point. It was then that I would need to be especially cautious of germs, open cuts, a sore throat, or fever.

Dr. Denver warned us that while on chemotherapy, any sort of infection needed to be handled with extreme caution. If I had a fever of 100.5 degrees or above, I was to page him immediately, any time of any day. If the fever persisted for more than an hour, he would send me straight to the emergency room. It turned out to be a very useful warning.

* * *

My family has an annual tradition on the day after Thanksgiving that involves lunch, shopping, and purchasing a Christmas tree. On our drive to lunch, I was so tired that I could barely answer the kids when they asked me questions from the back seat. I remember sitting in the car thinking about how exhausting it was just to open my mouth to talk. For someone who can talk pretty much all day long, I should have known I was sick. But I figured it was yet another chemo symptom I had to tough out, so I did. I pulled myself together and despite being unable to shake the nausea or fatigue, I had a lovely day with my family.

Brian had battled with the lights on our fake Christmas tree all morning before we left for our Christmas adventure and when we got home, he jumped right back into his fight. I collapsed into my healing chair—freezing with chills and feeling progressively worse—while the kids played at my feet.

When we gave the kids a bath, Brian checked my temperature—99.7 degrees. Not a problem just yet, but we both knew I was creeping closer to 100.5.

Once the kids were asleep, we checked again. 101.7. Crap. We paged Dr. Denver and he told us to pack a bag and come into the emergency room at the Brigham and Women's Hospital in Boston.

My parents immediately came over to stay with the kids and we arrived at the ER around 10 PM. I figured I'd be home the next day.

The ER team drew blood to check for infection. They examined my right arm, which was still terribly pained, red, and warm, and they took a chest X-ray to rule out pneumonia.

My selective memory had allowed me to forget how scary diagnostic tests can be when the stakes are high. Not only was I scared of the results of the X-ray, but I was scared that the process itself would cause my cancer to recur. As the technician lined me up for the test, I told him I was terrified that the radiation would make cancer grow again. He said he could give me some numbers to demonstrate that possibility, but I stopped him.

"Numbers aren't good for me," I explained. Of course, neither was the ER nurse's earlier explanation that pneumonia can be fatal when counts are low. If I had more energy, I would have told her that she should work on a more comforting sound bite.

Once they rolled me back into the ER, I was so hot and sick that I don't remember much of anything. I drifted in and out of a restless sleep as Brian sat or paced by my side. My temperature was climbing (by then 102.4 degrees), so they admitted me to an inpatient bed. My nursing team immediately began IV antibiotics which we prayed would fight off whatever my body couldn't.

Neither Brian nor I slept more than a few hours that first night, mostly because the IV machine beeped every time I unknowingly bent my arm. And because Brian's recliner ended at his knees.

I learned the next morning that the chemo had made me neutropenic. This meant my immune system was significantly weakened; particularly, my absolute neutrophil count ("ANC") was abnormally low.

Neutrophils are a type of white blood cell that mediates the body's ability to fight infection (or so I discovered). When those counts go down—and especially when they hit zero like mine had—we cannot fight off even the sources of infection that naturally occur inside our bodies.

While I felt guilty for not taking enough precaution against germs since my last infusion, I was oddly relieved to know that nothing I could have done would have stopped me from getting sick. With a zero ANC, it was inevitable.

For the next week, I lay in (and later roamed around) the hospital waiting for my ANC to rise. My doctors and nurses pumped me with antibiotics almost 24 hours a day. A few days after I was admitted, those antibiotics brought my fever under control. A few days after that, they helped bring my ANC up to a safe-enough range that I could be released back into the germ-filled wild.

In that week, I slept a lot, wrote a bit, and visited the gift shop more times than I can recall. Avoiding germs became my top priority, which wasn't a natural transition for me. Of all my phobias, none happen to involve germs so all of the neutropenic precautions were hard for me. Nevertheless, I abided by them.

Heading off to the Brigham and Women's
gift shop with Brianne – November 2012

When I ventured out of my room, I wore a mask and gloves, as required. I rolled my IV pole around by my side, and with my bald head and thin frame, I never looked so sick in my life. The funny part was that after my fever subsided, I didn't feel all that sick, aside from a sore throat and a gland that was so swollen it hurt to talk. I felt weak, but since I was well enough to wander to and from the gift shop, I was even more desperate to go home to my family.

One of the most difficult parts about that week was being away from the kids. That stretch was the longest I had ever been away from either of them, and I never even got to say goodbye. When I felt well, we video-chatted from my phone to Brian's, but I could never decide if those chats made things better or worse for me or the kids. It was so fun to see them through the bobbing little screen, but the "Call Ended" message felt like a crushing blow to my heart.

Once my ANC climbed up into slight existence, Brian brought the kids in to see me for an hour. We drew dog whiskers and funny faces on my mask before venturing to the cafeteria for dinner.

When it was time to go, Teddy got sad. *Really* sad. I faked that I didn't feel the same way, and proceeded to lay out the reasons why this would all be okay. But really, I just wanted to stomp my feet and bawl my eyes out right along with him.

At first, Annabel was fine with leaving me. She gave me a big hug and chirped out a "See ya," but I heard her wailing as she made her way down the hall toward the elevators. I figured Brian's heart was breaking just like mine was.

As I got back in my bed, I tried to think of anything that would give me the strength I needed to hold it together. I immediately thought of Ashley. Ashley was a 26-year-old beautiful and talented girl from Maine whom I met in the gift shop a few days earlier. She had battled cystic fibrosis her whole life and when she fell into respiratory failure, she waited patiently until a new set of lungs became available.

Ashley received a lung transplant several months before I met her, but the lungs would not prove to be the solution for which countless people had prayed. Ashley's new lungs contained a bacteria that caused her to have several strokes and the strokes necessitated brain surgery. When we met, Ashley was learning how to walk and talk again.

People toss around the word "inspiration" a lot, but Ashley was, and despite her eventual passing, still *is*, a true inspiration to me. For instance, as I listened to my kids bawling down the hallway, I told myself that if Ashley could tough out a hospital stay since June, I could certainly get through a few more nights.

Still, being away from my family was hard, and on the night before Brian's 33rd birthday, I couldn't help but break down in tears.

My friend Heather had called to beg permission to help with the kids, especially since Brian's hockey-coaching season began while I was in the hospital. Heather knew Annabel enough to know that she gives serious attitude to people when she first meets them. So Heather wanted to stop by the house when my family was there so Annabel could get to know her. I told her she could stop by the night after because Brian was coming in to visit me after his hockey practice. When I told Heather that day was Brian's 33rd birthday, Heather asked if the kids would like it if she brought cupcakes for them to decorate.

That's when I lost it. I sobbed uncontrollably over the phone, barely able to catch my breath. It was the first time I had cried that week.

Heather probably thought I was crying because I couldn't be there, and partly, I was. But I was really crying for another reason—I had stumbled upon a moment of such clarity that it reduced me to tears. I realized that we have friends and family who are so thoughtful, generous, and kind that they would make sure things didn't break, even though I felt like they had already broken.

The next day, Brian's 33rd birthday, brought us a precious coincidence—my ANC hit 33. I had a cake delivered to the hospital and we sat on my hospital bed together and had a piece. I worried about the germs that may have lurked on the frosting, but not enough that I didn't enjoy every last bite.

* * *

My doctors told me I could leave the hospital once my ANC reached 500. Fortunately, once the ANC starts to climb, it usually continues to do so. The next day, I was thrilled to hear it reached 171. The day after that, it hit 490.

When I heard the 490 number, I felt pure victory. I couldn't even believe it. "I'm getting out, aren't I?" I asked the physician's assistant who leaked the news to me. She smiled and denied the certainty of it, but I could tell—the answer was *Yes*.

I still needed one more two-hour infusion of antibiotics, but when that was done, they disassembled the hardware that was fixed to my arm and I busted out of the hospital like a caged animal.

Like most caged animals when they're released, I was quite apprehensive when I met the wild, or in my case, the bustling main lobby of the Brigham. It was packed with people, and all of a sudden, people meant germs. Germs meant fevers, fevers meant hospitals, and hospitals meant time away from my family. So while I had desperately waited for the moment I could walk the halls without a mask, I found myself at the information desk asking for one.

On the way home, Brian and I stopped at Legal Sea Foods and enjoyed a lunch that wasn't served by someone wearing plastic gloves. I was still in my pajamas, but we didn't care.

Still weak, tired, and sore, with a headache that just wouldn't quit, it was harder than I had anticipated to jump back into the hyperactivity of a typical night with the kids. Nevertheless, after baths, it was time to do what Teddy and Annabel had been waiting to do since the morning I left for the hospital—decorate the Christmas tree. So we did, and it never looked so perfect, even though all of the ornaments were loaded in two batches at the bottom of the tree.

In Sickness and In Health

Months prior to my November hospitalization, Brian and I had RSVP'd "Yes" to our friends' wedding in Portland, Maine. The wedding would take place at the beginning of December—in the heart of my chemotherapy treatment. Ever the optimists, we hadn't anticipated any of the complications that had plagued us. When the wedding rolled around, we had a million reasons not to go. But germs or no germs, we were going to Maine to celebrate.

At random times throughout that trip—from the romantic moments when we squeezed each other's hand to the times when we bickered about where to park—I thought about love and marriage. This was the first wedding we attended since my diagnosis, and like most "firsts" after such a life-altering event, this one was particularly meaningful. Plus, it's always fun to witness the marriage of two people who truly love each other.

Brian and I had also married in Maine, six years earlier, on a July day that was as hot as that December day was cold. Our wedding weekend had been marvelous—full of relaxation, celebration, and total debauchery.

I since have seen that weddings can get complicated—from seating arrangements to dress fittings—but ours wasn't complicated at all. I had my dress fitted a few days before we left for the wedding, and although there was only time for the tailor to tighten up one side, I figured one side was fine enough. I saw no reason to sweat the small stuff. I just wanted our loved ones to be with us in Maine and have tons of fun while I married my best friend.

Brian and I enjoyed personalizing our wedding ceremony, and the lovely reverend who married us encouraged it. We did not, however, write our own vows. Instead, we made a few edits to the vows that the reverend provided us, which we thought were quite nice.

To be honest, at the time, I probably wasn't mature enough to have written my own vows. If I tried to do so back then, I would have stuck to the basics—for instance, that I knew I was marrying the nicest, smartest, and funniest guy I had ever met.

If I had to write my vows now, they would have a lot more detail, and perhaps to some, seem much less romantic. My vows today would touch upon Brian's incredible patience in the vortex that is our kids' bedtime routine. I would talk about the fact that during his most important of hockey games, he never hesitates to give me and the kids a hug and kiss between periods. I would talk about Brian changing the drains that were sewn into my chest after my surgery and about his spirited attempts to sleep on hospital recliners. I would describe Brian's immediate instinct to put my well-being before any post-diagnosis fertility procedures and how, when I was bald, he told me I was beautiful every single day—and how crazily, I think he meant it.

I know that if a couple ever brought up cancer during a wedding ceremony, it would probably go over like a lead balloon. "In sickness and in health" definitely sums it up in a clean and concise fashion, so we all can stick with that.

Interestingly, however, back in 2006, we removed "in sickness and in health" from our vows. I don't remember exactly why we deleted it; perhaps it was simply because we couldn't fathom that either of us would ever get sick. Or maybe it was because we wanted to keep the ceremony full of only perfect visions of our future. Or maybe it was just because it sounded so generic.

Almost nine years later, I know that no couple's future will ever be perfect, no matter what their vows declare. Every relationship will be tested, albeit to varying degrees, by sickness, loss, or financial hardship. There is no doubt that cancer tested ours, and continues to do so. It added a great deal of stress to the regular challenges of raising a family and trying to make ends meet. Like any life challenge, cancer can strengthen a bond or it can break it. I am blessed that cancer strengthened ours. It showed me what *in sickness and in health* really means. Actually, the crux of it was pretty simple. It was this…

I found out just before our trip to Maine for our friends' wedding that I had graduated from the ICU and would be allowed to attempt my next round of chemo in the outpatient desensitization unit at Dana-Farber. The infusion would be long—about 12 hours—and I knew that despite our successful second round, this third one still brought with it the risk of anaphylaxis. Nevertheless, as I thought ahead to my next trip to the hospital, I didn't dread it. In fact, part of me looked forward to it, and the reason was simple—my husband would be there with me for the whole thing.

"Newlyweds"
July 2006 – Spruce Point Inn, Maine

"Less Hair"
December 2012 – Portland, Maine

Worry Woes

Worrying is carrying tomorrow's load with today's strength—
carrying two days at once. It is moving into tomorrow ahead of
time. Worrying doesn't empty tomorrow of its sorrow,
it empties today of its strength.
~ Corrie Ten Boom

I was a worrier long before cancer. In fact, I often think that it was being a worrywart that made me visit the doctor about the lump I found in my breast. Seriously, does a normal 32-year-old suspect a tiny lump to be an aggressive form of breast cancer? Probably not. But a hypochondriacal 32-year-old thinks just that.

Prior to cancer, I worried about all sorts of things, although terrorism and drunk-drivers usually took the top spots. Makes sense too, since those are two things over which I have absolutely no control.

Not that I like to give cancer credit for anything, but I sometimes joke that cancer focused my craziness. Where several different scenarios used to make me anxious, cancer folded up my worry and anxiety into a package of sorts. It was a monstrously big, heavy, nightmarish package with tentacles reaching out of every side, but at least it did have some bounds.

The dreadful package included, at its core, images of recurrence of my cancer or a bad gene I passed along to one (or both) of my children. While I was in treatment, even those nightmares seemed to remain at a safe distance. I usually didn't worry that I felt a recurrence; after all, I knew it was too early for that. Instead, as a worrywart, I dwelled on images and stories about what my medicine could be doing to me.

One of my biggest worries during my treatment was that the Herceptin would damage my heart. Dr. Denver explained that Herceptin carried with it a small risk of congestive heart failure. At first, I didn't worry too much about that possibility. Then I heard that Kristin was experiencing this symptom as she trudged through her own treatment. In full disclosure, her doctors believed it was the Adriamycin that caused the congestive heart failure, but the Herceptin likely furthered the damage. Unwittingly, I worried that I would follow in Kristin's footsteps and possibly have to make a choice that no one should ever have to make—(a) Herceptin, heart damage, and less chance of cancer, or (b) no Herceptin, a healthier heart, and a higher risk of cancer recurrence. These worries about my heart plagued me throughout treatment, as did the fear of another anaphylactic reaction. In the end, those fears helped lead me to a newfound clarity about the anxiety I had experienced for much of my life.

*   *   *

During the week I spent in the hospital dealing with neutropenia, I had a significant episode that I have yet to mention. It was nighttime, and my mom was sitting at the foot of my bed. We weren't doing much of anything when all of a sudden, I felt heat in my chest. Having remembered that feeling from my allergic reaction, I panicked. I became immediately convinced that I was going into anaphylactic shock, maybe as a result of something I was receiving through my IV.

I reached frantically for the emergency button on the side of the bed.

Within minutes of telling the nurse that I was having trouble breathing, a team of at least 10 people descended on my germ-protected hospital room. While a few students watched in fascination, the doctors and nurses moved quickly to stop my antibiotics and flow Benadryl and Ativan into my IV. They talked me through the episode and returned me to normal, or at least, my crazy version of it.

Over an hour later, once the crowd left my bedside, I fell asleep, perplexed as to why I almost experienced anaphylaxis again, but too tired to search for an answer.

The next day, the physician's assistant (Colleen) who was taking wonderful care of me referred to my near-shock as a panic attack. I was so confused. *Panic? I felt heat in my chest and I could barely breathe! That's got to be something more than panic!* But I didn't question her. I liked Colleen too much to argue. Plus, my doctors could think whatever they wanted to think. I knew that I was dealing with something much more than anxiety.

Less than a week later, Brian and I sat together immersed in an intense television show that someone with my crazy imagination (and fear of terrorism) should not have been watching. This particular episode of *Homeland* portrayed a character having a heart attack. I watched, and in an instant, I felt the devil's heat in my chest again. Then came the tightness. And the fire in my throat.

"It's happening," I told Brian, terrified that there was nothing he would be able to do to stop it.

Brian scrambled to shut off the television and get my medicine bag. I could hear him frantically rustling through the many pill bottles as I tried to calm myself down.

"It's the same as last week," I explained, bent over with my fuzzy head in my hands. I wondered if I should reach for the small lifeline device that my brother set up for me after my allergic reaction. *Is this the real thing? A heart attack because my heart has been fatally damaged by my medication?*

Knowing there was nothing else to do, I tried my best to convince myself that this was something far less serious. I remembered Colleen's explanation that I had suffered a panic attack in the hospital, and for the first time, I started to believe her. I remembered Colleen explaining that grown men often came into the emergency room mistaking a panic attack for a heart attack. I remembered the tests conducted when the river of scrubs flooded into my room—results showing my vital organs to be fine.

I started to convince myself I had control.

"I'm okay, it's not the shock," I assured Brian. "It's not my heart. It's panic. That's all. It's okay. It's okay."

A minute later, Brian rushed over with an Ativan pill and some water.

"This is what the doctors said to take," he explained. I had forgotten about that, but he was right. I swallowed the pill. Then he sat next to me on the sofa and held me tight.

"You're okay, you're okay," he repeated. I was, and this episode didn't escalate to the level of the one from the week prior. My legs and elbows never shook uncontrollably, and even though the heat in my chest and throat returned for a bit a few minutes later, I was able to convince it to go away.

About five terrifying minutes later, the devil receded to his hiding place.

Once I knew I wasn't going to die of a heart attack or anaphylaxis, I started to cry tears of relief, frustration, and anger.

Was this really what I had become? I couldn't even watch TV without enduring some ridiculous bout of drama? How long would all of this haunt me? Forever?

I told Brian I needed another image in my head—something much lighter than the heart-attack scene that was stuck on pause in my memory. Brian pulled out his phone and started to show me photos of the kids. It was a solid attempt at distraction, but it failed miserably. Those photos made me sick with worry—not the panic kind, but the sad kind. I scrolled through those pictures with a feeling of utter desperation.

I cannot leave them, I thought. *I absolutely cannot leave them.*

It was too hard to see those innocent little faces, so I stopped and asked Brian to put the phone away. My heart ached.

We sat together a while longer, staring at the Christmas tree.

A few minutes later, Brian got up to make the kids' lunches for the next day. I followed, and despite that making kids' lunches is one of my least-favorite parenting chores, this time I kind of enjoyed it.

Pink Envelopes

In the fall of my last year of law school, I accepted a job as a summer associate at a humongous corporate law firm. At the time, I knew very little about what the job entailed. I hadn't done much research on the position, which was just plain stupid, since in order to begin the new job, I had to resign from the teaching position that I loved.

At the time, my reasoning was simple—Brian and I were struggling financially and I figured that it would be wrong to pass up a job shoveling shit if it was for the amount of money that the Firm was going to pay me.

If I hate it, I thought, *I'll just tough it out for a few years, pay back all my loans, and go back to teaching.* In retrospect, this reasoning horrifies me in so many ways. Nevertheless, it's the truth.

There were a few other positives to the situation, aside from the quadrupling of my paycheck. Mostly, I was sincerely excited for a new adventure.

Looking back, I should have known much earlier than I did that I was not the big-corporate-law-firm kind of girl. Deep down I probably knew it immediately, but it took a while to register. Hefty paychecks have been shown to block logical thinking that way.

If I had to name one of the first times I started to realize that the Firm wasn't the place for me, I think I could. It was during a presentation by a woman I will call Nancy Swan.

The Firm had invited Ms. Swan to teach us everything we needed to know about proper business etiquette—from whether nylons were required for women's attire to tips for turning a cocktail party into a successful business initiative. For someone who thinks nylons are like a tourniquet and a cocktail party principally means free cheese, I wasn't picking up what this lady was putting down.

Enter utter ridiculousness.

While on the gripping topic of how to hold a drink, Ms. Swan cautioned us to never hold a drink in our right hand. Apparently a drink makes the hand cold and wet and we should always avoid a cold, wet palm while prepping for a handshake with our next best business associate.

Without time for my internal edit button to flick on, my arm shot up and I asked the first question I had ever asked in front of the whole summer-associate class, "So are you saying we aren't supposed to eat anything?"

"That's right," Ms. Swan answered, and she went on to explain why eating hors d'oeuvres at business events is a terrible mistake. I don't remember all of her reasons, but I do remember that while she lectured our eager little army of almost 200 new lawyers, I felt completely out of place. I loved boxing out my siblings when the chips and spinach dip hit the kitchen island, and I have never believed that plates are needed to eat pizza. I had no plans of passing up free cheese and fresh grapes, and if my new employer saw this type of etiquette crap as important, I was doomed.

In my mind, if people have good and honest intentions, things like nylons and cold palms should not make an ounce of difference. This attitude is probably why I never worried much about whether my bald head made people uncomfortable. Like no one has ever seen a bald head before? Funny, I see them every single day. They usually just happen to be on men.

Nevertheless, I'm not much of a social renegade either, and during my treatment, I often wondered if I were getting the cancer etiquette right. For example, I had no idea what to do with all of the plastic food containers and glass casserole dishes that we had gathered over several months from all of the meals people cooked for us. I saved every container, mostly with Post-it® notes inside bearing the name of the generous chef. But I never knew if I should really coordinate the massive return effort.

Then there was the how-are-you-feeling question that I know I still botch when it's graciously asked of me. During my treatment, I often felt terrible in all sorts of weird ways, yet I didn't want to burden the asker with too much information. At the same time, if I could fake a claim that I felt well, I wondered if I were doing a disservice to other chemo patients by portraying the whole process as something easier than it really was. In the end, I usually gave some middle-of-the-road answer and changed the subject.

Another piece of cancer etiquette that plagued me was the traditional thank-you card. Cancer has an incredible way of making almost every person you have known in your life reach out to you. Over the course of 32 years, that turned out to be a lot of people and I wanted to personally thank each and every one of them for so many different things. I was even given beautiful stationary on which to write such cards.

But every time I sat down to write my thank-you notes, I became overwhelmed by how much there was to say and how impossible it felt to say it. So I would stop and stare into space, wondering if anyone would care if I were to skip the whole process. Or perhaps it was like wedding etiquette and I had a year. I had no idea.

Like many people, I try to send out an annual holiday card (if I get behind, New Year's cards count). I thought that maybe during the first holiday season after my diagnosis, I would mail out a stack of hybrid holiday/thank-you cards. Was that cheating? Where was Nancy Swan when I needed her?

When it came to writing thank-you notes, or rather, *not* writing them, there was one set of gifts that stood out in my mind. Over the several months of my most intense treatment, an anonymous sender mailed one or two bright pink envelopes to me almost every day. The contents of the envelopes varied from jokes and quotes to 1980s song-lyrics quizzes. Some envelopes were inspirational, and some were just pure fun.

After a month or so I learned the identity of the anonymous senders, which, for my personality, made it even better. The senders were the children of one of my mom's most-special colleagues. I had never even met Billy and Annabel at the time they started sending me the pink envelopes, but Brian and I got the idea for our daughter's name from this Annabel, and I knew that Brian, Teddy, and Billy shared an unconditional love of hockey. Over the years, I also had become friends with Billy and Annabel's mom Lisa. Lisa is someone I strive to be like and I was touched that she would talk about me to her kids. I loved all the lessons that she was teaching them through the dozens of mailed envelopes, and the lessons they were teaching us—lessons about humor, thoughtfulness, and anonymous generosity. While the contents of those pink envelopes made me laugh and smile, they also reminded me of the pure goodness out there in the world.

The truth is, those envelopes were one of several instances of generosity that reduced me to tears and speechlessness. Each time I witnessed these acts of awesome kindness, I would collect myself, then stop and wonder: *What in the world could I ever do to properly thank this person?* A hand-written thank-you note simply wouldn't do the trick.

* * *

During the time I was receiving the pink envelopes, a friend shared this quote with me:

> Holy angels never draw attention to themselves.
> They typically do their work and disappear.

Throughout my cancer journey I've been surrounded by angels, and no holiday card, thank-you note, or poor combination of the two could do justice to the generosity those angels have shown me. That first Christmas post-cancer I tried anyway, and sent out holiday cards with a short, handwritten thank-you message. I decided it was the best I could do.

Eventually, however, I found comfort in the realization that maybe there is no real etiquette when it comes to cancer. Maybe we just need to leave etiquette to the summer associates at big corporate law firms. Meanwhile, the rest of us can ditch the nylons, keep the Tupperware, and eat lots and lots of free cheese.

Why

In December of 2012, I could see the light at the end of the chemo tunnel. I started to work more, although I scaled back during the period of each round when neutropenia posed the biggest danger. Exercise and writing remained a key part of each day, and while I still wrote mostly about my cancer concerns, I started to focus more of my writing on the lessons I softly wanted to impart on my children when they were ready.

* * *

On the morning of December 14, 2012, I sat at my computer in the kids' playroom, working intently on a blog post about how nervous I was to officially return to the work world when my medical leave ended in seven weeks. In that blog, I recounted the regimented routine that, prior to my diagnosis, I practiced every morning before catching my commuter train into the city. I wrote about the down-to-the-minute schedule I had to follow after Brian left for work—getting the kids up, dressed, fed, into the car, and to different schools before boarding the 8:07 AM train that (hopefully) hadn't already left the station.

At the end of the post, I included a photo of Annabel showing off the mittens (i.e., socks) that her teachers had given her on a cold winter day when I forgot to pack her a suitable pair of gloves.

Annabel at school – December 2012

The photo meant a lot to me. It reminded me that despite my mishaps as a mother, I could still raise happy kids without them getting frostbite.

After I published that post, I shared it on Facebook, as was my habit. It was then that I first learned of the gruesome tragedy that had taken place at an elementary school not unlike the one my children would attend, in a small town similar to ours.

While everyone else poured out their love, support, and tears for Sandy Hook Elementary School and Newtown, Connecticut, I was numb. Uncomfortably, queasily *numb*.

I didn't even cry.

I couldn't fathom what had happened there; better yet, I couldn't let myself fathom it, especially not as I stared at the photo of my daughter standing in front of the entry door to her school.

Numb or not, of course my sympathies were real. I sent the victims' families strength through my own sort of prayers. As I watched and listened to many people around me, those for whom the tragedy was also a distant one, I felt as if many of them were joining—albeit, temporarily—the world I had known since August 8, 2012. Where fear reigned. Where we understand, despite not wanting to, that at any moment we could be separated from those we love.

I read others' reactions—ones like *Hug your family tighter tonight*. But what were those of us to do when our hugs were already as tight as they could possibly be?

After a day of not being able to collect my thoughts or feelings enough to write, I sat down at my computer. I needed to make sense of something, even though I knew it would not be Newtown.

When I started to write, I suddenly became keenly aware of who may read what I wrote. I realized that what I would say to various audiences in the wake of such tragedy would be significantly different. Parents, teachers, school administrators, law enforcement officials, legislators, gun owners, the President, my friends, my husband, my kids—each conversation would be unique. If I tried to mesh them all together, I would fail miserably.

Brian and I talked about the Newtown shooting, but never in the context of "What should we tell the kids?" I knew that was because we both agreed that at five and two years old, Teddy and Annabel were far too young to know about it. Not that I judged anyone who made a different decision, but that was ours.

Nonetheless, I found myself wanting to write to my children that day, so I did. I meant them to read the resulting piece when they were much older, but I had some things to say to them and this was the time.

A Letter to My Children
December 15, 2012

Why?

It is one of the most important questions you can ask throughout your life. I hope that you ask it often and I hope that you listen thoughtfully to the answers. For instance, if someone asks you to do something that doesn't feel right, stop for a second and ask yourself—*Why? Why do I feel the way I do?* Maybe those questions lead you to a better decision. Maybe they save your life. Or maybe they just give you a minute to learn a bit more about who you are. Sometimes it's just time that you need.

I hope that this tiny yet monumental question helps you, but the truth is, there will be times in your life when it won't help you at all. Because sometimes there won't be a right answer. Or worse yet, every now and then, there won't be any answer at all.

I'm someone who needs answers. It pains me when I can't understand the *Whens* and the *Whys* and the *Hows*. It's not that the answers are always comforting, because oftentimes they are not. Still, I'm driven to ask those questions and seek those answers.

After September 11, 2001, I often found myself asking, *Why?* Sometimes I found reasons—ones that involved world history, politics, economics, or religion. But they weren't *real* answers. Probably because there won't ever be any of those.

I hope my generation leaves your generation a world without mass tragedies like 9/11. I am so fearful, however, that we won't. Even if we, by some miracle, could hand you a world without the complex international conflicts that contributed to those attacks, I know that you still won't find a world free of tragedy. Because even within the borders of a small town, there will be great sorrow.

I'm sure by now you know all about Scott Herr from the things your dad and I have told you about him and his family. Much of what I say here is likely what your dad would say, but I won't speak for him, especially because he had a much different relationship with Scott than I did.

I barely even knew Scott personally. I knew him like I know most of your dad's hockey players, which is to say that I knew his name, his face, his hockey number, and all the good stuff your dad had told me about him. I enjoyed talking with him and his family at team dinners, games, or functions in the town, but that was about it.

Nevertheless, when Scott died in a tragic car accident over five years ago, I was absolutely devastated. The emotional pain was so intense that I felt it physically. I remember thinking *I now know where the term "heartache" comes from.* Because I felt pain in my heart. A heavy ache. A darkness. No matter what time of day or what I was doing, it wouldn't go away.

For many months, nothing helped. I cried every day, mostly in the bathroom at work or on the train. I cried the moment that I thought about Scott, his brother, his father, and especially his mother. It all just felt so unreal, so unjust. *So* unjust. There was no answer to the question of *Why?* Sure, I had heard pieces of how it had happened—an icy highway, a heroic attempt to try to control the pickup truck as it lost traction. But none of that mattered. One of the most innocent kids I had ever met was gone.

Scott's death was the first time I truly comprehended that some questions have no answers. That realization is not an easy one. In fact, it's indescribably difficult.

Maybe some of you don't end up needing answers like I do, and part of me really hopes that's the case. Either way, at a certain point in your life, you will feel emotional pain so heavy that it hurts physically. I wish that weren't true, but it probably is—especially if you care for others and let them care for you.

I don't know how old you'll be when you realize that sometimes asking *Why* isn't going to get you anywhere. I don't know what event—perhaps good, but likely tragic—will lead you to that understanding. I just know that when it happens, you will hurt, and I'm so sorry for that.

When that hurt settles in your heart, I want you to know that you aren't alone, even though you may feel like you are. Others have felt your pain, and if you think it will help you, then find those people. Talk to them. Learn from them.

Or maybe talking about it is too hard, and at least for some time, that's fine too. Instead try to write, or read, or listen to music. Walk or run or hit golf balls really hard. Talk to someone—about anything—or find a quiet place that brings you peace. At first, none of this will help ease the pain. But if you're lucky, it will help you keep breathing when you feel like you can't.

I don't know what or who you will find that will comfort you in a time of great loss, and there is very little I could write here that will help either. Nonetheless, when the time comes, I want you to seek out a poem that has provided me solace in times of loss. It's by Maya Angelou and it's called "When Great Trees Fall."

Please read that poem. It's full of genius. Every word, line, idea, and emotion in that poem means something to me. I know now, as do millions of others, what it feels like to be "eroded by fear," to "breathe, briefly," to "see with a hurtful clarity." Indeed, at some point, your mind may "fall away." You may be "reduced to the unutterable ignorance of dark, cold caves." I hope I'm here, if nothing else, to sit with you in those caves. If I'm not, or if you would prefer to sit with someone else, I hope that person is there for you. Because even though the cave will still be dark and cold, it will be warmer and lighter if someone you love is in there with you.

Maya Angelou tells us that "after a period peace blooms, slowly and always irregularly." She doesn't tell us how long that period may take, or how much peace will bloom. Perhaps only time can provide those answers. Nevertheless, I cherish that poem most because while Maya Angelou understands the impact of great loss, she still finds hope in the most desperate of situations. She tells us that at some point, "We can be. Be and be better. For they existed." I don't know why, but I believe her. And more than anything, I hope that you do too.

Part Six

The End of Chemo

Never confuse motion with action.

Benjamin Franklin
(author, politician, scientist, inventor)

The Final Round

My last two rounds of chemotherapy were relatively uneventful. The desensitization team at Dana-Farber defied nature and through innovative protocols, guided the Taxotere safely into my bloodstream without causing an anaphylactic reaction. For that, I am eternally grateful.

The night before my last treatment, once again wired by powerful steroids, I sat in a hotel room across the street from the hospital while Brian and my mom slept nearby. A storm raged outside and given a questionable rain/snow line (and the fact that we had to arrive at Dana-Farber at 6:45 the following morning), we played it safe and booked a room at the nearby Best Western.

Well aware of the effect the steroids had on me, I didn't expect more than a few hours of sleep. Ativan eventually helped me drift off around 3 AM, but before that, I spent four hours quietly typing away at my keyboard, trying to quell the confusion inside me.

Truthfully, I hadn't anticipated being so distraught the night before my last chemo infusion. I figured by that point, the wind would be at my back, and I would coast to the finish line. Unfortunately, that kind of simplicity only happens in the movies and in sports montages. In real life, victory is a lot more complicated.

I knew the issue—I was scared to transition into a new phase. I would still be in treatment, with over nine months of Herceptin infusions left to complete, but the chemo—the heaviest hitters—would take a seat on the bench. Obviously I never, *ever* wanted to see them again, but that didn't mean it was easy to say goodbye.

Don't get me wrong—I never felt safe in chemo's presence. There were times when I thought my body couldn't tolerate much more of it, particularly when my nose was gushing blood and after I learned my inclination toward a zero neutrophil count. At the same time, chemo was the devil I knew. I could anticipate with great accuracy what I would feel in my mouth, stomach, or toes, and even when the nosebleeds would rear their ugly head. I wasn't even upset when my eyebrows fell out just before the last round because I figured that meant my Allies were defeating any cancer that remained. But the night before my last infusion, as the rain pounded against the hotel window, it became clear that the next phase—the "easier" one—wasn't going to be easy at all.

Mandatory last-round-of-chemo photo from the desensitization unit at the Dana-Farber Cancer Institute

Happy Birthdays

Annabel's second birthday fell a few weeks after my last round of chemo, and Teddy's fifth birthday came a few weeks after that. Long before cancer, I knew the days of my babies' births were more than significant. But after my diagnosis, the significance rose to a whole new level.

A few nights after Annabel's Cookie Monster-themed family party, I let Teddy stay up late so we could plan his party. Brian was at a hockey game, Annabel was already asleep, and I cherished time alone with my son. My favorite part was all of the "g-wate" ideas that he claimed he had to share with me.

Based on Teddy's love of the Disney movie *Miracle,* or better yet, of the famous 1980 USA-Russia game remade at the end of it, Teddy decided that he wanted a "USA Hockey pow-ty." And he wanted it at a place called Monster Mini Golf. Neither Brian nor I had ever been to Monster Mini Golf, but I learned that the place was an indoor, glow-in-the-dark miniature-golf course with, unsurprisingly, a monster theme. I let Teddy type the letters into Google and we confirmed that my four-year-old was right—they *did* host birthday parties.

We picked a date and paid the fee. A *Miracle*/Monster Mini Golf party it would be. Made sense to me.

Teddy and I discussed the party every day for the next few weeks. He was so excited, and for more reasons than he understood, so was I.

Thanks to chemo, my eyes were very watery around this time, but I admit I shed a few extra tears as I thought about both of my kids turning another year older and about being there to celebrate it. They weren't gut-wrenching tears, but rather, deeply grateful ones.

I thought back to August, when I wondered if I would be too riddled with cancer to enjoy my kids' next birthdays. There I was in January, healthy enough to run around after a roomful of kids flinging fluorescent golf balls at each other.

* * *

When it comes to cancer, *victory* feels like a loaded concept—far more complicated than a bunch of American college kids defeating Russian professionals in an Olympic hockey game.

Every so often, however, the concept feels simple—as simple as the realization that somehow, countless factors in my life aligned so that I could be blessed with healthy children and be there to watch them grow a year older. No gold medal was involved, but sometimes I was convinced that the sense of victory I felt rivaled the victory celebrated by Herb Brooks and his players when they beat Russia in 1980.

The day after I booked the party room at Monster Mini Golf, I remembered the craziest thing. When Brian returned home from the zoo on the day of my mammogram and ultrasound, we needed time alone to digest the cancer news. While Annabel napped, Brianne and Seamus took Teddy out for the afternoon—out on what became his first trip to Monster Mini Golf.

I will always love Teddy's persistence. Maybe he got a bit of that from me, because since August 8, 2012, Teddy had held onto the idea of Monster Mini Golf as the venue for his fifth-birthday party. And since that same date, I had held onto hope that I would be there to celebrate it.

Ten Years of Tamoxifen

At the same time Brian and I celebrated our kids' birthdays and the blessing that I was well enough to partake, we also grieved a related loss—the hope for another biological child.

Dr. Denver talked about fertility issues with me and Brian at our very first appointment with him, just five days after my diagnosis. He gave us the bullet points and referred us to Dr. Schmidt, the awfully apathetic fertility specialist I wrote about in Part One.

A key piece of information Dr. Denver delivered back in August was that while on Tamoxifen (the hormonal therapy to suppress my estrogen levels), I should not get pregnant. He emphasized the *not*, so I knew he really meant it.

At the time of my diagnosis, Dr. Denver described my Tamoxifen regimen as one that would last five years, thus ending when I was 38 years old. He explained that by then, the medications could have pushed me into early menopause and if that happened, having another biological child would be physically impossible. At the same time, he reasoned that at 38, there would be a good chance I could still attempt to get pregnant if I wished to do so. My instincts immediately told me that I would not have any more biological children.

At first, for reasons I have addressed previously, that thought didn't upset me. But a few months later, circumstances changed.

* * *

The month before Annabel's birthday, Dr. Denver had told us about a recent clinical trial regarding the efficacy of Tamoxifen. As he explained it, the results of the trial showed that women with estrogen-receptive breast cancers (like mine) would fare better with a 10-year course of Tamoxifen rather than just five.

Okay, that's fine, I thought while sitting in the windowless exam room. *Ten years of Tamoxifen it is, then.*

Distracted by a host of other issues we addressed at that appointment, and also by my upcoming infusion, the extra five years didn't register with me at first. But later that night, those five extra years hit me like a two-by-four across the forehead.

I worked out the math with a sick feeling in my stomach. When I finished the Tamoxifen (God willing), I would be 42 years old. While there would be a chance I could get pregnant at that age, I knew that 42 was too late for Brian and I to try for another biological child. Teddy would be 15, Annabel would be 12, and a new baby at that point in life probably wouldn't work for our family.

All of a sudden, I understood. Deep in my soul, I faced the realization— I would never have another biological child. I was crushed.

* * *

There was no way we could have known about the 10 years of Tamoxifen, or that the news would level us like it did. We sure never expected the blow to come that December night, particularly because Brian had a hockey game to coach. But it turns out that harsh truths pay no attention to high-school-sports schedules.

Brian has missed only two hockey games in his entire coaching career. The first was in 2009 when he came with me and my family to Long Island for my grandmother's funeral. The second was that terrible night after we learned about 10 years of Tamoxifen.

I'll never forget that Brian didn't leave me that night. Admittedly, we fought for part of it ("Go to the game! Please just go!"), but in the end, Brian sat with me on the sofa in our living room. We cried and we cursed a disease that at that moment seemed to have stolen something very precious from us.

In the months following, I went through a strange and unexpected grieving process. I worked hard at my job, wrote a lot, enjoyed my family, and exercised religiously. But whenever it came time to face the implications of the 10 years of Tamoxifen, I had to fight back tears and swallow the lump in my throat. I usually saved the outpouring of those tears for my meetings with Dr. Grace, as I didn't want to bother anyone else with them. In fact, I will never forget one particular meeting with Dr. Grace. It was the day I learned a significant lesson about grief and regret.

* * *

It was an April morning and natural light filled the consultation room at Dana-Farber. When the conversation turned to the baby situation, Dr. Grace asked me, "If you could go back, would you have made a different decision?" What she was really asking was, if I could rewind time and harvest my eggs prior to chemotherapy and Tamoxifen, would I have done so? Or would I make the same decision that I actually made—to refuse the whole process?

I don't remember exactly how I answered Dr. Grace's hypothetical question. My edit button was off and I wasn't shy about letting out the flood of tears I unknowingly had built up inside. I do know, however, that I essentially said, "Yes, if it were possible, I would go back and harvest my eggs." When I was done explaining why (and crying), I was exhausted.

Dr. Grace's response was just what I needed. Understanding. Empathy. Space to feel what I was feeling. It was so simple and so very therapeutic.

* * *

There were times during my treatment that I really did wish that I could turn back time and make a different decision about fertility treatment. During those times, I wished I had allowed a fertility doctor to pump me with hormones, harvest my eggs, and freeze our embryos so that one day,

Brian and I could have had more biological children.

Of course, I only would have done that if I knew what I learned months later—that in fact, my cancer had not spread. That the Tamoxifen would be a 10-year course instead of five. That Herceptin possibly could cure my cancer. But we didn't know all that then, and there was no way we could have.

During this time, I learned how intertwined grief and regret could be— because as I grieved the loss, I regretted the decision I had made to seal it.

* * *

Sometimes I grieved so quietly I didn't even know I was doing it. For instance, when I ran, I often found myself running through a nearby cemetery. I would visit Scott's grave, and the nearby stone bench dedicated to a high-school-friend's baby girl. I would stop running to take a deep breath in those two sacred places, and every time, I would sob for a few minutes. The strange thing was that it felt like a peaceful cry—one that felt oddly *right*. Obviously the passing of an 18-year-old and a tiny baby were so very *wrong*—so terribly unjust to them and the loving families they left behind. But there in the cemetery, surrounded by such tragedy, a part of me started to heal.

I never told anyone, not even Brian, about my trips through the cemetery. I wasn't ashamed, but it felt weird to acknowledge them: it was like I had an obsession with death or something. I had no such obsession, and for months I couldn't articulate what was drawing me there.

Eventually I figured it out. My secret jogs through the cemetery were my time to grieve—a way to accept the reality of losing a child that never had a chance to be. I knew my grief wasn't comparable to others' more significant pain. But I also came to believe what Dr. Grace had told me—that nonetheless we had experienced a loss of sorts, and we needed time to grieve it.

I gradually found peace with the fact that after my diagnosis, Brian and I had made the right decision for us, given what we knew at the time. We put my health first and played it safe in a scary situation. I decided not to regret that, but instead, to be forever grateful that I found myself a guy who insisted on protecting me.

Of course, deciding to feel (or not feel) a certain way doesn't always work. The feelings of grief and regret would surface for months to come and bring me down at times. Often, I found myself returning to a quote by Arthur Miller:

Maybe all one can do is hope to end up
with the right regrets.

I love that. Because even when I felt regret, I found peace in believing that at the very least, it was the right kind.

"Not That" and "Something"

After finishing my last round of chemotherapy, I felt cancer growing everywhere. Pain under my arms, aches in my back, tumors in my neck. Sheer terror at any sign of discomfort that I couldn't explain.

At my first post-chemo appointment with Dr. Denver, I wasn't about to reveal all of my crazy by disclosing my full laundry list of random aches and pains. So I picked the top one—the sharp on-and-off pain under my left arm.

I explained the pain with vague details. Dr. Denver asked some questions and I answered them. Eventually we arrived at the root of the problem. I tried not to tear up when I explained that I wasn't ready to talk about it, but a particular question had been haunting me.

"What would I feel if my cancer came back?"

I couldn't believe I had asked it out loud and I was embarrassed that I couldn't contain the flood of tears that followed.

Dr. Denver reached for a tissue and simultaneously responded with two words that were probably the most perfect two words he could have said at the moment.

"Not that."

Dr. Denver remained still, closed his mouth, and raised his eyebrows, as if to say, *That's all you need to know for now.*

He was right—it was.

*   *   *

I often wonder if oncologists know how many times patients like me replay their words after an appointment. (Answer: countless.)

Not that.

Not that.

Not that.

Every single time I felt pain under my arm…

Not that.

There were other words that helped me too. For instance, a few months later, Dr. Denver shared news that was so hopeful, I felt like I would float straight off of the exam table.

"HER2+ breast cancer will likely be the first cancer we cure in the metastatic state," he explained. He emphasized the in-the-metastatic-state part, although he didn't need to, because I already understood the significance.

"You mean, you could do something for me if it came back?" I asked (because selfishly, at that moment, it felt all about me).

"We would do something," my doctor replied.

It is impossible to explain what it felt like to hear that word—*something*. To know that even if my cancer came back, I would not die without a fight.

Something.

We would do something.

And sometimes, hope is *something*.

Detour: Some Thoughts on Heaven

Brian and I named our son after Brian's maternal grandfather who had taken the name "Teddy" when he first came to the United States from Albania. Our Teddy didn't ask us about Grandpa Ted's whereabouts until one night just before he turned five, which happened to be at the time of my life when I too was asking deeper questions.

I remember the night vividly. Brian, Teddy, Annabel, and I were driving home in the car when the conversation playfully turned to Grandpa Ted. Without skipping a beat, Teddy became serious and asked us where Gwampa Ted was now.

"He's in heaven," Brian answered before I could think of what to say. Teddy got quiet. He didn't ask any more questions although I knew his mind was churning. *What* it was churning, I had no idea.

Fast-forward to a cold afternoon a few weeks later. Brian was on a ladder reluctantly taking down the Christmas lights while Teddy, Annabel, and I were en route to Teddy's friend's birthday party.

Out of the blue, Teddy asked me from the back seat (still unable to pronounce his Rs), "Mommy, where is heaven?"

Goodness gracious—I needed some sort of warning before a chat like this. I swallowed and told my son that heaven was up in the sky—"so high up that we can't see it." *How dumb was that last part? I needed to pick up my game.*

"What do people do there?" Teddy asked.

Great question. I tried to think of a good answer.

"Whatever they want. Whatever makes them the happiest."

"Can they pway baseball?"

"Of course!"

"What do they use foe a bat?" This may have been the hardest question of them all.

"Hum, something like a regular bat?"

"Who's in heaven?"

"Lots of people. Mommy's grandma and grandpa, Daddy's grandpa. They are all together."

"People are to-gever in heaven?"

"Yep. People get to see everyone they love in heaven and be with them forever."

"Will you go to heaven one day?" *Gulp.*

"Yep, if I'm a good person."

"Will daddy?" *Do not register that thought.*

"Yes, because he's a really good person."

"Will I?" *This couldn't get much harder.*

"Yes, because you're such a nice person too."

"But not foe a weally weally long time, wight?" *Oh dear—I can't believe I hadn't clarified that from the start.*

"Right, because you're really young."

"Can we talk to people when they ah in heaven?" Teddy persisted softly.

"Yes, but they can't talk back like a person can. That doesn't mean they can't hear you though."

"Who will be my mommy and daddy when you ah in heaven?" At this question, Teddy's face scrunched up and he started to cry. Most remarkably, I saw that he was trying to hide his tears from me. I had never seen him do that before. I didn't even know that four-year-olds were capable of it.

My heart physically ached at the sight of him in my rear-view mirror. I never had to try so hard to be strong.

"We will always be your mommy and daddy, even when we're in heaven." Well shit, now I was crying too. I adjusted the mirror so he wouldn't see. "People don't have to be here on Earth for you to talk to them or for them to be your mommy or daddy." *Heavier gulp. Tears.* I couldn't take it anymore. "So are you excited for the birthday party?"

"Yep, can I have some vanilla cake?"

"Sure, buddy. And are you excited for your hockey game tonight?"

We continued on the hockey topic until we arrived at the party. Despite the distraction of 25 toddlers, I couldn't stop thinking about Teddy's questions. Maybe because I wondered a lot about those things too.

* * *

I didn't grow up practicing religion, and I never felt slighted because of it. Sure, there were times when it seemed as though I was the only one in my class not attending CCD or Hebrew school, but it didn't bother me to be different in that way. My parents taught me and my siblings about faith and values in other ways, and those ways made me feel complete.

Nevertheless, when I was 30 years old and trying to process several tragedies that had hit close to home, I was desperate for some sort of spiritual understanding. An explanation. A tiny ounce of justice. It was then that I started to believe in heaven, albeit loosely and disloyally.

The year after, for various reasons, Brian and I started attending services at the Unitarian Universalist church in town. We were eager to involve the kids in the religious-education program there, and figured we could use some teachings too.

Unitarian Universalism does not prescribe specific ways to think about things like heaven, which is partly why I was so drawn to it. The religion has Christian roots, and like my parents' lessons, it focuses on the importance of being a good member of our local and global community rather than on any particular religious text. Plus, our church closes for the summer and was lovingly forgiving of the fact that Teddy's hockey games took place every Sunday morning in the winter. The flexible culture worked for us. It also meant that we had to do some of our own thinking about heaven.

* * *

For years prior to cancer, I gathered bits and pieces to add to my evolving beliefs about heaven and the afterlife. I gathered some of those pieces from church, but most of them came from random other places including literature, funeral services, weddings, history books, poems, television shows, movies, and even science.

My conversation with Teddy was another significant source of my understanding, as it compelled me to write about how some of the pieces fit together. In truth, after Teddy's questions about heaven, I wanted my family, especially my kids, to know what I thought about it. By no means did I feel they needed to agree with me on the subject; I simply hoped that whatever they chose to believe would give them the same comfort that I felt once I ultimately put some of my thoughts together on the subject.

One such thought involved a newspaper headline that I read during my treatment. It was about some scientific report that there are hundreds of billions of planets in our galaxy. I didn't even click on the article to read more, mainly because I knew that I would never be able to comprehend the concepts discussed there and because I knew that if I tried, I would just end up scared and confused.

Hundreds of billions of planets? I couldn't even fathom the existence of a galaxy, never mind the enormity of hundreds of billions of anything. Perhaps the geniuses at NASA would scoff at me, but it seemed like there was a whole universe (or universes?) full of so much that we did not yet understand, and perhaps never could.

* * *

A few months prior to finding the article about all the planets, Brian and I stumbled upon the perfect chance to watch a movie together after the kids went to bed. It was the night before Thanksgiving, so the rest of the country was out gallivanting with friends. Brian and I weren't in the mood for that—me because I didn't feel great (and have always stunk at gallivanting), and Brian because he is a homebody who for some reason enjoys my company.

We sat together for a while flipping through the movie choices at our fingertips. In the end we decided that we could only handle something light so we chose the film *We Bought a Zoo*. It looked cute and bright—a sweet little family surrounded by zoo animals. Or so we thought.

Just a few minutes into the movie, we were both bawling our eyes out.

It turned out that the film, which was based on a true story, portrayed a young father (played by Matt Damon) raising his son and daughter while they all mourned the loss of the mother who died…you guessed it…of cancer.

By halfway in we had cried buckets, but I insisted that the sad parts would end and the happy parts would begin. They had to. Plus, we had already invested so much emotion (and $4.99) into the film, I figured we needed to stick around for some smiles. Unfortunately, those didn't happen.

At the end of the film, we literally couldn't collect ourselves. We sat on the sofa, crying in each other's arms. Our minds were now full of high-definition images of one of our worst nightmares—kids sobbing for their deceased mother, a good man mourning the loss of the woman he loved.

Sometime in the middle of my hysterical tears, a fit of laughter came over me. I don't know what started it. Perhaps it was the fact that we had picked *that* movie of all movies, or that we had become such a pathetic sight when we simply had tried to have a quiet night-in together.

Once I explained myself through the laughing tears, Brian started laugh-crying too. We laughed so hard our stomachs hurt and by the time we went to sleep, we were completely spent.

The next day I wrote a blog post about how I hate to give advice but I had one piece of advice for every young family going through cancer— never, *ever* watch the movie *We Bought a Zoo*. Seriously, *don't*.

Despite that I tried to forget that film, one part of it stuck in my head. I couldn't forget it because it had become a piece to my heaven-puzzle. It's crazy I know, because *We Bought a Zoo* is not exactly where one would expect to find a deeper understanding of the afterlife. But a key phrase in the film—just two small words—stuck with me ever since that tearful Thanksgiving Eve.

At the end of the film, there was a flashback to the day the young couple met. The handsome man finds the courage to ask a total stranger if she would like to go on a date with him.

She smiles and responds, "Why not?"

* * *

I know that I have scattered random puzzle pieces all over this chapter (planets, Matt Damon, etc.). It's by no means profound. But it's my explanation of the peace I have begun to find with respect to a concept that has long perplexed me.

After that talk with Teddy, or maybe during it, I decided that I really do believe in heaven. I don't have a clue what this heaven looks or feels like, and I doubt baseball bats are there. But I do believe that souls can somehow find their way to a place where they remain eternally happy. Where they can reunite with their loved ones. Where there is justice and peace.

Obviously it makes me feel better to believe all this. It makes cancer less scary. But that isn't the only reason for my newfound faith in the existence of heaven. I believe because in a universe so unbelievably big—so undiscovered—it *could* be true. So why not believe?

Really...*why not?*

Pain and Gain

No pain, no gain.

This old-school philosophy helped me during the worst of my chemo symptoms—the first night of awful nausea, the neutropenia, the nosebleeds. The pain was proof that my medication was waging war inside me and that proof helped at the time. Unfortunately, it also bit back hard when my most serious symptoms finally subsided.

No more pain, no more gain?

Perhaps it was a ridiculous spin on the philosophy, but it was a sincere worry that bred fear in me, particularly when my hair started to grow back.

Later conversations with my oncology team convinced me that the *no pain, no gain* mentality had no validity in the cancer world. First, they told me that patients should seek help for painful symptoms of chemotherapy. Granted, the potentially helpful medications often have side effects equally as nasty as the original problem, but still, there are options out there that one can consider.

Second, my team reassured me that the chemo protocol had excellent results and that the Herceptin and the Tamoxifen would continue to ward off a potential recurrence.

"But I don't feel those," I argued back at one appointment, referencing the non-chemo drugs.

"That doesn't mean they're not working," Dr. Denver responded. He went on to reiterate the remarkable successes of the drugs. As he spoke, I recognized a huge irony: I hated the terrible side effects of chemo, yet once they were gone, I missed them.

Linear Motion

Having cancer taught me that most people, including myself, like linear stories. Forward-moving. Simple. Bad becomes good. The end.

When a bad thing happens, we want to know *why* and *how*. We want to help, too—out of the kindness of our own hearts, but also because helping is a way to cope. We allow a sick or grieving person some time to wallow in struggle and self-pity because we know they deserve that. Then, not long after, we want to hear that they are better. That the struggle is over. Neatly wrapped up in a local-newspaper article, or maybe even a book.

In general, our attention span for another person's pain is short. We would much rather hear stories of healing, strength, and victory. Not only to celebrate those who suffered, but also so we can believe that were we ever in a similarly awful situation, we too could be victorious. It may sound like a selfish mentality, but I don't judge it that way.

The problem with our natural preference for linear stories is that real life can be so very nonlinear. We all find ourselves in a spiral sometimes—lost and dizzy. But people don't want to talk about spirals. They want to hear about the valley and the peak while safely avoiding the fact that a long and treacherous road winds for miles between the two.

* * *

At my oncology appointment before my last chemo treatment, I asked Dr. Denver, "Is there anything I can do to make sure it doesn't come back?" He thoughtfully cited several medical studies as I knew he would. He told me that eating well, limiting alcohol intake, and exercising have been shown to decrease recurrence rates. But I had done those things my whole life, which actually scared me more.

Sometimes I even found myself wishing that I had had disgustingly unhealthy habits prior to my diagnosis, then I would be able to make some meaningful changes. The fact that I was "healthy" when the cancer grew inside me made me doubt that there was anything I could do to stop it from growing again.

I struggled to make peace with the absence of something to *do* to fight the disease. There were no big diagnostic surgeries from which to recover. No nosebleeds to cautiously avoid. No nausea to wish away. No desensitization procedure to pray did not kill me or white-blood-cell counts to watch diligently. Just an effort to try to return to "normal." An effort to disconnect motion and action—two concepts that I had always assumed were equivalent.

Fear, Snow, and Ice

It is a familiar fun-fact that people living in places perpetually covered in snow and ice have many words for the different forms of those things. For instance, in an Inuit dialect spoken in Canada, there are over 50 terms for snow, including matsaaruti (wet snow) and pukak (powdery snow). Similarly, an Inupiaq dialect spoken in Alaska has about 70 terms for ice including utuqaq (ice that last for years) and auniq (ice that's filled with holes).

This fun-fact has a powerful connection to cancer because since my diagnosis I've felt like my world is perpetually covered with fear, yet I need a broader vocabulary to more accurately describe the many different forms of that fear. Indeed, sometimes what our language tells us is the same thing is not the same thing at all. Yes, snow is snow, and ice is ice. But anyone who needs to cross a frozen lake would learn quickly that decades-old, thick ice is very different than ice that has holes in it. Similarly, the cancer-related fear I feel one minute is often completely different than the fear I feel a short time later.

Whiteout-Blizzard Fear

Have you ever driven through a heavy snowstorm, like the whiteout-conditions, everybody-stay-off-the-roads kind? I vividly remember my worst experience in that kind of snow. It was the night of my maternal grandmother's funeral.

After the church ceremony, my family gathered at my late grandparents' house for food and drinks in celebration of my grandma's life. We knew that a blizzard had begun outside and the worriers among us vigilantly kept an eye on the fast accumulation. Despite not wanting to break up the party, a few hours later we knew we had to. Those of us not staying at the house shoveled off our already-buried cars and headed back to our hotel. My mom was driving, and I was in the passenger seat.

What I remember most about that ride along the dark and curvy Amagansett road was that it looked like someone had draped a thick white blanket over our car. We couldn't see a thing, and most of the time we could barely tell if we were still on the road. My mom had the headlights on, but somehow the more we tried to see, the harder it was to do so.

No doubt, that ride was scary. Like *really* freaking scary. I remember feeling like I couldn't get my bearings; couldn't tell which way was forward and which way was back. I remember telling myself to just keep breathing—that we would get there eventually. My legs were almost paralyzed by fear, so it's a good thing that I wasn't driving—I wouldn't have been able to find the gas or the brake, not that either were very useful anyway.

Luckily, I can count on two hands the number of times in my cancer career that I was paralyzed by fear in the whiteout-blizzard-conditions type of way. I can also vividly recall how I got through those times, because it was the same way I endured the snowy ride away from my grandparents' house: I focused on taking air into my body and pushing air out of it.

Once I mastered the breathing part, I added the monumental step of trying to count to 10. Sadly, in that sort of a state, it wasn't easy to do. When it proved to be too hard, I went back to breathing again.

In these difficult times, I learned something that I previously took for granted. I learned that time moves forward—even when the thought of the next moment is more terrifying than anything I could ever imagine.

Falling-Through-Thin-Ice Fear

In my rookie months of cancerhood, I was always walking on thin ice (or auniq, if you will). I would be shuffling along, trying to stay upright on the weak and unstable surface, when all of a sudden I would plunge into freezing-cold water. An example of this type of fear conveniently appeared while I was drafting the blog that became the foundation of this chapter.

One night, while cuddled on my sofa with my laptop (and Brian), my email inbox dinged. An email from Maggie popped up in the corner of my screen. It was a group invitation to an upcoming fundraising event where she would join forces with her prominent oncologist in order to raise money for Dana-Farber's Program for Young Women with Breast Cancer. I hadn't participated in any part of that program; instead I habitually tossed out all envelopes from the program coordinator because I thought I might learn something that would frighten me even more (assuming that were even possible). *This* email, however, was from my friend. I owed it to Maggie to read it. As I did, I felt the thin ice underneath me start to crack.

Fundraiser.

Wife and mother.

Lost her battle.

Breast cancer.

Age 35.

All of a sudden I was under water. I didn't enter with a violent *splash*, but rather with an eerie *slip*. The water was numbingly cold and for a minute or two, I felt like I may drown in it. The hair on the back of my neck stood up and I felt my insides freeze. I was paralyzed—suffocating and unable to do anything about it.

Then self-preservation kicked in. My instinct to swim. My instinct to fight to find the surface. Granted, these unconscious acts of survival couldn't bring me comfort, but they were least strong enough to tell me that I needed to find a way back up for air.

In silence, I grabbed onto some thicker ice (utuqaq, or my laptop). And somehow, I pulled myself up into the next paragraph.

Easy-to-Shovel Fear

A whole different form of fear is that which is easy to scoop up and shovel away (or pack into a snowball and throw at something). Luckily, most of the fear I experienced after my double mastectomy was of this variety. I was able to face it, reason with it, and displace it in such a way that it wouldn't become an obstacle to whatever else I found myself doing. The following is one example of this easy-to-shovel fear:

During chemotherapy, particularly after I learned of my severe allergy to Taxotere, I found myself worrying—*What if the pharmacy incorrectly prepares my infusion bag with too much of the drug and I suffer from a fatal overdose?* The thought was based on something real, and I felt the bitter cold of the fear every time I considered it.

Then logic (my shovel) kicked in. I would tell myself things like *They have procedures to ensure that the doses are correct. They will follow those procedures. Everything will be fine.* Soon enough, shovel by shovel, the driveway in my mind would be clear. Or at least, clear enough that I could back out the car.

One-Hour-Delay Fear

When my medical leave ended and I went back to work, I learned an important lesson about this kind of fear: don't bother trying to ignore it.

A client meeting had brought me to the same hospital where Teddy and Annabel were born. As I stood in the main lobby and waited to pay for parking, I looked around at the space that was etched into my memory for all good reasons. It was as if beautiful ghosts were acting out a scene there—my family waiting anxiously in the lobby for news on my C-section. I could see their faces—smiling sometimes, worried others, and beaming with excitement and relief when our baby was born.

I remembered holding my new babies a few floors up from that lobby—

the nervousness, relief, and joy of those first days with them. Then, as I inched forward to pay my ticket, a dark monster approached me. It was the reality that I would not give birth to another child—not in that hospital or in any other one.

I didn't fall through thin ice at this thought (thankfully, the ice is a bit thicker when I'm in work mode). I did, however, perceive a heavy sense of loss and disappointment—it suddenly felt as if dark storm clouds were rolling in all around me.

Alone in the car on the way back to my office, I cried. I knew there was only one thing that could make me feel better—one tactic that could fight off that monster. I desperately needed to write.

Unfortunately, in a job that bills by the hour, I didn't feel the freedom to open my laptop and write during work time. Instead, I settled into my office and forced myself to tend to my assignments.

I was productive that day, but in a stubborn way. I was like that superintendent who should have delayed school-opening, but insisted everyone start on time. It's silly, really, because ultimately, everyone's still going to be late.

The next day, I still hadn't transferred my thoughts into a solid piece of writing. I arrived at work anxious, distraught, and covered in matsaaruti. In an attempt to learn from the day prior, I tried a different approach.

I called for a delay. Not a two-hour-delay-with-no-afternoon-kindergarten, just a simple one-hour delay. In that hour, I wrote. In order to form coherent sentences, I untangled emotions that had been storming inside me since I stood in that hospital lobby the day prior—when I had seen the ghosts and the dark monster. Each sentence brought me some clarity, and every paragraph brought me some peace. By 10 AM, I had exorcised my thoughts and was ready to get back to work.

Schools-Are-Still-Open Fear

This is the kind of fear with which I operate on a daily basis. It's a light snow that falls on and off all day. It's not a pretty, glistening type of snow, but it doesn't make the day dark and dreary, either.

This kind of snow doesn't accumulate. School principals take note and continue to monitor it, but they don't cancel school or call off afterschool activities. Is this type of fear distracting and sometimes inconvenient? Absolutely. But if I navigate carefully through it, I can still get to where I'm going.

Granted

Another important lesson I've learned about fear is that at some point in our lives, we all have to face it. I have never been comforted by that truth per se, but it has given me some much-needed perspective. In fact, I have an amazing woman to thank for a great deal of the perspective I clung to during my treatment. That woman is one of my clients, Maureen.

I met Maureen a few years before my diagnosis when my friend (and colleague at the Firm) Hannah and I teamed up on a new pro bono immigration case. We knew very little about Maureen's circumstances when we agreed to assist her—just that she had fled her African nation after facing the brutality of a government that wouldn't tolerate her political opinions (opinions that emphasized peace and democracy, by the way).

The immigration court system in Boston faces a perpetual backlog which is very unfortunate for the thousands of people whose lives hang in the balance of that system. In the fall of 2011 when Maureen, Hannah, and I appeared in court, the judge assigned Maureen an individual hearing date a year and a half later. Now that I know how hard it is to wait for a day that will change the course of your life and that of your family, I can't even fathom how Maureen waited for February 5, 2013.

*   *   *

While I hadn't been able to keep up with my corporate work during medical leave, I nevertheless kept up with Maureen's case. Given the relationship we had forged and the sensitivity of her traumatic experiences, I didn't even consider handing her case off to someone else. So with Hannah's help and help from another Firm associate, I did what I needed to do to prepare for the hearing. With great courage, Maureen did the same.

By sheer coincidence, February 5, 2013 was my first official day back to work from medical leave. It also ended up being one of the proudest days of my short legal career. Because on that day, hundreds of hours of reading, writing, researching, meeting, practicing, photocopying, emailing, praying, and traveling to and from law offices around Boston all came down to one handwritten "X" made by the pen of an immigration judge on a final order:

> The Respondent's application for asylum was
> (X) granted   ( ) denied   ( ) withdrawn with prejudice.

*   *   *

Maureen and I were both born in 1980 and we both gave birth to a child in 2008—I had Teddy, and thousands of miles away, Maureen had a little girl who I will call Robin.

On Halloween 2010, Brian and I took Teddy trick-or-treating around our neighborhood. While we skipped around collecting candy, half way around the world Maureen was saying a painful goodbye to her daughter and her husband, not knowing when (or if) she would ever see them again. Maureen then fled her country to this one, with little more than a few hundred dollars in her pocket and the name and phone number of someone she had never even met. All of this because she had peacefully opposed a corrupt government.

With certain exceptions, the United States provides political asylum to people who are unable or unwilling to return to their home country "because of persecution or a well-founded fear of persecution on account of race, religion, nationality, membership in a particular social group, or political opinion" (that's straight from the federal law). This means that the U.S. will protect these people by giving them legal status as asylees and eventually giving them the opportunity to become permanent residents and years later, citizens. But first, each individual must prove to an asylum officer or an immigration judge that he or she meets the legal requirements of asylum. On February 5, 2013, I was honored to help Maureen do just that.

Maureen is one of the most appreciative people I have ever met. Back in 2011, just a few months after we met, Maureen told me how grateful she was to have found attorneys to help her (her case had been delayed several times when the judge instructed her to find legal assistance). I also remember how upset and disappointed Maureen was with herself because she couldn't pay us. I explained to her that we still collected a very good salary from the Firm so she shouldn't worry about anything. Then I told her that seeing her daughter get off a plane in Boston would be better than any amount of money I could ever be paid. I believed that then and I believe it even more now.

Of all of my many meetings with Maureen, one stands out as perhaps the most difficult. It took place a few months before my diagnosis; back when February 5, 2013 still felt like a lifetime away. Maureen was devastated about not being able to work and more so, about having to wait (and wait and wait) until a judge would decide her destiny. Maureen also didn't know if she would be able to testify about the tragic things she had experienced. She contemplated giving up on her asylum claim to return to her country. "If I'm killed, I'm killed," she told us, staring into space, eerily matter-of-factly. I remember telling her that she wasn't doing this for herself; that she was doing this for her daughter. I remember that because it was the one thing I said that day that I know made a difference.

In his book, *Man's Search for Meaning*, Viktor Frankl wrote:

> A man who becomes conscious of the responsibility he
> bears toward a human being who affectionately waits
> for him, or to an unfinished work, will never be able to
> throw away his life. He knows the "why" for his
> existence, and will be able to bear almost any "how."

Before my very eyes, Maureen proved Mr. Frankl's words to be true—for her daughter, Maureen bore the immense weight of a long and lonely *how.*

There's no doubt that the corrupt government in Maureen's country stole so much from her. Maureen couldn't speak, write, read, gather, or travel with the freedoms that we take for granted every day. She was brutally abused in ways I can't even bring myself to write about, and she never got to watch her daughter pass through the toddler years.

When she came to the U.S., practical realities limited Maureen, too. Sure, she could travel where she wanted to. But Maureen wasn't allowed to work while she waited for her hearing, so she had no money, and it's hard to travel, or do anything really, for free.

Another part of Viktor Frankl's book reminded me of Maureen:

> Everything can be taken from a [person] but one thing,
> the last of the human freedoms—to choose one's
> attitude in any given set of circumstances, to choose
> one's own way.

No matter what had been taken away from her, Maureen never let anyone steal this last sacred freedom. Over two years after she was granted asylum, we're still working to reunite her with her family. Nevertheless, every day Maureen chooses her own way—an optimistic and hopeful one—and in doing so, she has helped me more than I could ever help her.

Part Seven
Birthdays

The older you get,
the more it means.

Bruce Springsteen
(musician, singer, songwriter)

My Therapy Lady

By March of 2013, just seven months after my diagnosis, I physically felt great. I had gained back all of the weight I shed unintentionally when I was worried sick. I could run, lift weights, and even do push-ups despite Dr. Lee's warning that those were banned for good. My hair had grown in enough so that I didn't look like a cancer patient, but rather, like a woman who couldn't be bothered with as much as a comb.

Oddly enough, my hair seemed like it meant a lot more to others than it meant to me. Several times a day, someone would remark, "Your hair is getting so long!" I would respond with a calm and polite "Thank you," but my internal voice worried, *If my hair can come back this fast, does that mean that the cancer could too?* I knew that was a negative spin on a positive comment, but I couldn't help it. Which brings me to the purpose of this chapter—the importance of my therapy lady.

* * *

To best describe my meetings with Dr. Grace, I would reference the end of a game of Connect Four®. My kids and I have not actually *played* that game but we have dropped the yellow and red chips into the plastic grid a thousand times. At the end of the game, once all the pieces are lined up in the holder, Teddy or Annabel releases the bottom and all of the chips fall into a heap on the table. There is no slow or neat way to do it—to clean up, you need to make a big messy pile first.

That was me with my therapy lady. I would seem calm and collected in the waiting area. I would enter the consultation room with all of my little pieces lined up. Dr. Grace would shut the door, sit down, and ask me how I was. At that moment, it was like she released the lever on my mind and a million random pieces fell into a messy heap at her feet.

I never felt like I needed an edit button with Dr. Grace. I could dump any thought onto her table—no matter how dark or scary—and I didn't have to worry about making her sad or fearful. I didn't need to worry that she would worry, and perhaps this was why she was so helpful to me.

Of course, it wasn't that Dr. Grace had no feelings because I knew she did. I just knew that she had so many pieces dumped, placed, or even thrown at her feet in those consult rooms at Dana-Farber that my pieces would not cause her any harm.

I liked Dr. Grace so much because she didn't try to connect all the pieces into neat lines during our 50-minute sessions. Instead, she tried to look at one or two of the pieces and find the right place for them. Her approach made everything feel more manageable.

I remember one meeting in particular when we talked about the piece that was my writing. I told Dr. Grace about how much I wrote and how much it meant to me. I can't remember if she asked why my writing meant so much or if by that point, I was literally asking myself questions and answering them. Either way, I remember exactly what I told her. "Because if I die, my kids will know me." It wasn't the only reason, but it was what I blurted out with my edit button shut off.

Indeed, I discovered healing powers in writing. When I sat down at the computer, I began like I began with Dr. Grace—dumping out a pile of emotion and worry, joy and pain, confusion and clarity. Then I would pick up one or two pieces and look at them more closely.

Sometimes I would find a connection between an earlier part of my life and a later one. I often understood issues related to my cancer better when I viewed them from a different stage of my life. I would experiment with how the pieces looked from different angles, how they fit nicely next to each other, or why they didn't fit at all. Occasionally I would approach an issue like a math problem—a puzzle that I needed to solve before I could walk away. Other times, I let myself wander in circles and was pleased even when I didn't discover anything new. Either way, by the time I was done writing, I had put a piece or two in place and the other ones felt lighter.

It was this discovery that led me to found a nonprofit organization, Writing Saves Lives. At the time this book went to print, the organization had received its 501(c)(3) status, proving that as much as I hate to fill out forms, I can do it if I really want to. Someone with no website-making experience (me) had created the webpage and we hadn't even started to solicit donations. Nevertheless, I have very high hopes for the organization, mostly because I know what writing can do for many people who haven't yet realized its miraculous healing powers.

I believe that the medications I received and the surgery I underwent saved my life. But so did Dr. Grace, and so did my writing. I've heard others speak of music, running, or volunteering in the same way. Whatever it is, I hope that others find their outlet, their way to express thoughts and emotions that would otherwise combust inside.

Luck and Water

In the first few months after my diagnosis, I didn't think much about why a tumor had grown in my breast, probably because I was so focused on getting rid of it. But once the cancer was—knock-on-wood—gone, I found myself constantly wondering *Why?*

What had caused the stupid cancer? I had no family history. Was it something in the air? Pesticides on my fruits and vegetables? Hormones in my milk? Chemicals in my deodorant? The birth-control pill? Microwaved plastic containers? A faulty gene? Lack of sleep? I found myself wandering in circles around these questions every day, not out of pity, but because (if possible) I wanted to stop doing whatever it was that had caused the cancer in the first place.

To best describe how the mystery of *Why?* can resonate with a cancer patient, let us take something simple, like drinking a glass of water.

Before I was diagnosed, I drank a glass of water without any thought beyond *I'm thirsty.*

After cancer, however, the thoughts that stomped around my brain were something more like this:

I'm thirsty. But I can't have tap water because there could be some mineral or metal residue or chemical in there that could ignite another tumor. Are there any bottles of water left? Wait, what if that water bottle was in a hot delivery truck and the plastic melted just enough to put plastic carcinogens into the water? That would be bad. But they must make sure that doesn't happen. Could they air condition the backs of trucks? Ah, yes, that's called a fridge. Right. But I bet they don't put the water bottles in refrigerators.

How about a Nalgene bottle? If it says "BPA free" it must be okay. Or are those recycle numbers on the bottom what matter? Darn it, I can't remember which numbers are safe and which are toxic. Okay, I'll use that metal bottle Brian brought home from a golf tournament last year. "Made in China." Eek. Are they as thoughtful about cancer in China as they are here? I have no idea.

Alas, glass! Yes, that must be the safest way to go. Unless the soap from the dishwasher could cause cancer. I'll just fill up my glass from the big blue bottle they deliver to our house every month. Crap. Those bottles are recycled. And I got some crazy email from our water company last month about how they meticulously check those bottles before they recycle them because some people use the bottles for things like gasoline. Gasoline?! Excuse me!? I never even thought about those bottles being recycled, never mind that there could have been gasoline in them! Then again, I would taste the gasoline, wouldn't I? I hope so, because gasoline is sure to cause me cancer. Oh sweet Jesus. I'm thirsty.

Now take that ridiculous (and exhausting) exercise and apply to, well, pretty much everything. I had no idea *why*, but the question quickly became a terrible burden.

* * *

When I finally asked Dr. Denver why I got cancer, he smiled and told me it was "the billion dollar question."

"And the answer *is*?" I persisted.

"No one knows," he replied, visibly disappointed that he had nothing more to tell me. "Bad luck?" he offered, knowing full well that it was an empty answer.

I wanted to ask more questions. *Did that mean once the cancer was gone, my luck button was reset? Would I need to have a second, totally separate bout of bad luck for it to return? Or was I predisposed to the disease so that my luck button could never get a full reset?* But I just smiled and kept those questions to myself. I knew Dr. Denver didn't have the answers.

* * *

Many people believe that everything happens for a reason. A subset of such believers have repeated the philosophy to me, implying (I think) that my cancer will lead to good things. In some ways it has, and it may continue to do so. But whenever someone tells me this, I want to ask *Would you say that again if cancer killed me?* I'm half-joking and I never actually say it out loud. I just hold my tongue and smile, curious if they've pondered that train of thought as much as I have.

I didn't believe everything happens for a reason before I had cancer and I don't believe it now. Instead, I believe that a million things happen—some good, some bad, some epic or tragic, and some seemingly plain and neutral. These things happen because of countless factors including nature, circumstance, and decisions apart from our own. Many happen for a reason we will never know and could never understand.

I sincerely believe that we can control some outcomes by learning and thinking and making good decisions. But I also know that I must accept that many outcomes will unfold no matter how much I learn or think or make the perfect decision. And so the issue transcends *Why* and becomes *How. How will we react and respond to what we find before us?*

That *how* is probably a whole bunch of seemingly small things. The decision to get out of bed and shower, to call the doctor, to join a family dinner. The decision to say yes or say no, to lie down or get up, to speak up or stay silent. The decision to laugh, cry, tell the truth, or lie. The *whys* can be hard to find, but the *hows* are all around us. We may not notice them at first, but they are there. And when we put them all together, we have something monumental: We have our life.

Steady Ground

The cancer worries that plagued me after my diagnosis weren't just about my own health; they were about my kids' health too. After Teddy and Annabel's pediatrician, Dr. Michaels, assured us that genetic testing would not lead us to answers that would indicate we should *do* anything to protect them from childhood cancers, we decided to forego the tests the genetic counselor had offered us. A bad result would mean only torment, and until such a result could be followed by an actionable next step, we weren't interested.

In this phase of heightened worry, Annabel started to complain about her leg. At random times over a period of a month or two, she would tell us that her "weg hut." Initially, I didn't think much of it. She was keen on jumping off sofas and chairs, and was always playing rough with Teddy. I figured her pain was a typical little-kid injury.

Then came the day she told me she couldn't walk. I plunged into icy waters as I watched her limp around the house. *Was this it? Was my worst nightmare coming true?*

But a short while later, she looked fine again. I was puzzled, and I didn't like it.

I told Brian I was scared and wanted to take her to the pediatrician. He said he was nervous too, and when I asked him what he was scared about, he immediately responded that he wasn't nervous about cancer. Clearly he knew that I was.

I was calm about Annabel's appointment in the days leading up to it, but on the ride over to Dr. Michaels' office, my mind ran amok.

I tried to tell myself that it was nothing, that she would be fine. But I had said the same things to myself on the drive to have my lump examined. Plus, I couldn't erase the geneticist's voice from my head ("…risk of childhood cancers…") or her follow-up letter suggesting that I schedule an appointment to discuss further testing for me and the kids.

At the appointment, Dr. Michaels held Annabel's legs and assured me that we would figure everything out. She said she wanted to take X-rays so we could rule out things like sarcoma. A few months prior, I wouldn't have known the meaning of that word. But just before Maggie began her new job treating sarcoma patients, she told me about the disease. Unfortunately, it's a brutal type of cancer.

When we reached the radiology department, I lifted Annabel onto the cold, hard X-ray table. She looked as small and innocent as I had ever seen her.

The radiation technician entered the room, looking down at her clipboard. Without so much as a "Hello," she asked me if I was pregnant.

I laughed out a "No," remembering the repeated times that Dr. Denver told me that I should absolutely not become pregnant while taking Tamoxifen.

"I do have cancer, though," I blurted out, too scared for my edit button to be functioning. I felt terrible the moment those words dove out of my mouth. I wished I said, "I *had* cancer," but perhaps it was just semantics. Either way, the tech didn't care. Cancer or not, I had to stay in the room with Annabel. The woman with a stone heart wrapped me in a heavy apron and a neck guard, then gave me a pair of solid gloves that looked like they belonged to someone involved in falconry.

When the tech left the room to press buttons, my mind started racing. *Is this safe for me? Should I stop it all and call Brian so he can come take my place? Could the exposure spark a tumor in me? Is my apron enough to stop that from happening? I should go tell the lady not to press the button. No, I'm being crazy. It's fine. But what if it isn't? I'm being so selfish. I need to make sure my baby is okay. If she's not, my cancer is the least of my worries. But...* The first image was done before I could finish processing these thoughts.

Three images and a bit of crying (by Annabel) later, we were done. Annabel selected an excess number of stickers from the basket before we climbed upstairs to discuss the results with Dr. Michaels. As I reached for the railing, I realized that my hands were shaking.

We took our seat in the waiting room and Annabel immediately began to play with the toys. I took note of her actions, but only with a small part of my consciousness. The rest of my mind was on another planet. A very, very dark planet. One on which I faced a sarcoma diagnosis in my baby girl. In those 10 minutes, while Annabel played happily, I felt like the ground was falling out from underneath me. Again.

"Annabel S."

Gulp.

Hold breath.

Wait.

Knock.

Hold breath.

"Normal."

On the ride home, I felt like I do after I wake from a nightmare. Obviously there was relief, but there also was a dark, lingering shadow of that terrible dream.

* * *

Long before cancer, I would have been nervous for those X-ray results of Annabel's legs. But there was something new that made it all so much worse. I felt compelled to figure out what that was. *What had cancer done to me?* Gradually, with the help of my therapy lady and my writing, I uncovered a few pieces of the puzzle.

One piece was the revelation that we are all vulnerable. Now I knew that one moment, one decision, one doctor's appointment could change everything. A split second could mean lasting pain. How utterly disconcerting.

Another piece of that puzzle had to do with what I call "steady ground." Prior to cancer, I had planted my feet on the firm belief that nothing mattered as much as good health. *Everything else could be fixed*, I thought. I didn't tell myself this only when something went wrong. I thought it when everything went right, too.

When we discovered that my "good health" wasn't very good at all, I felt like I lost my footing on this Earth. Eventually, I found a way to plant my feet again. My loved ones helped, as did my hope muscles and my instinctual belief that I had a medical team with the heart, brains, and science to cure my cancer.

The crazy thing was, this new ground was a lot like the old. It was based on absolutes—that everything would be fine as long as I didn't have a recurrence and my children didn't get cancer. Unknowingly, I had steadied myself on potentially hollow ground.

The potential hollowness of that ground was what made waiting for Annabel's X-rays and hearing stories of cancer recurrences so hard. I knew what utter betrayal felt like and I really didn't want to feel it again.

Over more time (and at first unknowingly), I started to build a foundation of steadier ground. It was a foundation based on faith—not faith that everything would go precisely how I wanted it to, but faith that even if it didn't, things still would be okay. I began to realize my faith in the human spirit.

Footprints of My Faith

Have you ever heard the story about God and the footprints? There are several different versions, as well as some debate as to who authored the first one. Nevertheless, the essence of the story is as follows.

The speaker has a dream that she (or *he*, but I will use *she* for now) is walking along the beach with God. Scenes of her life flash before her and she notices that during most of those scenes, there were two sets of footprints side by side in the sand—one for her and one for God. The speaker realizes that during the difficult times in her life, there was only one set of footprints. She is upset by this and asks God why He would abandon her during the hard times. God explains that alas, it was during those times that He carried her.

If others draw strength from this story, that's wonderful, but I don't find strength or faith in it. In fact, I reference this story only as a way to explain what my faith is *not*.

*   *   *

I admit, many times during my cancer treatment and its aftermath, I would have *loved* to believe in a God like the one in the *Footprints* story—a God who could have picked me up and carried me to the next minute or even the next month. Heck, I may have even gotten Him a wagon and He could have pulled me. But like Paul Tillich, a philosopher and theologian whose work I admittedly just barely know, I have never believed that God is a being who can effect events like mortals can. I never believed that God gave me cancer, and I never entertained the idea that He could take it away.

For me, the concept of God is a bit more complex. Or maybe it's simpler—I really don't really know.

I do know, however, that there is a difference between religion and faith. Anyone can have a religion. But faith is something that must be sculpted and cared for. Religion can be taught and practiced, but faith must be earned and protected.

*   *   *

In the film *Life of Pi*, the main character (Pi Patel) explains that "faith is a house with many rooms." My house of faith includes a blog and this book. Early on, my blog gave me a place to start sculpting my beliefs. It became my assurance, or perhaps my *insurance*, that if something happened to me, my kids and their kids could still know who I was. Writing was, and continues to be, my sanctuary.

Immediately after my diagnosis, the foundation of my faith was, in all honesty, modern medicine. I know that some people speak of science as the opposite of faith, but I don't see it that way. If faith is trust in something that cannot be seen and has no proof, then it makes sense that I would need to have faith in science and the people who dedicate themselves to it. After all, I will never know more about cancer than Dr. Denver does, and I cannot wake up each morning and confirm that cancer isn't growing in my body. I have never been able to feel what the Herceptin (hopefully) has done to save my cells from forming a new tumor. And like every other human being, I have no proof that anything I hope for in the future will actually happen, save that the sun will rise the next day.

In the months immediately following my diagnosis, I started to build my house of faith on the belief that the best modern medicine, at the fingertips of smart and dedicated people, could save me from cancer.

But I didn't stop there, as Pi Patel implies we shouldn't. I started to add on rooms, because even though a solid foundation is key, most of us don't want to live in the basement.

Thanks to the people around me, I was able to add on to and even decorate my house of faith. For instance, I added a room for music and I wandered there when no other room could help me. I remember coping with some indescribably awful minutes by repeating over and over the lyrics to Bruce Springsteen's *Waitin' on a Sunny Day*.

I also added a room for education, because I have faith that education is the beginning of all progress in the world. I started to believe that every student in a science classroom could have in his or her young mind pieces of the answers we need.

My house of faith was small, new, and modest, but surprisingly sturdy.

Then came my anaphylactic reaction to Taxotere. With that, the foundation of my faith cracked.

As I wrote about in Part Five, the weeks that followed that dreadful Halloween were some of the hardest of my life. I worried that my cancer was regrouping while I waited for answers from the allergists. I worried that my carefully-crafted treatment plan had been altered to my devastating detriment.

In those weeks, I nervously paced and even dragged myself around the rooms of my house of faith. More than ever, it would have been nice to believe in a God who could carry me. But I didn't.

Instead, with the help of my family and friends, I found a way to stand on my own two feet. To repair the cracks in my faith. To get back to building my foundation and the walls above it. Maybe I would need a new treatment plan, but if so, I came to have hope in it.

* * *

As time went on, I continued to decorate the rooms of my house of faith with beliefs formed from a variety of different places, from my church to my hospital room. I shaped my faith over my kitchen sink as my nose bled, and I shaped it in the car with my mom driving to and from my treatments. I shaped it while eating dinner with my family, while cheering on Teddy during his tee ball games, and while watching Annabel chase her big brother around the bus stop or the backyard. Through writing, I realized that if I believed in a God who carried me, I would have missed discovering my own, deeper faith.

Please don't get me wrong—I don't mean to judge or question those who believe their God can carry them through difficult times. My point is that every person needs to discover his or her own faith. It just so happens that I wasn't raised to believe that someone, or even God, would carry me. Rather, I was raised to trust and to see in practice that I would be surrounded by love and support while I figured out how to walk on my own two feet. That is the message I want to give my children, too.

And that is why I love Pi Patel's concept of faith. Because I don't believe that I can sit in one room, no matter how sacred it is, and find all of the answers I need. I'm claustrophobic in real life, and claustrophobic about my faith. I need to be able to build onto it, knock down part when it's not working, and decorate it with all sorts of unique ideas from countless people, places, and experiences.

* * *

Over two years after my diagnosis, cancer is still almost always on my mind. Admittedly, my house of faith still gets dark sometimes (even, every now and then, pitch black). But I *do* believe in God, and ultimately, that helps bring back some light.

Paul Tillich explains:

> The name of the infinite and inexhaustible depth
> and ground of our being is God.

Cancer is really freaking awful, but it has helped me scratch the surface of the depth of my being. Which I guess means that it introduced me to God.

I think of my God as a sort of spirit that pervades the house of my faith. He has not picked me up and carried me through my cancer journey but He has helped me build a multi-story house of faith. That house has been marked by many different footprints including, even in the most troublesome of times, my own.

Vital Passengers

I don't know much about being the caregiver to someone with a serious illness and for that I feel blessed. I have, however, watched my own caregivers from my healing chair, my hospital bed, and my seat at the dinner table. From them, I have learned a few important lessons. This chapter covers one.

* * *

Just after my first surgery, as Brian, my mom, and I carefully weighed different chemotherapy options, I had an appointment with my primary-care physician at the time, Dr. Thomas (who happens to be my mom and my dad's doctor too).

As Dr. Thomas washed her hands and prepared to examine me, she made doctor small talk—*How was I recovering from my surgery? How was I sleeping? How was I eating?*

Prior to breast cancer, Dr. Thomas knew of my hypochondriacal tendencies and attributed almost every symptom to stress. I didn't usually agree, but there was no use arguing with her.

I held my breath while Dr. Thomas felt around my neck. When she asked me about my chemotherapy plans, I was forced to exhale.

Dr. Thomas's questions struck me as so odd—she knew such detail about the options we were considering for chemotherapy, despite that I had never spoken to her about them.

When I left the exam room, I told my mom about how much Dr. Thomas knew about my situation; that she referenced details I knew were not in my medical record. *She must read my blog,* I thought at first, but that made no sense. *How would she know about my blog?*

My mom figured it out right away. "I think your dad told her," she explained as we left the doctor's office. *Ah ha. Yes.* My father had been in for an appointment recently. My heart sang and cried at the very same time.

* * *

My dad and I almost never talk about my cancer. During my treatment, he always asked how I was feeling, but we'd quickly move on to something lighter like work or the kids. He gave me love and support, but when it came to playing the role of the caregiver, my dad took a back seat. Not necessarily because he wanted to, but mostly because there wasn't any more room up front.

As much as I've written about how hard my cancer was on my mom and Brian, I haven't written enough about how hard it was on my dad. He was in an awkward position—obviously wanting to do anything he could to fix me, but knowing that Brian and my mom were there to pick up the pieces before they even fell out of my hands.

Early in the treatment process, I thought my dad was in denial about the seriousness of the situation. I didn't fault him for it, though I worried that he didn't really get it. But the moment I learned of his discussion with Dr. Thomas about my chemotherapy options, I realized that he knew most of the details we were weighing even though he and I had never discussed them. It was then that I knew my father wasn't lost in denial (at least, not completely). He was suffering too. I learned that day how seeing cancer up close is hard, but that doesn't mean seeing it from a distance is any easier.

* * *

Sometimes when I drive by the local pharmacy with my mom, she recounts the story of my dad on the day after my double mastectomy. I don't remember any of it, but apparently the other pharmacy up the street didn't have the medications I needed when my dad went to pick them up. My dad wasn't going to take no for an answer.

A few hours and several trips through town later, my dad secured the pills I needed to keep my pain in check. While most people would burst into the house venting about their frustrating adventure, my dad simply rushed in so he could hand my mom the medications for me. He just wanted my pain to subside.

My dad is incredible in that way. When I ask him for anything—to be at one of the kids' school events, join us at Teddy's tee ball or hockey game, take me to a treatment, anything—my dad says yes. Then he does it, no questions asked.

* * *

Partway through my treatment, my dad and brother started a new company. My dad is an entrepreneur down to the bone (or in his case, the artificial joint) and I know why. He is a visionary, a dreamer, a doer. He sees things bigger than I could imagine, then he builds them. He doesn't consider failure an option, or if he does, he doesn't show it.

So while my mom's calendar included all of my medical appointments, my dad's calendar was, I believe, focused on his lifelong dream—to put his children and grandchildren through college. He and my mom had already achieved the first part and despite the fact that their three children all chose outrageously expensive schools, my parents somehow made sure that all of us emerged from our undergraduate years without loans to worry about. I know that wasn't easy for them, and I hope that's part of why they're so proud of it.

* * *

It isn't easy to drive a car barreling down the road of cancer treatment. For Brian and my mom, riding shotgun wasn't easy either. But there were all sorts of challenges for my dad, as there are for anyone sitting loyally in the back seat. Sometimes those passengers need to be quiet when they want to scream. Sometimes they need to wait while the driver pulls over to a rest stop and cries on someone else's shoulder. They need to watch to be sure the exhausted navigators are heading in the right direction, but they can't always see clearly out the front window. These passengers need to be ready at any moment to change a tire or trek five miles for gas. Or sometimes they need to suggest that someone in the front turn up the music.

I hope these brave and loving passengers know how important they are. I worry they think that from the back seat, they somehow mean less to the driver. But that couldn't be further from the truth. Because even if they aren't seated right beside us, they are nevertheless vital to our journey.

Baby Dolls

During and after my treatment, Teddy and I talked openly about cancer and related topics. I answered his questions about everything from my hair to heaven to my terribly weak fingernails (he often noticed me grimace in pain when I caught one the wrong way). Annabel, however, was a different story.

At two years old, my little girl was still so young that I often wondered what, if anything, she understood about what we were going through. But then, if I watched closely, I could see that she picked up a lot more than she got credit for.

I remember one weekend in particular, about a month after chemo ended, when I saw a small but significant glimpse into what my cancer meant to my daughter. She was playing with her "bee-bees" (her dolls), only because Teddy was at a friend's house. (When Teddy was around, Annabel did everything he did—play knee hockey, build Lego towers, belt out Aerosmith's *Dream On*.)

That afternoon, I watched my two-year-old care for her baby dolls. She put "butt cweam" on their behinds and wrapped them in her own diapers. She made sure they had their "pacies," taught one of them to pee on the potty while she sat and watched, and put them down for naps in her crib— even remembering to turn the night light on for them.

After one of her babies woke up from napping, Annabel held her and kissed her several times. Then in her sweet little voice, she repeated, "Es o-key, bee-bee. Mommy go to doc-a today. Es o-key." She was so deeply entrenched in her own world of motherhood that she didn't even know I had overheard her. But she was right: it was okay. Mainly because she thought so.

My 33rd Birthday

When you're bald and fighting cancer, people are really nice to you. It's one of the perks of holding the cancer card (the little blue Dana-Farber card in my wallet). On my 33rd birthday—March 10, 2013—I got to thinking more about the cancer card as I hopped over puddles on a run up and down the main street in my hometown.

It was a glorious day and I was feeling great. My legs moved faster than they had in a while, and for that, some pride welled up in my hopefully-healthy heart.

I passed the police station and then my church when a carful of high-school-age boys drove by. Their windows were down and they screamed in my direction—a mean and nasty "c" word, and I don't mean *cancer*.

The loud profanity startled me, providing a stark contrast to the beauty of the day. As the boys drove off, I said out loud to myself, "Well *that* wasn't very nice." I vividly remember my next thought, something like—*I look enough like a girl that they would call me that word?* Because makeup-less (and thus essentially eyebrow-less), with my blue running jacket, very short hair, and black pants, I sometimes wondered if I could be mistaken for a guy. Obviously I didn't care enough to do something about it (except, I guess, get the boobs), but I was happy that even to a car of juvenile idiots, I still looked like a female.

My mind churned on. I thought about those kids, the word they said, and the energy with which they said it. Then the craziest thing happened. I started to run faster. I felt awesome. In fact, not a single part of me felt sorry for myself. Yes, it was my birthday, and I was innocently enjoying a run inspired (as most of my workouts are) by my oncologist's message that exercise decreases the rate of cancer recurrence. Sure I probably looked like a startled deer to those kids (and they probably got a kick out of that), but I didn't care about being so startled initially. Because inside, I felt *strong*.

As I covered four more miles, I thought a lot about those boys. I wondered how they felt before and after they yelled at me. They probably felt fine. Hell, most of them likely forgot about it almost immediately. But who knows? Maybe one of them felt guilty. Maybe one was going through his own terrible time. Maybe one of their moms had cancer, too.

I continued up the street, still fixated on "c" words, when I passed another runner. That was the first time I was really bothered by that Nissan Maxima. I wondered if the boys had screamed at her too. I wondered if she had my feeling of sheer resilience, and I hoped she did. I was sad at the thought that maybe she didn't. Then again, she could have been thinking the same of me.

Lending further evidence to my theory that the boys' journey was motivated largely by boredom, the Nissan passed me again, this time, coming up from behind. Again a violent blast of the "c" word, and again I was startled (you'd think I'd learn). This time, my instinct was to ask "Why?" with my palms facing the sky.

As if I couldn't get any more nerdy, I finished my run powered by how much I believe in the power of writing. I would love more than anything to sit down with those kids and ask them to write about their trip in the blue Nissan Maxima that March Sunday. About what they saw, what they said, and what they felt (or didn't feel) when they said it. I would love for them to be forced to think about the people on the other side of their words. What thought were they startled out of when the boys drove by? What made them get out there and run that day? Pain, happiness, fear? A complex combination of all of those things? I know, I may be nuts, but I really would love an hour with those kids.

* * *

The cancer card is a funny thing. The literal one gets you great parking rates at Dana-Farber. The metaphorical one is more complicated. Because on my 33rd birthday, I couldn't decide if I wanted to throw the card against the windshield of the blue car or hide it proudly in the pocket of my running jacket. On one hand, I wanted those kids to know they just picked on a cancer patient and I wanted to believe they'd feel badly about that. More so, I wanted them to know that if I was strong enough to fight cancer, I was sure as hell strong enough to keep my head up after being called a *bleep*. On the other hand, however, I wanted to hide that card and bask in the glory that maybe, just maybe, on my 33rd birthday the world didn't see me as a cancer patient anymore.

The Nightmare

A few nights after my birthday, I had a nightmare. It wasn't just any nightmare—it was *the* nightmare. I would have preferred one of my typical bad dreams—you know, the ones about earthquakes, tsunamis, and terrorist attacks. I'm used to those disasters slipping into my subconscious while I sleep, and I know how to push them out of my brain in the morning. But this nightmare was different, perhaps because I can't ever fully wake up from it.

In this nightmare, I found a lump. Unlike the real lump, however, this one was visibly protruding from my chest. A mass of death. Like the one Mary showed me the last time I saw her.

The rational part of me knew this nightmare was completely ridiculous. I would certainly notice a lump long before it grew to be the size of a baseball. But like most nightmares, the absurdity made it worse.

I woke up just before 5 AM, sweating, shaking, and absolutely terrified. I put my glasses on to try to get my bearings. I felt around my chest to see if the lump was really there.

It wasn't.

I checked again to be sure.

I was such a wreck that I wondered if I should take an Ativan. I couldn't remember when I last took one, but I knew where they were in our closet. I decided against it only because I knew I had too much to do at work to risk falling asleep at my desk.

I thought about waking Brian up, but that felt unfair.

I thought about writing, but I was too distraught.

So I got up and went to the 5:30 AM exercise class I frequented—not at all interested in doing so, but too scared to stay still. As I drove there, I wondered if I would even end up going in.

I did go in, and that hour of lunging across the floor, lifting stuff, and jumping up onto a box helped steady me. It strengthened my hope muscles.

On the way home I was still shaky with fear, but I was also a tiny bit proud that somehow, from the depth of my falling-through-the-ice fear, I had found a way to surface.

Wanting

I wasn't surprised I had that awful dream when I did. I had been more anxious around that time than I had been in a while. The worst anxiety crept up on me when I least expected it. In those moments I wrestled with fear (the whiteout kind), doubt, and anger. Once those feelings passed, I became frustrated that I still had them. I was back to work and (to others anyway) "back to normal." I wasn't supposed to be having such a hard time, or at least that's what I thought.

Meanwhile, I didn't want to bother anyone with my persistent struggles. *That story must be getting really old for everyone by now,* I told myself. *Leave them alone already. Your time to cry is over.* But it wasn't over.

I needed to figure out why my anxiety was on the rise again. For weeks, I refused to face the question head-on. Instead, I chose to do what preschool teachers do when kids cry at drop-off—I "redirected" myself.

That strategy worked for a short time, but eventually I needed to get to the bottom of it. If I redirected myself any further, I'd find myself in Mexico.

At first I thought maybe my birthday had induced the stress—not the celebration part because that was wonderful, but the milestone part. In ways I have already explained, my birthday was an awesome milestone that made me indescribably proud. But in other ways, my birthday was completely overwhelming. How had reaching 33 become a huge accomplishment? Maybe I wasn't ready to think about reaching annual milestones.

But it wasn't just about my birthday. There was something else, too—an intense feeling that came with a tinge of anger.

I finally started to recognize this feeling one night when I got home from work after the kids had gone to bed. I visited Annabel's room first and gave her a kiss. I repositioned her blankie and her Cookie Monster (the only two things she would allow in her crib). She was so peaceful, innocent, and adorable that my heart ached.

Then I visited Teddy. It was a miracle that Teddy even fit in his bed since he shared his mattress with at least 25 stuffed animals, 10 books, several blankets, two pillows, Brian's championship ring his hockey team won a few years prior, and during Christmas-time, tree ornaments. When I asked him once why he needs all of those things in his bed, he told me they "keep him safe." *Ouch, that hurt.*

In response I told Teddy, "Me and daddy will always keep you safe no matter what's in your bed." But it didn't matter—he still wanted his odd collection of little protectors.

When Brian or I aren't home at bedtime, Teddy adds another thing to his bed crowd—a picture frame of whichever one of us is absent. That late work night in March, as I unloaded the books from his bed, I found the photo of me and Teddy at his first Red Sox game the summer prior.

A crazy thing happened in that moment. Whereas before my heart would have ached at the thought of missing future Red Sox games with my son or not being there to tuck him in at night, now I felt something totally different. I felt an intense *wanting*—not wanting to avoid something, like cancer or death, but wanting to secure something, like more years of life.

After I recognized this unexpected shift, I found myself thinking less and less about how much I didn't want to die and more and more about how much I wanted to live. I know they may be two sides of the same coin. But trust me, they feel like very different sides.

Saying Goodbye

Once my medical leave ended, it was harder to find time to see Mary. In fact, the easiest days to visit my friend were my treatment days because I usually had a few hours after my infusion and appointments before the kids got home from school.

I emailed Mary's husband Cong on the afternoon before a March treatment day, to see if Mary was back safely from a trip to Vietnam and up for a visit. I figured that it could be the last time I saw Mary, and I thought it would be helpful to have Brian there for the teary drive home. Plus, I really wanted him to meet the couple I had talked so much about for almost two years.

Over email, Cong explained that Mary was not doing well and the next day wouldn't be a good day for visiting. "I take her to Dana-Farber for treatment in the morning," he explained. My heart jumped when I realized that I would also be there then. I told Cong about my own appointment and we made a tentative plan to meet up.

The next day, after my oncology appointment, Herceptin infusion, Brian's platelet donation, and my session with Dr. Grace, Brian and I wandered around Dana-Farber in search of Mary. She and I had missed each other several times between all of our different appointments and even the people at the front desk were trying to help us connect. Brian wanted to go home, but he also knew that I wasn't leaving before we found Mary. Finally, we did.

When I first saw Mary, a nurse was taking her vital signs in the same area where another nurse took mine hours prior. Mary looked drastically different than the last time I had seen her. She was in a wheelchair, unable to walk or sit up straight. One side of her face looked especially weak and hollow, and she could only barely open one eye. Before she saw me, I also noticed she was vomiting into a small bag that she could barely hold. When I saw that Mary's vomit was red, I wanted to cry and run away. Thanks to months of training to *not* run away and cry while at the hospital, I didn't flee the floor. Instead, I greeted Cong and the interpreter. It was crowded, and despite Mary reaching for my hand and motioning for me to stay next to her, I said I would move to the waiting room until the nurse was done.

When Mary's vitals were complete, the nurses moved her to a private room with a bed in the infusion suite. It was the same kind of room where I received my last two rounds of chemo.

Mary was alone when we reached her bed. The blankets were pulled up to her chin and she looked like she was sleeping. Before we could turn to leave so she could rest, Mary woke up and welcomed us in.

I sat down on Mary's bed and she held my hand. Her hand felt thinner, softer, and colder than it ever had before.

At that time, Mary's cancer was deep in her brain and it was affecting her ability to think straight. She spoke in Vietnamese to me, smiling as widely as she could. A few minutes later, I could tell that she realized she was speaking a language I couldn't understand. Mary laughed and apologized. I nodded and rubbed her hand, trying my best not to cry.

When Cong joined us, he gave me his usual gracious and enthusiastic greeting. He was so happy to meet Brian. Cong's English wasn't great, so the conversation was far from smooth, but at least with him there, Mary and I could exchange basic ideas.

Through Cong, Mary asked me the same question she asked me the last three times I saw her. "Where is your cancer? On the bone?" Then she pointed to her chest. Like last time, she unbuttoned the top of her shirt to show me her tumor. And like last time, I couldn't look away. I also couldn't believe how much bigger the mass was since a few months prior. The protrusion from Mary's tiny frame made me want to scream from the rooftop of the hospital how much I fucking hate cancer. Excuse my French, but I really do.

I tried to lighten up the conversation a bit and that worked for a short while. We talked about Mary's trip to Vietnam and how well her daughter and son were doing in school. I told her what I had told her a hundred times—that I would not lose touch with her family.

At the next break in conversation, Mary switched gears to a topic I never dreamed she and I would ever discuss. Sex. Yep, Mary started talking to me and Brian in broken English about *sex*. I blushed, probably because sex was the last thing I would ever have thought about within the walls of Dana-Farber.

I tried and failed to follow what Mary was trying to tell me, so I made a joke about how she was supposed to be a proper Catholic lady and here she was talking about sex. It was a bad joke in English and I'm sure once translated, it was even worse. Mary laughed anyway.

Eventually, the one with the common sense (Brian) chimed in from the chair behind me. He whispered to me that Mary was telling us not to have any more children. Mary lit up at the realization that Brian understood. I hated the third-child topic, and truthfully, would have much preferred an awkward conversation about sex.

After more struggle to understand each other, we arrived at Mary's strong belief that pregnancy and hormonal shifts would be bad for my cancer. She didn't have any clinical evidence to support her theory, but she was very adamant about it. With a lump in my throat, I told her we would not have any more biological children. "So don't you worry about me," I smiled through my tears. She was pleased with our decision.

Mary's timing on this topic was amazing because a few hours earlier, I had completed a survey asking if I would be willing to participate in a clinical trial for young breast cancer patients who wanted to get pregnant.

The first sentence of the survey was an unwavering statement that being pregnant has not been shown to increase breast cancer recurrence. It even said something about pregnancy possibly lowering the chance of recurrence. Talk about confusing. I had no idea what to think, but ultimately declined to take part. The study would involve stopping Tamoxifen after 18 or 36 months, trying to conceive, then restarting the Tamoxifen sometime later. As I wrote on the paper, I was too scared that being pregnant had contributed to my cancer. Dr. Denver denied that it had, but even his certainty didn't change what I felt in my gut.

At the same time, I'm not suggesting that pregnancy causes cancer. What the heck do I know? Nothing. I just feel what I have felt since my diagnosis—that after what I went through, it would not be good (assuming it were possible) for me to have another biological child. I found it remarkable that out of the blue, Mary told me that she thought the very same thing.

Mary received her very last cancer treatment the afternoon after Brian and I left her bedside. She then spent several days in the hospital before the doctors sent her home with hospice.

JJ and Mary

One week later, on my way home from work, I picked up dim sum takeout at Mary's favorite place and went to visit her and her family in their Dorchester apartment.

Since Mary could no longer sit or stand up, Cong had moved her bed into the living room so she could get more sunlight during the day. Mary was so happy to see me, as I was to see her. I could tell she had declined significantly even from the week prior.

Cong bustled around the room plating the food, filling glasses of water, and making sure that the family photos he had taken over the years ran in a loop on the television. We laughed at the old photos and smiled quietly at the newer ones. But I must admit—considering the situation, all of them made me sad.

As I sat on the folding chair next to Mary's bed and tried to avoid having to eat more dim sum, I heard my cellphone chime with several new text messages. I didn't want to be rude, but I leapt up to view the texts. This was a special exception to my no-texting-at-mealtime rule—Brianne had checked into the hospital that morning to deliver her first child and I was anxious to hear news about baby and mother. Indeed, the texts alerted me to the fact that Brianne and Seamus's firstborn son had arrived. James Joseph, or "JJ." He was perfect.

When I told Mary and her family about the baby, everyone erupted into cheers. I showed Mary the photo of Brianne holding the baby bundle. Mary rubbed the screen of my phone lovingly, as if she could touch the baby through it.

I will never forget that moment as long as I live. On the verge of death, Mary beamed at new life. It was overwhelmingly tragic. And indescribably beautiful.

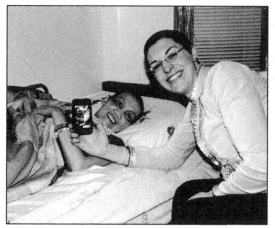

With Mary celebrating JJ's arrival – March 27, 2013

Part Eight

Reconstruction

Allow for the greater possibility
of your own survival.

Anonymous
(blog reader)

The Rearview Mirror

In April 2013, eight months after my diagnosis, three months after my last chemotherapy infusion, and two months after I had returned to work from medical leave, I met with my plastic surgeon to discuss my next surgery. The surgery would be the second part of my chest reconstruction.

Since she had inserted the tissue expanders back in September, Dr. Lee had gradually inflated the expanders with saline. Now that my body was able to heal wounds and fight infection, it was time to switch out the expanders for silicone implants.

When I met with Dr. Lee in the pre-op appointment, I assured her that I wasn't nervous for the procedure. However, I did have one question.

"Have you ever opened someone for this surgery and found more cancer?" I curled up in preparation for the answer.

"Never," she responded with confidence. I wanted to hug her and cry happy tears, but Dr. Lee is so classy that I tried to emulate an ounce of her grace. I contained myself, smiled, and let that be that.

When it came time for the surgery I was calm and collected, which felt good (and rare). The general anesthesia made me sleep while the plastic surgery team traded out my expanders for implants. It was uneventful, which is precisely what I had hoped for.

Over an hour later, I woke up in the recovery room with my new boobs. I had several conversations that I don't remember, and just a few hours after that I was heading home to reclaim my position in my healing chair.

Compared to the bilateral mastectomy, the pain I felt after this second surgery was mild. I didn't even use the prescribed painkillers since ibuprofen was strong enough to do the trick. Still, I had to rest, and I must admit, I really suck at resting.

I learned that week that I especially suck at resting when I can't see clearly. It turns out that most forms of entertainment involve seeing, but once again the anti-nausea patch I wore behind my ear to combat the dreaded side effect of the anesthesia made my eyesight very blurry.

Bad eyesight—really bad eyesight—runs in my family, so I'm not a rookie to blurry vision. Since we met in college, Brian has always loved to poke fun at my visual disabilities. His favorite trick early in our relationship was to steal my glasses and hide them while I wandered around feeling surfaces for where they could be. Often, he'd be wearing them. He got such a kick out of me looking straight at his blurry figure telling him what a jerk he was, all while my glasses sat just above his mean little grin.

A few days after surgery, my ability to see long distances improved. But I still couldn't read anything up close unless I took my glasses off and placed the text an inch from my face.

At first, my blurred vision didn't bother me. Hunched over in my healing chair, I could type with one hand while holding my laptop a few inches from my face with the other. I was sore after writing for hours in that position, but I felt satisfied to have found a way to work around my limitations.

A day later, however, I lost my patience. Not being able to write or read was definitely the worst part. Not being able to exercise, shower, pick up my kids, drive, or essentially do anything productive turned me into a total grouch.

The entire time that I was in a bad mood, I knew how ridiculous I was being. I knew I should have been thankful that I already wanted to do all of those things again, uninhibited by the fears associated with cancer. I knew how lucky I was and how simple this surgery had been compared to the last one. But none of that helped me shake myself into a better mood. Eventually I just let myself wallow in my own grouchiness.

While I was happily surprised by the lack of physical pain associated with the reconstructive surgery, I was unhappily surprised by the significant emotional impact that the procedure had on me. But why? Why was this surgery so hard? Gradually, I figured it out.

* * *

Despite some setbacks, I have been blessed with a relatively linear battle with cancer: diagnosis then surgery then treatment then recovery. I took huge steps forward with each move, and those steps fit my personality well.

My second reconstructive surgery was another step forward, but in the subsequent days, I couldn't see it that way (no pun intended). Instead, those days felt like an unwanted flashback to a world I had worked so hard to move beyond—a world full of wounds and gauze and unwanted rest. A world where I couldn't see clearly (literally and figuratively).

In those days post-surgery, my mind was fuzzy. As I dozed in and out of short naps (another feeling I hate), I had to determine over and over again whether my surgery had already happened or if I was still preparing for it.

During this time, I also had several *very* bad and *very* vivid dreams. The combination of those nightmares and my surgeon's instructions to rest suddenly thrust me back into the Kingdom of the Ill.

One night, while moping around that kingdom, I returned to a comment that an anonymous reader had shared on one of my blog posts:

Tara,

Your blog has been a new place with familiar feelings for me. I am an eight-year survivor of Stage 3 breast cancer (briefly bumped to Stage 4...long story). We are informed by mortality-rate pies that do not reflect the amazing progress we have made with this disease. When I was first diagnosed I asked a friend, a survivor, if there was ever a day, an hour, a moment, that she did not think about cancer. She was 10 years out and she said "months go by." I couldn't believe it. It took some time for that to be true. You will grow old. You don't have to be more grateful than anyone else for the privilege. Be proud of your brave fight and allow it to get smaller and smaller in the rear view mirror.

You are so alive, and your writing reflects that. I think the instinct is to try to appreciate each moment (bald, with mouth sores and nosebleeds...and the constant threat of your own mortality...hah). Allow for the greater possibility of your own survival. Live as if....isn't that how it was before? Being wrong then didn't change that. The quality of your life returns when you can embrace the probability, just as you did before diagnosis, that you will be a gray-haired old granny.

I have every confidence that you will prosper. I am now, very recently...a granny.

This comment helped restore some hope in me at a time when my hope muscles had atrophied. It also made me believe, for the very first time, that one day my mind could be free of the running cancer commentary that so burdened it.

* * *

If someone asked me before my second surgery if I had put cancer in my rear-view mirror, I would have answered with a resounding "No way!" I would have said that cancer's big ass was still planted in my passenger seat, and worse, that it refused to put its seat belt on so the warning alarm was relentlessly dinging. But those grouchy, blurry days after the implant surgery made one thing clear—I *had*, in fact, started to pull away from the real throes of cancer.

I returned to work the next week in my Velcro® surgical bra and loose-fitting blouse. My chest was fragile and the scars were fresh, but so long as no one bumped into me on the train, I was okay getting back to my routine.

Several weeks later I realized that if I looked back, I could once again see cancer getting smaller in my rear-view mirror. If I looked to the side or to my back seat, I could see my family and friends still with me on the crazy ride. If I looked down, I could see my new boobs. And if I looked forward, I could see myself. Not only did I have hair, but even better…I think it was gray.

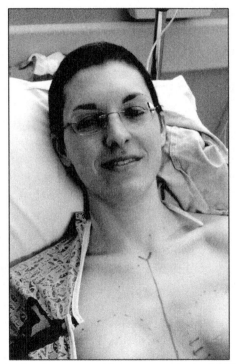

Preparing for my second breast surgery in April 2013 –
Dr. Lee had drawn up her plans on my chest

She Is Here

The year Teddy was born, my mom and I started a Mother's Day tradition. Instead of buying each other gifts, we escape for a night together. We leave from our offices on Friday night and drive somewhere simple and peaceful—like New Hampshire. We have a nice dinner and fall asleep in comfy beds with lots of pillows. We spend the next day shopping and exploring, then arrive home before dinnertime. It's not a long or wildly adventurous trip, but for both of us, it's indescribably precious.

In most respects, my first post-cancer Mother's Day trip wasn't much different than the trips before it. My mom and I talked most of the way up I-95. We munched on snacks, listened to music, and sat in traffic—the latter of which didn't even bother us. In at least one way, however, that Mother's Day trip was so very different.

It started on the train ride from North Station to the Winchester stop near my mom's hospital. As I sat squished next to another commuter for the 18-minute journey, I thought back to same ride exactly one year ago. Then my mind jumped to next year. *Would I be on that train again? Would all of the treatment have worked? Would my mom be okay if it hadn't?*

All of a sudden, I felt completely overwhelmed. My mind continued to run amok. *Would my children grieve for me when a future Mother's Day rolled around? Would the holiday mean sadness and loss for them? Would they ever recover from that?* I realized that despite how far I had come in believing that I had a future, the idea of that future still terrified me.

* * *

I have several friends, relatives, and former students who have lost their mother. Of those tragedies, I know very little. Sure, I know the disease or the basic circumstances that took their mothers too early. But I don't know how those survivors coped with such a significant loss. I just know that they continued breathing and living.

On that Mother's Day train ride, after wallowing in my own fear and misery for a few minutes, I realized a huge irony in the way I was behaving. There I was, en route to New Hampshire with my mom, and I was letting my fear ruin it. I was letting my fear of next year damage the joy of this year. The fact that I had recently published a blog post about living in the moment made me feel like a terrible fraud, and a spoiled brat for mistreating a day for which countless others would pay a small fortune.

I fought to pick myself up from these depths. Once I found the surface, I decided it best to redirect my mind. How does one redirect with just a few minutes left of a train ride? Meditation would have been good, but I didn't know about that yet. So I did the opposite of mindful meditation: I checked Facebook.

As I scrolled through my newsfeed, I came across a photo that my friend Lauren had recently posted. It was of a Mother's Day gift her young son made her at school—one of those fill-in-the-blank worksheets where the kids answer a few questions about their mother, and then color around the text before they cut it into the shape of a flower.

My mom is ___. She likes to ___. Her favorite food is ___.

The last fill-in-the-blank brought tears to my eyes:

The best thing about my mom is ___. Lauren's son had answered: "That she is here." I swear, little kids often find the words that I couldn't find if I sat for hours in search of them.

As my mom and I checked into the hotel and relaxed in the room for a bit, I couldn't stop thinking about that answer. Even as I turned the light off that night, I was still smiling at the clarity that the answer brought me— that the best thing about *my* mom is also *that she is here.*

I hope that decades from now, my kids can say the same—that their mother is here. But if for whatever reason they can't, I hope they can answer the question without overwhelming pain in their hearts. And maybe even a smile. *That she was here.*

Blessed

Spring in our suburban neighborhood means the start of many wonderful things—wiffle ball and street hockey games, impromptu gatherings in a driveway or on a porch, and lawns cared for by proud and humble homeowners. We are blessed to participate in all of these things, but let's focus on the last one for a bit. Let's talk about "the lawn."

All of our neighbors know how much my husband loves our lawn. (Brian usually calls it "the lawn," but sometimes he slips and calls it "my lawn," which seems perfectly justified to me.) When it's not covered in snow, Brian spends hours working outside on his lawn. He built a shed to house the many tools and machines involved in the lawn's maintenance, and he battles a constant case of poison ivy to make sure that the surrounding brush is just right.

I sometimes wonder why Brian loves caring for the lawn so much. As the parent of two young kids, he may just cherish the quiet escape. But since there are much easier ways to avoid us, I'm pretty sure it's something deeper. Whatever the reason, Brian is proud of the lawn, and it looks proud in return.

Brian is an educated consumer, and after buying bags and bags of fertilizer and laying it down several times a year, he figured out that lawn-care companies can fertilize the grass for less money than it takes to do it himself. So a few years ago, VeryGreen began to visit our property every few months.

Brian loved VeryGreen, not only because the lawn always looked awesome, but also because the VeryGreen guy always left behind notes telling Brian to "keep up the good work." He's easily flattered.

Teddy used to love using his plastic lawn mower to "help" Brian mow the lawn. He would put on ear phones just like Brian and scoot around behind his dad. Sometimes Annabel would help too, but she hates loud noises so usually she could be found screaming that the "yawn mow-wo is too youd!"

* * *

Prior chapters likely have made it clear that cancer can change a person's perception of just about everything. For good or for bad, our lawn was no exception.

Where I used to focus on the lush color and beautiful feel of the grass, cancer pointed me to the little yellow sign that VeryGreen left behind after each fertilizer treatment—you know, the one with the faceless little family circled and crossed out, and the warning that people and dogs should *Keep Off.* Perhaps naturally I became scared that some sort of lawn chemical could contribute to a recurrence of my cancer—or worse, cause cancer in my children.

* * *

During an appointment with Dr. Denver in the spring after my diagnosis, I asked him if Brian and I should reconsider the chemicals we put on our lawn. Dr. Denver said that we didn't have to bother, although he did mention that when his kids were young he thought about these issues, too, and at one point, he even made some significant changes in the name of all-natural. In the end, however, Dr. Denver told me that as long as I didn't eat the grass (I don't), he wouldn't worry about it.

I recounted the conversation to Brian later that night. He didn't say much in response, and I assumed that his silence meant that he thought I was being crazy. I probably was, so I didn't argue or push him to talk. I figured that the conversation was closed and that I would have to make peace with the little yellow sign and the VeryGreen chemicals that came with it.

The next day, Brian texted me out of the blue: "VeryGreen out ... NaturalGreen in. Spoke to guy for a while on the phone. All-natural, organic treatment of lawns." I cried when I read that.

In the following months, I heard from several people who had tried organic lawn care that their lawn never looked the same again (none of them meant it in a good way). I relayed this news to Brian. I wanted him to fully understand the potential sacrifice. I warned him that his four years of hard work may be erased by the switch to NaturalGreen. But it didn't matter. Brian had made up his mind.

* * *

I don't know if it's the cancer thing, the writing thing, or my anxiety medication, but sometimes I have precious moments of clarity—moments when one tiny concept makes so much sense that somehow, for a split second, the whole world makes sense too. Brian's NaturalGreen text provided one of those moments.

That text, and our ultimate shift to NaturalGreen, showed me that those who are truly blessed are not people who successfully avoid fear or pain. No one can do that. Those who are truly blessed are not the rich, or the beautiful, or those who live to be 97.

The truly blessed are those surrounded by people who love them with honest depth and devotion. The truly blessed are surrounded by people who would sacrifice for them—in big ways and in small ones. They're surrounded by people who declare (sometimes silently), *I will do anything to make you better.* And then they go ahead and do it.

What Scans?

As the one-year anniversary of my diagnosis came into focus on the calendar, I felt like an experienced cancer patient. I had picked up a decent amount of medical lingo, and could rattle off names of several chemotherapy drugs like they were my phone number. I knew the ins and outs of Boston's Longwood Medical area, and knew when to put my arm out for the check-in person at Dana-Farber to tape the ID bracelet around my wrist.

Then again, there still would be times when I felt like I didn't know crap about crap. One of those times happened in June of 2013 when an acquaintance asked me about my "most recent scans." Um…*What scans?*

Sometimes when I try to think back to what I did yesterday I blank out for a moment or two. That happened pre-cancer, too—although less so pre-kids—so I'll go ahead and blame the kids and not the cancer. Even so, when faced with the scans question, I had to stop and think if I was missing something. Again, *What scans?*

A few seconds later, I convinced myself that my gut reaction was correct—I had no recent scans. Of course I knew why they didn't scan my breasts—there was no tissue left to check. But I didn't know why they didn't check the rest of my body for metastasized cancer. Obviously, this made me wonder.

If (Heaven forbid) my treatment was ineffective, wouldn't it be good for them to find the new tumor(s) as early as possible? Or maybe, I thought, they wait until after the year of Herceptin infusions to start the scanning? I was curious, but at the same time, I didn't know if I really wanted the answers.

At my next appointment, I built up the nerve to ask Sydney why I don't get scanned. I braced myself for the answer.

Sydney explained that for patients like me, there's no difference in life expectancy if they find the metastasized tumor earlier from a scan, or later as a result of me finding a lump. *Well, shit.*

Sydney stressed that they hope to have destroyed all of the cancer cells with chemo, and Herceptin does the rest. She also explained that most people have one or more odd growths somewhere inside their body. While those masses are not necessarily dangerous, for a cancer patient, they would cause much anxiety and likely lead to unnecessary biopsies.

"We also don't want to expose you to anything when there's no data to show it's useful," she concluded. I figured she was referring to the rays in the MRI, CT, and X-ray machines.

It wasn't easy to digest what Sydney told me—that metastatic cancer would be a tough haul no matter when we found it. Still, it felt oddly liberating to have asked a question that terrified me, and even more so, to have found the guts to listen to the answer.

Backfired

In a church sermon a few years ago, I heard a short story about Ryan White's mother Jeanne. Ryan White was a hemophiliac who contracted HIV/AIDS through a blood transfusion in the early 1980s. When he was diagnosed in 1984, Ryan was given only months to live. Nevertheless, he bravely battled AIDS and the terrible stigma that came with it for almost seven more years. Jeanne was her son's biggest advocate.

I remember hearing in the sermon that one part of Jeanne's day—both before and after Ryan's death—was sacred to her. That time was each morning when Jeanne made her bed. Apparently that ritual, that time alone to focus and breathe, convinced Jeanne that she could keep going despite all of the pain, loss, and confusion that she and her son had to endure.

This tiny part of Jeanne's story—the precious making-the-bed routine—resonated deeply with me during certain parts of my cancer journey, including in June 2013 when in the same week I threw out my back at the gym and caught a stomach bug.

At the time, I was more than halfway done with my Herceptin infusions, and physically I felt great. The mental part was more difficult, and I had developed my own routines to cope. I had slowly discovered what helped me and what hurt me. Of course, writing still helped the most. Second to writing was my morning hour of exercise.

The hour I spent exercising before the kids woke up became sacred to me. It was my time to focus and breathe; to repeat to myself that everything was going to be okay. Without even intending to, I came to rely heavily on that hour for my mental well-being. As I walked, ran, rowed, or lifted weights, I thought to myself, *If I can do this, then I must not be sick.* I loved the confidence the routine gave me to start my day. I cherished it.

The problem with my sacred morning ritual was that when I didn't feel well, it came back to bite me. And I learned the hard way that it had really sharp teeth.

*   *   *

As I struggled without my morning ritual, I knew I shouldn't complain. I knew there were people who had it so much worse—who were confined to a wheel chair for life, whose heart failed after chemo. I just had a tweaked back and a bad stomach. It shouldn't have been a big deal, but it sure seemed like one at the time. Because in that week of aches and nausea, cancer crawled all over me. I felt it everywhere—in my back and my chest, in my arms and legs, even in my ear. I wish I were joking, but I'm not.

Gradually I understood that it wasn't easy to lose suddenly the precious way by which I set my day on course. It was frustrating to think that others didn't understand. Except for Jeanne. She definitely understood.

One thing that helped ease my fear that dreadful week was the fact that Teddy had puked three times in one day—once in Brian's classroom, then at a sandwich shop, then in Brian's ear when they were at the dentist. Sadly, Teddy's puking was a source of great comfort for me in those days when I didn't feel well either. I know—what kind of mother thinks that, never mind writes it?! What kind of mother is comforted by her five-year-old's stomach bug? The terrorized kind, that's who. The kind who needs to blame aches, nausea, and fatigue on something other than a cancer recurrence.

Around this time, I also found myself wondering, *Why didn't someone tell me that this part would be so hard? Was this a little cancer secret that everyone successfully kept from me?* Maybe I was just looking for someone to blame. Seriously, did I really want Dr. Denver to warn me before my treatment began, *You think this part is hard? Ha! Just wait about six months after chemo when you don't feel well. Wait until you see how much that's going to suck!* Maybe it's similar to why few of us bother telling a tired, pregnant woman what's in store for her. One day at a time, right?

Part Nine

Anniversaries

As I grow to understand life
less and less, I learn to live it
more and more.

Jules Renard
(author)

In Peace

By the last week of June 2013, I knew that Mary was about to die. She was no longer able to eat and was essentially comatose. I selfishly wondered how her family would tell me. I figured it would be via email or text message, since that was how we usually communicated.

Midweek, I texted Ngan to tell her that I was thinking of her, her mom, and the rest of their family. *This must be a terrible time for you all. I'm so sorry,* I wrote.

Ngan texted me back a few minutes later to thank me. Then she told me when and where the wake and funeral would be.

For some reason, I was shocked. Despite that I had anticipated this news since the day I met Mary a few years prior, the real thing felt like a devastating surprise. I wondered if Ngan and her family felt the same way. I prayed that they didn't.

* * *

Earlier that week, thanks to the idea from a friend and fellow blogger, I spent some time writing about bucket lists. When I started brainstorming about this topic, my gut told me that a bucket list wasn't really my kind of thing. After thinking more about it, however, I revised my work and shifted some of my ideas. I remembered a book I had read a few years back when I was on maternity leave with Annabel. It was called *Creating Your Best Life,* and I dug it out of my basement the week before Mary died.

It turned out that the first chapter of that book was all about bucket lists. My subconscious may have remembered that but my conscious had totally forgotten it, probably because back then a bucket list was as foreign an idea to me as cancer. But I *had* remembered the main messages told over a few hundred pages: (1) by writing down our goals we are better able to achieve them, and (2) achieving our goals leads to happiness. I got the point, and a few months later on the train home from work, I made a list.

It wasn't a bucket list. It was just a plan for the next few years—when we would have our third child (summer 2013), when I would leave the Firm (January 2015), how much money we would have saved by each milestone (a hell of a lot more than we had actually saved). When I recalled that list in 2013, the piece of paper had been in a file cabinet in my basement for over three years. It must have been laughing at me.

Nevertheless, by the end of writing the bucket-list blog, I decided I should draft a new list—places I wanted to go, things I wanted to see. I had no idea how we would ever afford these things, but I would dream about them anyway. It wasn't a cancer-thing—it was just a fun-thing.

Cancer, however, made me hesitant to put the list down onto physical or virtual paper. I worried that if I died and never made it through my list, my family would find it one day when they were cleaning out my things and be crushed that I had dreams left unfulfilled. So I thought the list was dangerous, even if it included a most important caveat: that these things were just gravy—small items on a silly list—because I had already been given life's greatest gifts. Ultimately I decided I would create a mental bucket list. No danger in that.

The next day, however, I learned of Mary's death. It changed me. Suddenly, the idea of a bucket list, even a mental one, made me feel guilty, spoiled, and totally misguided. I was back to my gut reaction—no bucket list for me. Just day-to-day appreciation of the simple things. Perhaps it was cliché, but I didn't care because I sincerely believed it.

Surprisingly, the whirlwind of emotion I had over Mary's death had very little to do with *my* breast cancer. When I first heard the news, I just wanted to scream for Mary and her children. But I didn't scream. I just stared beyond my tears and through my office window toward Boston Harbor.

Then I became angry. It wasn't even at cancer either; I was angry at a former New England Patriots football player who, at the time, faced murder case being built against him. I knew it was a ridiculous and random reaction, but it was the truth. *Why did he get to walk on this Earth and Mary didn't? Why was he strong and healthy enough to shoot people and play football and Mary was dead?* I was aware that I was mostly just being nuts, but as I broke my no-crying-at-work rule in the privacy of my own office, I was furious that someone so good was taken so early. Injustice can fill me with such pain that way.

A few minutes later, after I collected myself and realized that the awful NFL star and Mary were not exactly related issues, I was just sad. So very sad that Mary never got to make a bucket list of adventures and travel destinations. She wasn't even well enough to go to Ngan's high-school graduation, and I know how much she had wanted to be there. My heart ached, physically *ached.*

I tried to work that day, and somehow I managed to pull myself together and get a few things done. But when I left work, my heart still felt broken.

On my commute home, I just sat on the train and thought about things. But I found no clarity. No words of wisdom. No idea of how I could ever even partially reconcile that tragic situation.

Now I realize that it isn't right and never will it be. I shouldn't have bothered to search for any explanations to the contrary.

* * *

The next night, desperately in search of comfort, I returned to the stream of text messages between me and Ngan. I don't know why I went there, but when I did I found Ngan's message with funeral arrangements. In my shock that Mary was gone, I had glossed over Ngan's last sentence in that message—"My mom left in peace."

At first I internally scoffed at those words. *She did* not *leave in peace*, I asserted silently. *I saw her. She was coughing up blood. She didn't know her own name. No one could die from cancer in peace.*

Then I thought more about Mary. I thought about how organized, calm, and brave she was when Liz and I first met her. How she always smiled, sometimes even when she was crying. I remembered how she had come into the cramped office at the back of the health clinic in Dorchester with a small Hello Kitty notebook full of her most perfect Vietnamese penmanship. How she had documents in worn but well cared-for envelopes. I remembered the first time she removed her wig in front of me—how free and how sick I thought she looked, and how scared I felt. I remembered how Mary sat with us for hours. A tiny woman on an colossal mission.

What Mary wanted from Liz and me was simple, albeit next to impossible—she wanted the father of her children to be with them when she died. No bucket lists. No skydiving. No trips to the Grand Canyon or Paris in the spring. Mary just wanted to be sure that her children had their dad; that they would not be alone when it was time for her to go. We knew that only then could she die in peace.

Mary's children were not alone that summer morning at 7:19 AM when Mary passed. Their father was with them. I felt an ounce of comfort when I remembered that, and a tinge of pride when I realized that I had something to do with it.

* * *

Over two years later, I'm still a long way from finding peace with Mary's passing. I do, however, now know that it's not about me. Just because I think that Mary's passing is so tragically unfair doesn't mean that Mary had not found peace with her reality. Deep down, I honestly believe that she had.

In the end, my gut instinct was right—I'm not a bucket list kind of girl. I'm more like Mary. I don't need to travel the world or bungee jump or finish a marathon. I just need to know that my family would be okay if anything ever happened to me.

Impossible Justice

I didn't think a lot about Mary's funeral until the drive there. I had planned to mentally prepare myself for it during a morning run, but once I had my sneakers on, Annabel woke up and begged me not to go (obviously, I didn't). Instead, around 7 AM on the morning of Mary's funeral, I took my little girl for a short walk around the neighborhood in her stroller. She alerted me to every "bow-d" or "skwa-wel" that flew or hopped past and I tried to maintain enthusiasm even though by the tenth (okay, the third) squirrel, it was hard to fake it.

Mary was a devout Catholic. In fact, part of the reason she moved to the United States was that the communist government in Vietnam did not tolerate Catholicism.

I'm not Catholic, although lots of my family and friends are. Through them, I have been to several Catholic weddings, funerals, and way back in high school, even a Christmas Eve mass. I have to admit that Catholic churches have always intimidated me a bit. Nevertheless, when the priest starts preaching, I listen to every single word.

Cong, Ngan, and Ngan's brother Hy were all at the back of the church when I arrived for the funeral mass. I hugged them before I took my seat. Hy's hug was strong—kind of what I would expect from a teenage boy who just lost his mother and was trying to be a man about it. Ngan's embrace, on the other hand, was so desperately weak—as if she needed someone to hold her up. She probably did.

The service went on for almost 90 minutes, which made it the longest mass I have ever attended. Except for a two-minute *Thank You* from Mary's uncle, it was entirely in Vietnamese.

The language barrier was tough because I so desperately wanted to hear how the priest tried to explain this tragedy to a church full of grieving people. I wanted to understand how he could make sense of the fact that Mary's beautiful photo sat atop a small wooden box that held her wounded body. I wanted some guidance to fill my hungry stomach and some comfort to ease my aching heart.

When I finally accepted that I wasn't going to be able to understand a word of the mass, I started to really listen—to music, tone, inflection, volume, and even silence. I had never heard music more beautiful than the choir's songs. Those songs weren't solemn, despite that they had every right to be. Instead, they were bold and humble. Reverent and strong. Sympathetic and hopeful. Just like Mary.

I watched the priest pace at the front of the stage, trying to comfort people that he seemed to know personally. His tone fluctuated from one posing delicate questions to one posing possible answers. I felt some peace in watching this man who seemed, so sincerely, to want to help.

And I saw cameras—two video cameras and one digital zoom. The Vietnamese cameramen recorded every part of the ceremony as I had seen videographers do at wedding ceremonies. How fascinating—a culture that saw a funeral as a life experience worthy of being immortalized in this fashion. It felt so very honest.

In the end, Mary's funeral was one of the most spiritual experiences of my life. I cannot even rightfully explain it, but there was something surreal and even meditative about those few hours of Vietnamese prayer and song in the middle of Dorchester.

* * *

When I got home from Mary's funeral, my brother had just come off a three-hour video-game binge with Teddy. Somehow my conversation with Sean turned to the jersey swap that the New England Patriots had organized for fans like us who no longer wanted a game shirt stitched with the name of a murder suspect. (Santa had brought Teddy the #81 replica the Christmas prior, as an effort to ease the little lad's pain over the injury to his favorite player, Rob Gronkowski.) I told Sean that we were going to take the Patriots up on their offer to make an exchange.

When Teddy overheard Sean and me talking about the jersey swap, he lost it. "I don't want you to take my Aa-win Hew-nandez juw-sey," he wailed hysterically. (For context, Teddy completely freaks out when he thinks that something is gone forever even if that thing is as small and replaceable as a golf ball.) To calm him down about the jersey swap, I told him that I wouldn't take his shirt and that we would talk about it later. But I knew that was just a temporary fix and that if he continued to push back, I would have to explain to him that I would never let him wear that jersey ever again.

* * *

For some reason, I couldn't seem to separate my anger about the football star murder suspect from my anger over Mary's death. After Mary's funeral, I clicked past a radio station that was talking about the Patriots' football-jersey swap and about how the ex-football star was essentially being erased from history. All of a sudden, the ridiculous juxtaposition that previously felt so unfair to me felt different—not at all *right*, but the tiniest bit *just*. We could effectively negate a former #81 by swapping out a bunch overpriced shirts. But Mary's spirit would live on in those of us who were blessed enough to know her.

One day, I'm sure my kids will understand that most of the world's greatest heroes never got a jersey with their name on it. They just had kids and loved them—so much so that they attempted the impossible for their children, and didn't give up until the impossible came true.

Keeping the Faith

When we were little, my sister and I often suffered from what we called "Sunday-night feeling." You probably know the feeling I'm talking about— it often surfaces after a weekend or a great vacation. It's the awful feeling that everything good is in the past.

As a child, my Sunday-night feeling sometimes escalated to a helpless fear. Now I realize it was a classic case of young anxiety, but at the time I had no idea. I just remember feeling so overwhelmed that I didn't know how I'd make it to the next minute.

Usually it was thoughts about death—my parents' death in particular— that worked me up into this terrible tizzy. The thought of losing my mom or dad suffocated me like a dark, heavy tarp thrown over my head. I could lie still in my bunk bed, but inside I was terrified that the awful feeling would never go away. Thankfully by the next morning, it always did.

I remember one of those nights as if it were yesterday. I remember being dreadfully embarrassed to tell my parents what I was feeling, so while my dad watched TV and my mom read, I asked them a bunch of questions. I had probably done the same thing the week before and the week before that. I remember framing my questions in terms of natural disasters which for some unknown reason were the things I feared would kill my parents.

"Could we ever have a tornado here? A tidal wave? How do you know that it wouldn't wipe away our whole house? Or you?"

My parents reassured me. "Tornados and tidal waves don't come to Canton. We'll be fine. We're not going anywhere."

I went back to bed, wishing I were satisfied.

But I wasn't, and I returned sometime later. I'll never forget what my mother told me on my second attempt for comfort.

She said something like, "Even if we did die, you'd be fine. Human beings are amazingly resilient and they bounce back. You'd be okay."

As the parent of a child who asks 20 questions before bed, I realize that my poor mother was probably just exhausted and frustrated that her more-conventional answers hadn't gotten me anywhere.

Still, at the time, her answer shocked me. *How could she even reference death with such nonchalance? Especially the death of the two people that were the center of my universe? And how could she ever think that I would be okay if something happened to them?* I knew I would not ever be okay if my parents died, and that was that.

* * *

When I said goodbye to Mary for the last time, I couldn't stop crying. I'm embarrassed to admit it, but at that moment, Mary, unable to even sit up, comforted me. She told me that she trusted God. I held her hand and listened. I could feel the peace that her God brought her. Part of me was relieved by it. Another part was jealous.

I continued to cry like a fool.

I later found myself thinking more about my own faith, and wondering if I could ever learn to trust God the way that Mary did. I wasn't sure and still am not. Nevertheless, I do know this:

I have faith in people. I have faith that they've studied hard to learn about biology and chemistry and that their advances with proteins and antibodies could save my life. I have faith in the teachers who taught them and the books that they read. I have faith that progress is being made every day in laboratories and in hospitals.

I have faith in my doctors, and in the laws that they follow. I have faith in the beams that hold up the buildings where I was treated. I've seen the names of pediatric cancer patients spray-painted on those beams, and I've seen the love that went into crafting those letters.

I have faith that good ultimately outweighs bad, although sometimes we may feel like the scales are tipped in the wrong direction. I have faith in the generosity of our loved ones, and also that of complete strangers.

I have faith in my family. I have seen their strength—how, when they fall, they pull themselves back up again. I've also seen indescribable grace in families who have lost a loved one. They've shown me what my family would be capable of if ever they were to lose me.

I have faith in the music and the literature that carried me through some of my darkest moments. I have faith in words and sentences and paragraphs.

I have faith in friendship—old and new and undiscovered.

I have faith in love. I don't believe that it comes along only once, no matter how much Brian hates when I suggest that he would (and should)

225

find someone else if I were no longer around.

I have faith in myself, in my own resilience, and in my body that I thought had betrayed me. I have faith in my own mind that has trudged back from the dark recesses of caves to find light again.

And I have faith in miracles. I believe that things happen that we cannot explain—perhaps mystical or even magical—that could be influenced by factors so big and complex (or so small and simple) that we could never begin to comprehend them.

*   *   *

I have my doubts—far more often than I'd like to admit. Those times are hard. Those times have made me reread this chapter and consider deleting it. Do I really have faith in something if at times I doubt it? I've decided that I do.

In a prior chapter ("Footprints of My Faith"), I reflected on dialogue from the film *Life of Pi*—Pi Patel's explanation of faith as a house with many rooms. When asked if there is room for doubt, Pi replied:

> Oh plenty, on every floor. Doubt is useful, it keeps faith
> a living thing. After all, you cannot know the strength of
> your faith until it has been tested.

After my cancer diagnosis, and later, my allergic reaction, I doubted a lot of things; like whether my cells could remain free of cancer long enough that I could raise my children. In those dark times, without even realizing it, I had started to build my house of faith.

I've already described many of the rooms in my house of faith. But there's one last room that I want to tell you about. Those who know me may think this room is dark, but it just may be the brightest one of all.

Okay, admittedly there's a dark and painful hallway leading up to this room. That hallway whispers to me what I have come to learn in the past few years: that life can change in the blink of an eye—by finding a lump or driving down the highway or watching marathoners cross a finish line. I learned that even without cancer, we are all vulnerable and our tomorrow is never guaranteed. So I'm building an awesome room at the end of that oft-dreaded hallway. The bricks are sculpted from my faith in human resilience.

In that room, which I visit only rarely, is the faith that I married a truly remarkable man and that he could raise our kids without me if he had to. In that room is the faith that there exists someone else out there who would love my husband like I do, and whom he would love, if I could no longer be here. Brian and I never talk about this room, not because I won't, but because he can't. Which is fine. Because if nothing else, with this chapter, he'll know that such a room exists.

Let me tell you a bit more about this most important room. It houses my faith in the relationships that we've helped our children form with their aunts, uncles, grandparents, and most of all, with each other. I have faith that the wonderful women in Annabel's life would teach her how to be strong and independent, and that they'd help her pack for college and plan her wedding if I couldn't. I have faith that my son will love baseball and hockey and that he'll do his homework even if I'm not there to watch him. I have faith that my family would still put gifts under the Christmas tree and blow out candles on birthday cakes, and even that Brian would learn to clean out the fridge without me (okay, it would have to *really* stink of rotten food before he cleaned the fridge, but I have faith it could happen).

Ultimately, I have faith that though they'd be really sad if cancer took my life, my family would eventually find peace in the fact that we were all so lucky to have had the time together that we did.

Even if I died, they'd be fine. Human beings are amazingly resilient and they bounce back. They'd be okay. I have the deepest faith in that.

The Power of Words

Throughout 2013, my Herceptin infusions continued every three weeks. Most of those infusions were uneventful, but a few led me to write for solace. For example, there was a Wednesday in July.

Every few months during this phase of my treatment, a nurse in the lab drew my blood so that Dr. Denver could keep an eye on my counts. It was an easy part of my treatment and I didn't worry about it.

After the usual waiting in the lab area, a cheerful, middle-aged nurse (who I will call Elaine) called out, "Tara S."

I told my mom I'd be right back.

Ten minutes later, I emerged in a state of total disarray. It took a few minutes before I could even explain to my mom what had happened.

First, let me be clear—Elaine was very kind. She was talkative and good-natured and she meant well. But Elaine had one flaw—she didn't understand the power of her words.

When I sat down and she looked at my chart, she asked me how many treatments I had left.

"I'm done at the end of October," I explained, and even though that sounded far away, given the three week increments it meant only about five more treatments.

"Wow! That's so exciting! Congratulations! You must be so happy!"

"Yes, I am," I said with some reluctance. *Pause.* "But it's scary too. It's hard to think about being without the Herceptin."

"I know, that is scary. It's scary to think about what you've had to put into your body. I mean, it's all poison and the chemo *can* do real harm down the road. I've seen many cases of that. But then again, what's the alternative?"

I froze. Elaine chattered on while she inserted my IV and drew six or seven vials of my blood. As she stuck the little printed labels of my information onto each vial, I watched her. I didn't hear her, although she was still talking. I had become a ghost again—body in the chair, arm extended, mind on another planet. I felt terrified and defeated—the word *poison* on repeat in my head.

When I returned to the waiting room, I held it together (barely) because I had an errand to run—to donate the wig I never wore. But while my mom and I waited for the lady to whom we'd hand off the wig, I broke down and told my mom what Elaine had said. My mom felt so bad, but I was too upset to sympathize.

When we left the little shop and reached the hospital foyer, my mom hugged me and apologized for what Elaine had said. I explained to her how scared I was that the Herceptin would end up being toxic to my heart or that there could be some other terrible side effect that they discover years down the road that would land me back in treatment. "Herceptin is so *new*," I argued from my dark place. "They don't even know what it could really do to people!"

My mom didn't argue, but she did explain that she thinks they *do* understand the biology of Herceptin. Then she said something even more helpful. "Hon, I could walk outside right now and get hit by a car. None of us know what's going to happen tomorrow." It wasn't exactly something that I would have expected to bring me comfort, but it did. A real sincere sort of comfort.

I later wondered why that was—why my mom's comment helped me so much, especially since if I really thought about it, my mom being hit by a car would send me into a mental tailspin. But I didn't really think about it. I just felt better. Later, I decided that was because my mom had reminded me that we're all vulnerable, and also that I'm never alone with my particular vulnerabilities. And I finally understood one thing that was more difficult than facing my own demons—facing them alone.

*　*　*

I know that people like clean and happy endings; I love romantic comedies too. I knew back then that Elaine and everyone else (including me) wanted the end of my infusions to feel like pure victory. Sometimes it did feel that way. But no story—at least not one that involves cancer—is ever that simple.

I still wonder if Elaine appreciates how hard the end of treatment can be. I wonder if she knows the power that she holds as she taps patients' arms to find their best vein. I'm not saying her job is easy, because it absolutely is *not*. Anyone who works with vulnerable populations hold more power in their hands than the CEO of a Fortune 500 company, at least in my humble opinion. Because those who work with patients, children, teenagers, the mentally or physically disabled, the elderly, or the poor have the power to give someone hope or give them doubt. When we're feeling scared and weak, nothing is more valuable than hope. And nothing is more debilitating than doubt.

I know that in some ways what Elaine said was true. I've heard Robin Roberts' story, and I know that my chemo could cause me more cancer down the road. I've met several women who were treated for lymphoma years ago and, as a result of their treatment, have battled breast cancer or been forced to take drastic steps to avoid it. I know what Herceptin could do to my heart. And I know that there was no good alternative to the drugs I accepted into my body to fight the cancer. I also know that sometimes, hope is more important than truth.

Maybe Elaine just slipped up, just as I have done countless times before. Or maybe she, like so many of us, just needs a gentle reminder of the sheer power and resonance of words.

Rainbows and Puppy Dogs

When I got home from that mentally tumultuous treatment, I tucked the kids into bed and then wrote a blog about Elaine's *poison* comment. I wrote the blog for the same reason that I usually wrote (and write)—to help me organize thoughts that would otherwise swirl down destructive paths in my brain. I never expected, and certainly never intended, that the blog would do anything more than help me cope with my mental mess.

Then again, I should have remembered that my mother is my mom.

For my mom, the issue of what Elaine had said to me was far from over. My mom wasn't mad—she's far too professional for that. Instead, she was motivated. She wanted every doctor and nurse in the world to stop and consider the power of the words they choose for vulnerable patients like me. "Chemotherapy is not poison," she insisted, "and no one caring for cancer patients should ever refer to it that way."

Since she knew reaching the whole world was an ambitious goal, she at least wanted to reach the health care providers at Dana-Farber. So she went online to find out who she could contact to discuss the issue. When she found the email address for the president of the hospital, she asked me if she could use it. She wanted to share my blog.

I was hesitant about my mom's idea. I hadn't written the blog as something that anyone at Dana-Farber would read. But my mom has always believed that none of us can improve if we don't get positive *and* negative feedback. I completely agree with her, but so often I lack the guts and the grace to give negative feedback (and even more so, to receive it).

After some discussion, I gave my mom the green light to share what I had written. I didn't think anything about it after that, probably because I figured that nothing would happen. Shame on me for underestimating Dana-Farber.

Within hours (*i.e.,* around midnight), the head of the breast care program responded to my mom's email. I was impressed solely by the fact that the president had read the message and forwarded it to the leader of the breast care program, and that this prominent oncologist had taken the time to reply. But I was even more impressed by the doctor's actual words, which I found to be thoughtful and productive, mostly because they opened the lines of communication if my mom wanted to talk further. I was also comforted by the doctor's words that "Herceptin is an amazing medicine..." Personally, that's all I really wanted to hear. In my mind, the case was closed. To others however, it remained open.

The top nursing administrator at the hospital called me the week after. At first, I had no idea why, but I soon realized that she wanted to discuss the incident in the lab. In fact, she wanted to meet me when I was in for my next treatment. I felt embarrassed—like I had blown something way out of proportion; like I should have had a thicker shell when Elaine had casually spoken to me. I blamed myself, which I have a tendency to do.

Then it dawned on me that my records had led the administrators back to Elaine. *How could have I have been so stupid to have assumed that using a pseudonym in my blog was all I needed to do to hide "Elaine's" identity? Of course the hospital could see who had inserted my IV that day—it was in my chart!* A terrible feeling crept into my stomach—the one I get when I hurt someone. Because I knew that I had hurt Elaine.

*   *   *

The week after that encounter with Elaine, I read a commencement address by George Saunders that he had delivered at Syracuse University a few months prior. I encourage you to Google the 2013 speech—it's excellent.

In that address, Saunders discusses his biggest regrets in life, which he has decided were "failures of kindness"—"those moments when another human being was there, in front of me, suffering, and I responded...sensibly. Reservedly. Mildly."

Mr. Saunders reminds us that it's so much easier to respond mildly to something uncomfortable and keep quiet when we see something wrong. This is part of why I pretended to Elaine that her comments hadn't hurt me—it was just easier to reserve my emotion and smile as if nothing had just happened. But something *had* happened. And even if my thoughts were not sensible—at the time, those thoughts were terrifyingly *real*.

In his speech, George Saunders explained:

> Who, in your life, do you remember most fondly, with
> the most undeniable feelings of warmth? Those who
> were kindest to you, I bet. It's a little facile, maybe, and
> certainly hard to implement, but I'd say, as a goal in life,
> you could do worse than: Try to be kinder.

After googling the definition of *facile*, I'm reminded of its meaning. *Appearing neat and comprehensive by ignoring the complexities of an issue.* I agree that the goal of trying to be kinder does sound "neat," and I like that Mr. Saunders explains, "Kindness, it turns out, is hard—it starts out all rainbows and puppy dogs, and expands to include...well, everything."

George Saunders's explanation of the importance of kindness provides yet another reason why I love my mom—I don't think she *ever* fails at kindness. Sure she may think babies (and probably rainbows) are boring, and she wouldn't even pet a puppy dog. But my mom will dive gracefully into uncomfortable waters if she thinks that doing so could help someone. She will have difficult conversations in order to make things better. My mom will ask questions and listen to the answers, and she will expect others to do the same in return. Yes, my mother has high standards—not in a snobby sort of way, but in a let's-improve-this sort of way.

To be honest, the sensible, reserved, mild part of me just wanted to give Elaine a hug and tell her that I was fine—that she didn't need to worry about having hurt me. I know that my mom would have encouraged me to do that if it would have made me feel better.

But my mom has taught me something more about kindness, or better yet, about the messier stuff that's beneath the surface of it. She taught me that real, true kindness takes more than just a smile and a hug. It takes courage to bring an issue to the forefront and intelligence to determine how best to address it. Kindness triggers the empathy and awareness that allow us to be productive as we walk the very fine lines that present themselves in difficult conversations. Most of all, kindness takes selflessness; as Mr. Saunders reminds us, keeping quiet is *so* much easier.

George Saunders tells us that we'll remember most fondly those people who were kindest to us. I agree, and I would go even further. Because I believe that we will remember most fondly the people who had the guts and the grace to stand up and say, "This could be better, for you and for others after you." Often those people are not the rainbow or the puppy-dog type. But they *are* those who would find us a rainbow or a puppy dog—whatever it takes—if we told them those things would make us feel better. *Those* are the people I will remember most fondly. And obviously, my mom will be at the front of that precious pack.

A Part of Life

I either love driving in the car with my kids or I'm basically numb to the shit-storm of complaints, commands, and spills from the back seat. Fortunately, the majority of the time, it's the former.

A few days before my one-year-diagnosis anniversary, on an enjoyable ride to another birthday party, my conversation with Teddy and Annabel turned to some silly talk about babies in bellies. Teddy was fascinated by the idea that he was once in my belly, and every now and then he would ask me questions about it. Annabel, the budding jokester in the family, loved to make us all laugh. With a little smirk on, she told me and Teddy things like "Mama was in *my* beh-wee!" We laughed and I reached back to tickle her chubby thighs.

That afternoon, Teddy asked me when we were going to have another baby. "Vee adopted one," he clarified. I couldn't believe that he even remembered the word "adopted." I told him that I didn't know when we would have another baby and that it takes a long time to make a baby. (I left out the part about how long it takes to *earn the money* to adopt a baby, as I was still trying to grasp that unfortunate reality myself.)

The natural opportunities to talk about adoption with the kids didn't come along often, and even though I felt uncomfortable talking about something that I didn't know with certainty would happen, I didn't want to let those chances pass. So in the car that day I talked to the kids about how much fun it would be to have another baby in the house and how it didn't matter if the baby didn't come from my belly.

As we sat in traffic at a stoplight, Teddy got quiet. A minute or two later, he told me that if we got a new baby, we would have three kids in our family like our neighbors, the McCreadys. Then Teddy reminded me that the youngest child in the McCready family (Annabel's best friend, Tabitha) was *not* adopted.

"You're right, she wasn't," I responded. "But all families are different."

Then, referring to Tabitha's mother, Teddy asked me, "When will

Debbie get her bwest can-sew?"

There are a select few times in my life when my heart literally felt like it melted, but that was one of those times.

I stammered through an explanation that not every woman gets breast cancer. We listed lots of women in his life who never had it, and a few others who had. He asked me why I got it.

"I have the same exact question!" I told him with far more delight in my tone than I actually felt. "And as soon as someone tells me the answer, I promise I'll tell you!"

Glancing at those two curious little faces in my rear-view mirror, I felt such love that my heart physically ached. Soon we arrived at the party, ate cake and ice cream, and went swimming together.

* * *

When will Debbie get her breast cancer? I learned so much about my son by that little question, including the fact that deep down, Teddy thought of breast cancer as a part of every woman's life. And clearly he believed that every woman would move past it. On the one hand, his assumptions made me proud. On the other, they made me realize how much work we still have to do to cure cancer.

The One About August 8th

On the evening of August 7, 2013—364 days after my diagnosis, I was full of emotion and yet awkwardly empty. I was scared and frustrated and proud. I was tired and wired; strong and weak. Part of me had no idea what to think about *one year later.* And another part of me found such clarity in the milestone.

Until the night of August 7, I had never realized how helpful tradition can be. Of course those traditions vary and evolve, but nevertheless they provide a solid structure for how to celebrate important life milestones. Or at least, the good ones.

But what about the bad ones? What about the anniversary of a loved one's passing? A divorce? A miscarriage? A cancer diagnosis? How are we supposed to treat those milestones?

In the weeks preceding it, every time I thought about August 8, adrenaline rushed through me. But August 8, 2013 was also a workday. A Thursday. A summer day. A regular day to everyone else.

I pondered how to treat the anniversary of my diagnosis. Should I start some sort of tradition—perhaps something as simple as a morning walk with my best friend? Then I wondered if I may have been giving all of it way too much thought. Or maybe too little thought. What if another date deserved my attention? Should I instead celebrate my one-year anniversary of being cancer free? But when was that? December 27—my last day of chemo? Or since the chemo worked its magic for some time after the last infusion, should I celebrate a few weeks later? Or maybe the real milestone was September 12—the day Dr. Nadia extracted the tumor. Then again the stupid HER2 protein was the ultimate enemy, so tumor or no tumor, Herceptin was the key. Maybe the real one-year point was the day of my last Herceptin treatment, which wouldn't be for another few months. I was confused.

On the eve of this big day, frustration set in. It was a deep frustration, and at the same time, it was so very shallow.

*   *   *

Throughout my treatment, I always found it interesting when people told me that my writing inspired them. I wondered what they really meant by that, and sometimes I wanted to ask. Of course I never did, as I never wanted it to look like I was fishing for a compliment. But still, I wondered. Did my writing make them think something like, *Well, shit, I won't complain about my bad haircut anymore*? Or maybe it was nothing more than *Damn, that sure sounds like it sucks. My life sucks a lot less!* By no means am I judging these sentiments, as I've had them myself at various times in my life.

Once I got cancer, however, I would find myself employing the same train of thought after someone complimented my strength or my courage— *How in the world is* this *impressive? What* would *be impressive is if I* chose *this. But this was just thrown on me. So really, I'm just dealing with it—like someone deals with wiping dog shit off his or her shoe. But thank you so much anyway.*

As August 8, 2013 approached, however, I started to realize something a bit deeper about what it meant to *deal with it*. Of course I didn't start to think that cancer smelled like roses (it still smelled like dog shit)—it was just that I started to grasp that at some point in our lives, we all have to deal with something awful that we never would have chosen of our own accord. Granted, the degrees of awfulness vary greatly, but in a cave, darkness is darkness.

When the darkness sets in—however suddenly—everything we built aboveground crumbles. We can't eat, sleep, work, or even carry on a conversation that we're certain to remember. Breathing becomes an overwhelming chore, laughing nearly impossible. It's a truly terrible series of moments that can stretch across days or months or maybe even years. But on August 7, 2013, I understood it can be a pretty awesome series of moments, too. Because as clichéd as it may sound, I realized that those terrible times are when we find our foundation…our core…*ourselves*.

We may not recognize it right away, but in time, we'll see. We'll see the family and friends who would do anything to make us better, and those who never even called. We'll see the truth (or lie) behind a marriage vow and how much our kids really mean to us. We'll recognize strengths and weaknesses we never knew we had. We'll learn a lot about how we value ourselves, or perhaps how much we need to work on doing so.

When our bodies betray us, we have to start over—rebuild our relationship with our own cells so that we trust them again. We have to reexamine things that we took for granted—our breasts, our fertility, our birthday. Our next August 8.

This act of rebuilding is much easier for some than it is for others. I was blessed with a humungous head start—a support system, a job, health insurance, access to great health care, and countless other reasons to be happy. I know it's not like that for everyone and that this world is full of injustice.

Still, on August 7, 2013, I felt so proud and so grateful for how I'd been able to *live*—not just *survive*—over the year prior. That summer night, I understood that I was one of the lucky ones because my foundation had allowed me the precious chance to rebuild.

Part Ten

The End of Treatment

I suppose in the end, the whole of life
becomes an act of letting go.
But what always hurts the most
is not taking a moment
to say goodbye.

Pi Patel
(character from the film *Life of Pi*)

The Hands that Held Me

A few months prior to my last infusion, I sat down for lunch with my new friend Courtney. Courtney was just a few years younger than me and she had been a patient at Dana-Farber 14 years ago when she was treated for Hodgkin's lymphoma at age 19.

At our lunch, Courtney and I talked as if we had known each other for years, despite that it had only been months. Cancer has a funny way of bringing people together like that.

One topic of our conversation was how much we appreciate Dana-Farber and our doctors there. We talked about how safe the place can make us feel, which is ironic given the scary experiences we both had there.

During our lunch, Courtney told me something that I will never forget. She told me that the first few times she visited Dana-Farber after her treatment was complete, she wanted her scans to reveal cancer. "Not *a lot* of cancer, and *definitely* something that they could fix," she explained smiling. "But if they found cancer, I could still be treated there, and I would be safer with them watching over me."

I laughed with Courtney about this, not because I thought she was nuts, but because I so sincerely understood. The truth was that while every fiber in my body wanted to be cured, part of me was afraid of being without the people, the medicine, and the institution that had cured me. At Dana-Farber, I knew I was in the very best hands. So maybe it was only natural that I didn't want those hands to let me go.

Taming the Beast

A few nights before my last infusion, Brian and I miraculously got both kids to sleep before 7 PM. I admit, their early bedtime wasn't so much because *they* were exhausted, but rather, because *we* were.

There is an awesome irony in the fact that a few hours into the peace and quiet of that evening, I asked Brian if he wanted to do a little bit of adoption research together. He agreed to, and on our respective laptops, we started our first real research about how we could bring another baby into our family.

As I've described before, Brian is the steady one in our pair. He's thoughtful and purposeful and he doesn't usually let his emotions get the best of him. Naturally Brian's starting point for research was the process, the facts, the things we would need to have and do to adopt our third child.

I, on the other hand, found myself immediately wrapped up in the emotional details. I clicked my way to adoption sites to read the profiles of couples and single people introducing themselves to birth mothers in hopes that the prospective mother would choose them to be their child's adoptive parents. I had no idea that domestic adoption worked this way.

For an hour or so, I read profiles and looked at photos of the would-be adoptive parents' homes and extended families. I read about their religion, their favorite books, and whether they had a gender or a racial preference. I read about how much they all wanted to bring a baby into their home and about why they turned to adoption to accomplish that. And I realized, about 30 profiles in, that none of them mentioned cancer. Clearly we were different, and not in a good way.

This realization brought me to the verge of tears. I didn't want to interrupt Brian, so I tried to hold it all back. I watched in amazement as my husband—calmly and collectedly—moved between adoption-agency websites and fantasy-football stats. It was a perfect dose of normalcy mixed in with something completely foreign.

Still trying to pretend that I was as stable as he was, I decided to shift my research to the international adoption route in hopes that I would find something more encouraging. I read up on several countries and their individually complex situations. I learned the very basics about the adoption situations in Guatemala, Uganda, Ghana, South Africa, Bulgaria, and Haiti. I learned that adopting a child from a foreign country usually involves both parents making two trips there—the first, a three- to four-week "bonding trip" and then a second trip, some weeks later, focused on completing the legalities and bringing the baby home. (We've since learned that international adoption is next to impossible with a cancer diagnosis.)

One word kept coming up in my research that night—*volatile*. Several sites explained, explicitly or implicitly, that the process of adopting a child can be a volatile one—with many unknowns, starts and stops, and oftentimes, significant disappointment. I knew that having a baby the natural way or through fertility treatments could involve all of the same, and I tried to keep that perspective.

After a while, I couldn't contain myself anymore. With a huge lump in my throat, I told Brian that this was way harder than I thought it was going to be and I trudged upstairs to bed in an angry, sad huff.

I turned on the Sunday night football game on our small bedroom television (those games have helped ease my anxiety ever since I was little girl). Since it was October, of course there was pink everywhere. Brian joined me and a few minutes later, we listened to the announcers explain the extraordinary progress that's been made in treating breast cancer. I couldn't see the game through my tears.

One thing that was so hard about that night was that I could barely articulate why I was so upset. Partly, I just wanted to scream in frustration that just when I thought I had made progress, the terrible beast would rear its ugly head again. *Would I ever get better?! Would the beast ever go away for good?!*

I managed to get just one thought out to Brian before I fell asleep. "No one would ever pick a woman with breast cancer," I finally told him, thankful for his patience.

"But you don't have breast cancer anymore," Brian argued.

"Yeah, but no one knows the difference," I asserted and cried some more.

Then came the most tragic realization of all.

"If I were a birth mother, I wouldn't even choose me." More tears.

Brian just hugged me.

In my half-conscious state before sleep, I considered taking my whole blog down, lest it crush any possible chance we had at a birth mother choosing us. I cried myself to sleep in Brian's arms not long after that. It had been a while since I had worked myself up into such a state. Beasts can be tricky that way.

* * *

Before I was diagnosed and for some time after, I equated cancer with a death sentence. I know that some people still think of it that way, because I hear it in their voices when they talk to me. I also know that some cancers or stages of cancer don't offer patients a whole lot of hope for lots more time. But from what I've seen, in many cases, breast cancer is different. Thanks to the millions if not billions of dollars that have been poured into breast cancer research, fortunate women and men with aggressive triple-positive, triple-negative, and even Stage 3 and 4 breast cancers can still hope for time.

I know that Octobers have a lot to do with that enormous sum of research funding. The pink that was all over my television screen during that football game helped raise awareness, and awareness matters. But awareness is an interesting concept that we should all think about more. *Awareness of what?* Awareness of how many people have, or will get, breast cancer? Awareness of how much money and work is still needed to cure the disease? Awareness of how much it sucks to get cancer? Of how many people die from it?

After that terrible night viewing adoption profiles, I realized what awareness really meant to me—that it would help convince just one birth mother out there that a lot of life can be lived after a cancer diagnosis.

Letting Go

I received my last Herceptin infusion in the exact same chair in which I had my anaphylactic reaction almost one year prior. When the nurse led Brian, my mom, and I back to that chair on a bright October morning, I couldn't help but laugh at the sheer coincidence that this would be only my second time in that particular infusion suite.

"Back to where it all began," I remarked. We found ourselves sarcastically singing the song "Memories" just a few minutes later.

The process of inserting the IV into my arm had not been an easy one in my prior infusions. Three weeks earlier, the infusion nurses dug a needle around in my veins five different times before (45 minutes later) they found a route into my bloodstream. It wasn't fun, but it didn't cause any harm (I could certainly handle four small bruises). I also knew that it was mostly my own fault—the day prior I had traveled for work and I hadn't focused on drinking water like I usually did the day before an infusion. My veins were dehydrated and tired and screaming that they'd had enough.

I drank so much water prior to my last infusion that the IV went in on the first try with only minor needle-digging. The Herceptin bag made its way up from the pharmacy soon after, and so began what I hope will be the last infusion necessary to successfully treat my cancer.

* * *

My last infusion was uneventful, which is always a good thing in that building. Brian caught up on one of his (previously) secret fascinations— *People* magazine—and my mom faked that she was taking care of a work issue while she coordinated a surprise gathering of my family eight floors down in a conference room. I didn't do much more than sit back and feel the cool liquid flow into my arm.

When a patient's bag of chemotherapy or biotherapy medication drips down to empty at the end of an infusion, the computerized machine attached to the bag starts to beep. A half-hour into the Herceptin, I knew the beeping was imminent.

Suddenly, everything around me seemed to fall quiet. I leaned by head back on my chair and looked up at the near-empty bag of Herceptin. I watched the drug drip into the tube attached to my right hand. I caught it at just the moment that the very last of the liquid traveled out of the bag. My teary eyes followed it, and the air bubbles that trailed, as it moved along the clear tube and into my vein.

I will never forget watching the clear liquid fall through that tube, or the air bubbles that playfully chased it. I will never forget how time froze at that moment and how, as odd as it sounds, I stumbled upon a precious moment to say goodbye.

It wasn't easy to say goodbye to something that saved my life. That's why I love the *Life of Pi* quote so much. Despite weeks of trying to mentally and emotionally prepare for the milestone of my last treatment, I never anticipated that I'd be blessed with a moment like I somehow was able to capture that day; a moment to silently be thankful—at a cellular level—for every minute of work, every penny, and every sacrifice that went into making it possible for my chemotherapy and my Herceptin to give me more life.

Before the nurse came in to turn off the alarm and the machine, I also got a minute to smile through my tears at my mom and my husband—to hold their hand, thank them, and tell them I loved them.

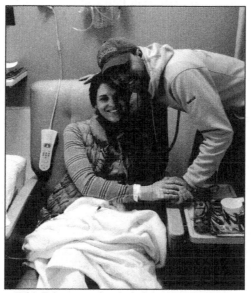

With Brian at my last infusion – October 2013

The Magic of a Moment

I've never been one who likes to make a scene. When Brian proposed to me on the steps of the art museum on Bowdoin's quad, I even hoped that the two girls sitting on the grass a few hundred yards away didn't notice us. I just wanted to have our moment, alone, without any special attention. Brian and I have never talked about that part of his proposal, but I know him enough to know that he felt the same way.

My family members typically don't like to make a scene either, but they most certainly do like to celebrate when something deserves to be celebrated. This was why a few days prior to my last treatment, it dawned on me that they may have something planned.

At the time, I wasn't in the mood to celebrate. Ambivalent about ending treatment and terrified about being released back into the wild of the world that gave me cancer, I also knew that there were patients in that infusion suite who would never be cured, who would only end treatment when that treatment became a useless weapon against their cancer. Through an email to my immediate family, I came clean.

I told them that I just wanted to keep it simple at my last infusion. I didn't want anyone taking off work to join us for it. I just wanted to walk in and out with my mom and Brian as quietly and peacefully as possible.

* * *

After that last infusion, Brian, my mom, and I walked unceremoniously to the elevator. I tried to take it all in, and at the same time, I tried to just keep moving.

Since our car was parked in the parking garage, I expected us to get off the elevator at Level P1. But we didn't. At the last minute, my mom told us that we needed to run a quick errand so we should get off at the ground level.

As we walked through the lobby, I could tell that something was up. Brian and my mom led me to the Volunteer Services suite and before I could ask why, the door to a conference room in the back opened.

Surprise!

I was in shock—the good kind. Despite that we had dropped the kids off at school just a few hours prior, they were there, as was my dad, my siblings, their significant others, Kirsten, and Helen. I hugged them all and started to notice that the walls were adorned in Mickey Mouse and Minnie Mouse decorations.

When we settled down, my mom handed me a piece of paper with an itinerary. In three weeks, all of us were going to Disney World.

*   *   *

The week before we left for Disney World, a six-minute video went viral. The video—of a young breast cancer patient dancing in the operating room prior to her double mastectomy—hit very close to home.

The main character in the video was a doctor herself—Dr. Cohan—and I was fascinated as I watched this woman, now a patient, dance to Beyoncé with her surgery team just prior to her operation.

First and foremost, the setting fascinated me. Given my terrible eyesight, I never saw the inside of the operating room before my surgery. Plus, I was already so drugged up that if I had tried to get up and dance in the OR, I would have face-planted into the table with the surgical tools.

On my first viewing of the video, despite my little peach pill, some heavy anxiety crept up on me. I couldn't help but wonder, *Should the surgeons and nurses all be this relaxed before such an important procedure? Shouldn't everyone be more focused?* Sure it all looked fun, but I'll be honest, if my airline pilots were dancing to Beyoncé as they prepared for takeoff, I'm pretty sure that I wouldn't board that plane.

Once I dug deeper, I also realized that the Dr. Cohan dancing clip also made me feel personally inadequate. I'm not proud of that reaction, just like I hate to admit that when I see a woman's tiny waist, I sometimes feel the need to pinch my own stomach rolls. But as I watched that video again, I found myself comparing my own state prior to my surgery—drugged-up and nearly blind—to this beautiful, brave, and joyful woman. *I am* so *not fun*, I thought, disappointed in myself.

Granted, I often default to far-too-serious mode. Nevertheless, on my third time watching that video I realized that I was doing to Dr. Cohan what I try so hard never to do to anyone. I had taken the six minutes of her life that she let me see, then proceeded to make it into her whole story. I thought to myself, *She mustn't even be scared! Look at her! It must be because she's a doctor…*

Maybe Dr. Cohan wasn't scared while she shook it out to Beyoncé. But those six minutes were just a small sliver of a much bigger story, one that I knew next to nothing about.

Thanks to social media and our love of bravery in the face of terror, we know that Dr. Cohan can dance. We also know that not long after that video was shot, a surgical team removed her breasts to save her from cancer. Does that surgery make her heroic? Maybe not. But what *does* make her heroic, at least in my mind, is that despite the fear and the angst that I'm certain she felt before and after those six minutes viewed by the world, she still decided to let loose—to remind cancer that while she fights, she'll still get her groove on.

The day before 10 of us left for Disney World to celebrate the end of my treatment year, Dr. Cohan gave me a precious gift. She reminded me that closure or no closure, clarity or confusion, fear or fearlessness, there is often a way to escape into a moment to find a magically good time. It can happen in the operating room before a double mastectomy or it can happen 14 months later…upon descent into Orlando.

Along for the Ride

Our four days in Disney World were everything I had dreamed of and more. The trip was the ultimate escape—the very opposite of cancer treatment, if there is such a thing.

The night after we returned home, after tucking Teddy into bed, we heard whimpering from his room. Brian ran up and I trailed.

"What's wrong, buddy?" we asked.

"I'm so sad vat Disney Wo-wd is ov-o," he bawled hysterically.

We had been there before, following other family vacations or sleepovers at Nana and Papa's house, and we had partly anticipated this meltdown. Still, it was heartbreaking.

I usually take the lead on these rounds of kid therapy because when I was younger, I felt the same way. But that night, Brian played therapist and I listened while I unpacked our suitcases.

Brian explained to Teddy that there were so many fun things to look forward to at home and that if we stayed in Disney World, we would miss all of those things—hockey practices, hockey games, hockey team dinners, Thanksgiving, Christmas, playing with his friends. Despite the shameless references to his favorite winter sport, Teddy wasn't buying it.

A few minutes later I peeked into his room. He was still crying. "Should we plan another trip to Disney World, then?" I asked thoughtlessly while I hugged his teary little face.

"Yes," he replied. Then he started crying more. "But I want ev-wee-one to come wiff us!" he wailed. I totally understood and I said that we would work to make that happen one day. Then Brian circled back to the more-realistic solutions (hockey). Eventually, Teddy calmed down and fell asleep.

* * *

Most of the time on our Disney trip, I didn't reflect. I just enjoyed the ride (often literally). Sometimes, even for a whole hour or so at a time, cancer felt like a distant relative. We danced on the street in the Magic Kingdom when the parade came around, and we went up and down the hotel waterslide *maybe* 80 times. I thought about the most basic things, like keeping track of my family in the crowds and what kind of ice cream I wanted for my next snack. And I enjoyed every moment of watching how adorable the kids were as they took it all in.

Of all the little wonders of the trip, if I had to choose my favorite, I would choose this one. Whenever our large group approached a ride, Teddy would plot who he wanted to sit next to. Brian and I were usually at the bottom of the list, and one time Teddy found himself sitting next to me, he whined, "Oh nooo! Can I sit next to someone on this ride?" Five years in, I guess I still hadn't earned my spot as "someone." But I definitely got an "A" for effort.

Seriously though, I accepted long ago that Teddy is a loyal guys' guy, and that his grandfathers, uncles, and of course his father would always come first. Still, I know how much he loves me by the subtle things (my most favorite being that when he goes to bed before I get home, he always cuddles up with a framed photo of me and him together).

My brother, who Teddy and Annabel absolutely adore, is very sweet about encouraging our kids to like us more when he's around. For the first day or so in Disney World as we approached a ride, Sean told Teddy, "You should sit with your parents, buddy." He was almost embarrassed that Teddy always wanted to sit with him.

For the first day, I repeated, "No, no, don't worry. Sit wherever you want, Teddy," and Teddy chose to sit next to Sean. Of course Sean loved Teddy's company, but I could tell that he felt like he was stealing time away from us.

The truth is that Sean wasn't stealing time away at all, nor were any of my relatives stealing anything whenever the kids chose to sit with them. A day or two into the trip I explained this to them as we all boarded the boat ride in Epcot's Mexico. I told my siblings how much it meant to me that our kids love them as much as they do. And I explained that when they have kids and those kids choose me and Brian over them, I will happily accept all the love they give me and won't apologize for any of it.

I can't rightfully explain what it means for me to know how much my kids adore their aunts and uncles and grandparents. I can't describe how my heart melted when Teddy drew a picture before we left for Florida that said "I love my Papa and Nana and my house" and tucked the note safely into his Mickey Mouse backpack. On our trip, I cherished watching Annabel sit across the table from me on Auntie Lauren's lap at dinner, wearing Lauren's fancy jewelry and practicing her "A for Annabel" on the paper placemats. I loved how much Annabel laughed at The Lonely Island's "I'm on a Boat" remake that Rachel invented while we rode the ferry to dinner that night (Annabel obviously had no idea that Rachel was replacing profanity with the words "Cookie Monster"). And I love that Teddy would ride the scariest of roller coasters if it meant that he were more like his granddad or his uncles. Finally, I don't know if there is anything that melts my heart more than watching Annabel tell my mom a story. My mom talks to her like a real person and Annabel loves it, so she just keeps talking and talking and talking. Kind of like I do, I suppose.

The funny thing about the cancer lens is that from behind it, tragedy and sheer joy often feel intertwined. Because for me, as a young mother just out of cancer treatment, my kids' love of their extended family was so much more than a cute photo opportunity. It was proof that my kids can enjoy the ride. Even if they aren't sitting next to me.

Detour: Some (More) Thoughts on Anxiety

When I packed us all up for Disney World, I was very good about bringing only the bare minimum. I didn't even bring my purse; instead, I took the essentials out of the worn little bag and left it in the closet. The essentials of my purse turned out to be just five things—my cell phone, my credit card, my license, my lip balm, and my blue Dana-Farber card. I hid the last item in the side pocket of my travel bag, embarrassed (even to myself) about the fact that I needed it with me.

My reasoning was ridiculous, I know. *What if I find a lump while I'm there and the only way I can calm myself down is to go to the hospital and for some reason, at the hospital, they need that card?* That was about as remote a possibility as me visiting the all-you-can-eat breakfast buffet just once, but still, it was possible.

* * *

Although I had dealt with anxiety for many years, I never I thought it deserved any attention. In fact, no one aside from those closest to me even would have known it existed. I'm blessed that my anxiety doesn't hold me back or hurt me physically. But still, it's hard sometimes.

Thinking back to my earliest memories of anxiety, I recall the first day of summer camp during elementary school. Feel free to laugh, but I'm not joking. My parents sent us to one of the best day camps in the area and the camp offered more activities than one could count—carpentry, Indian Lore, music, flag football, arts & crafts, rocks & ropes, gymnastics, boats, track & field, tennis, and video production, just to name a few. In fact, there were so many activities that every hour on the hour (except for the two hours a day spent swimming), each camper got to choose which activity he or she wanted to attend from a group of three or four options.

The first day of camp, the head counselor always held a clipboard with a fresh sheet of paper that laid out the "Choices." For most kids, that paper was a chart of a whole bunch of fun stuff they could do that summer. For me, it was an agenda.

Some people may interpret this chapter to mean that I didn't enjoy camp, but that couldn't be further from the truth. I looked forward to camp so sincerely and I absolutely loved it. Nevertheless, intertwined with that anticipation and excitement was a feeling that I now understand to be anxiety. It was an overwhelming feeling of *How will I ever get everything done that I want to get done?* What would a third grader possibly need to "get done" at summer camp. Gosh, so many things!

First, I had plans to go to the Olympics for track & field *and* gymnastics so I needed to attend every session of either one of those Choices (obviously that 45 minutes once a week with another camper's parent is where champions are born). But what if one of those Olympic training sessions conflicted with arts & crafts...then when would I make a vase for my grandma for Christmas? And I could *never* miss Indian Lore because that was when I would make the beaded necklace for my sister's birthday and I had to go to ropes to conquer the "spider web" and I had to go to tennis to practice for our family's summer tennis tournament. I could go on. In retrospect this all sounds very amusing, and if you're spared a photo of how terribly nerdy I was, it may even sound cute. I assure you, however, that at the time, I was very serious about it. And I was *not* cute.

One may assume that my parents pushed me to become this way but I assure you they didn't. I just was how I was, and since it was the only world I knew, I had no idea that others didn't feel the same way. Of course, my adorable little sister—the lighthearted one that all the counselors wanted to take home with them—offered me plenty of evidence that I should chill out and have fun, but I just wasn't wired to be chill. Plus, I *was* having fun. As long as I was producing something, getting better, achieving—that, to me, was fun.

Since those earlier years, my anxiety has come in waves. Sometimes it's almost nonexistent and other times it's particularly bad. For instance, when I was a teacher, my anxiety was largely in check. In my classroom, I was where I wanted to be and I never felt overwhelmed. Law school added some stress, though not in the I-need-to-do-well sort of way. I was oddly okay with not excelling there, probably because I started with no plans to leave education, and I never thought of myself as a law student or a lawyer. Ironically, this nonchalance was probably part of why I ended up doing well.

Life at the Firm was a different story. For the most part, I really didn't want to be there. Despite how much I tried to fight it, I all-too-often fed off of, and maybe even contributed to, unstable energy. I generally didn't stress about meeting my target billable hours or insignificant stuff like that.

But I did stress about how I would fit a six- or eight-hour assignment into a Saturday without missing any time with my kids (if you sleep just a few hours, there are ways). I worried about how I would get to their school parties on a weekday and how I would keep my house clean, my fridge stocked, and clean clothes available. I even got anxious about how I would find time to go to the doctor if I needed to.

When I moved to a smaller firm, my anxiety settled into a comfortable place. Sure, I worried about terrorism and drunk drivers and cancer (doesn't everyone?), but generally, my mind was at ease. It was a honeymoon for which I was grateful.

Still, anxiety is something that happens on the inside, sometimes without much regard to what's happening on the outside. When I feel my worst anxiety, it feels like I'm trying to swim in the ocean during a strong riptide. The waves are huge, or maybe they're small but they feel huge, and no matter how hard I try to swim out beyond the point where those waves break, I can't get there. I wouldn't describe it as *frustrating*, because being frustrated requires feeling some control over a situation—some belief that *I could do it, if only...*

The most significant anxiety I have experienced is more paralyzing than that. It's more like *This is all so big, so strong, so powerful, that I don't know how I will face it.* And the funny thing is, the thing that feels so big is usually, to a person on the shore, actually pretty small.

Compared to others, I know that my anxiety is mild, and maybe that helps me feel comfortable enough to talk openly about it. Or maybe I feel freer because of that little blue cancer card that I packed with me on our trip to Disney World.

Truthfully, the cancer card gave me something for which I'll always be grateful. It gave me the confidence to admit that I have things wrong with me—both when it comes to cells in my boob that wanted to kill me and when it comes to wiring in my brain that made me stress out about summer camp. Cancer also gave me an easy and safe reason to say *Yes* to anxiety medication.

Sadly, it took cancer to show me that while our culture finds bald chemo patients quite lovable, we rarely feel the same about those with mental illness. I'm certain that I have it so much easier as a cancer patient than I would as a person with schizophrenia or depression, for instance. But why? I'm sure a person wants to be schizophrenic or depressed about as much as I want to have cancer. And they likely won't have people bring them dinner and spoil them with gifts after their diagnosis. In fact, the opposite likely happens—instead of being showered with love, they are shunned and forgotten.

This chapter is not about patients with serious mental illness—I'm not qualified to write about that. I can, however, speak from personal experience and admit that even relatively mild forms of anxiety can feel daunting.

Enter a little peach pill called Effexor (drug name venlafaxine). From the little I choose to understand, Effexor treats anxiety, depression, and panic disorders (among other issues). For many cancer patients, it is part of their daily medication regimen. I take it every morning with my Tamoxifen and aside from one side effect that I can't bring myself to write about in a book my father might read, I've found no negative implications. Meanwhile, it's greatly helped to lessen my anxiety.

Of course, there is a great irony to all of this—that my anxiety is, in a way, *better* since cancer. I should explain.

To me, fear and anxiety are not the same thing. Fear is more logical and tangible, while anxiety can be completely illogical and impossible to grasp even when it's front and center.

I want to be clear that my anxiety medicine does not take away my fear of terrorists or drunk drivers or cancer, and truthfully I don't want it to. If it did erase those fears, I would feel less human and I don't want that to happen. My medicine simply helps me believe that I can handle the waves. It doesn't make me think that I'm Brianne Nyad or anything, and I don't fool myself into thinking that I'm so strong and so brave that I can swim beyond the point where the waves break. My little peach pill just makes me able to better focus on the wave in front of me and worry less about those that will come next. I know those waves are there, but usually I'm strangely okay with that. I no longer feel like I need to deal *today* with the would-be challenges of tomorrow.

I am not a paid consultant of whichever pharmaceutical company makes Effexor (Pfizer, I think). I'm just a regular person who never recognized anxiety for what it was until cancer handed me a card that made me comfortable admitting that sometimes my brain wiring goes a little sparky. I'm grateful for a little peach pill that calms those sparks down a bit; that helps me appreciate that summer camp (and life itself) shouldn't always feel like an agenda.

The greatest irony in all of this is that I will forever thank my anxiety for helping to save my life. I believe that my sparky neurons helped lead me to check for lumps in my breast and have a doctor take a look at the mass that I found.

Before I give my little peach pill too much credit, however, there's one important caveat to share. Yes Effexor helps, but if I had to choose between writing and my little peach pill, I would choose writing any day of the week and twice on Sunday. Because for me, nothing steadies my mental state like sitting down to write about it. And what's more, there's not even a co-pay for that.

Truth, Lies, and Flu Shots

Unlike during chemotherapy when getting my children a flu shot felt like a lifesaving measure which had to be taken as soon as possible, the year after, I totally procrastinated the chore. When I finally decided that it was time, I discovered that I could get the kids' flu shots at a local pharmacy and one Sunday morning, the kids and I headed there. Brian had to coach his high-school hockey practice, so I was on my own. I pretended I could do it alone.

I didn't want to ambush Teddy and Annabel, so I introduced the idea of the shots when we were halfway there. I had seen a sign at another pharmacy about some national flu-vaccination week, so without much else to go on, I ran with it. I told the kids that "everyone" was getting their flu shot this week, so I figured we would too.

"Is Liam getting his shot this week?" Teddy asked, referring to his best buddy.

"I think so," I lied.

Annabel then asked about Uncle Sean and Auntie Lauren.

"Yep, them too," I lied again. But it didn't matter—Teddy and Annabel both started to cry.

Once I could raise my voice over their wails, I took a different tactic. It wasn't one that I'm proud of, but it was a sure bet. Since I was outnumbered, I felt I had no other options.

"Okay, so since you guys have been good today, if you *want*, I can take you to the one pharmacy that I know gives the shots that don't hurt." I didn't like the way I felt while I said this, but they both stopped crying and looked at me interested in hearing more.

I had already done my research, and we were simply headed to the nearest pharmacy to home that administered shots to kids, but I pretended like I rerouted us after they expressed their deep desire that we go to *that* particular pharmacy.

I went on to explain that there were some shots that "took a long time and hurt a lot" but then there were a few others that "were really quick and felt only like a small pinch." Teddy told me that pinches hurt, so Annabel repeated that too. I agreed that yes, pinches sometimes hurt, but we were really lucky to have a pharmacy nearby that could give them the quick version of the flu shot.

My strategy was a wild success and tears gave way to smiles. As we headed down Route 24, Annabel referred to the flu shot as a "food shot" and once Teddy and I laughed, she didn't let up. We discussed what types of food they wanted in their food shots and I agreed to buy them a sweet treat after their "short pinches." We all arrived at the pharmacy in good spirits.

I liked the concept and the cute rhyme of a "minute clinic" but that term was lying just as badly as I. It took what seemed like an eternity to get all of our information into the computer, then we waited for the man in a white coat to invite us into the little room for the shots.

When we got in there, Annabel completely lost it. Even the PEZ candy she had started to devour did nothing to calm her down. She wanted out—just a tad more than I did.

Teddy, however, played it cool. He liked that I was telling the man how brave of a big brother he was, and Teddy wanted to fill the role he saw laid out for him. When Teddy mentioned something to the man about getting the shot that didn't hurt, I thought I would have to subtly explain, but the guy wasn't even listening enough to any of us to register Teddy's request. Since tuning out noise must be a very useful skill for someone who administers flu shots to scores of uneasy children, I didn't judge.

I got Annabel to stop crying by explaining that Teddy would go first. Then I did something *really* stupid—like gambling-with-the-mortgage stupid. I told Annabel that if Teddy thought the shot hurt then she wouldn't have to get it.

Teddy, however, was convinced that it wouldn't hurt. That was probably what made me feel the worst because let's be honest, it kind of does, at least to those who don't get poked in the arm every few weeks.

My little guy was so very brave, but when the actual stick stuck, his face turned red and he started to cry. "It hu-wts!" he wailed. Annabel followed. In the midst of the madness, there was a knock on the door. I figured it was a manager wondering if murder was taking place, so I just ignored it. But the knock persisted and despite the chaos, I answered.

It was my knight in shining armor—Brian in his coaching gear, straight from practice. I don't know if I've ever been happier to see him, save (maybe) walking down the aisle seven years prior. Teddy calmed down as soon as his dad surprised him.

With a newfound strength, we swiftly moved onto Annabel and after physically restraining her, she was poked and we were out. She ate PEZ the whole way home while she repeated to me that she never wanted to get a food shot ever again.

Flannery O'Connor once said:

Truth does not change according
to our ability to stomach it.

I thought about that as I reflected on December's national flu-shot week. And I realized once again that as a parent with cancer and young kids, I had a complicated relationship with truth.

An Odd Little Comparison

I have drawn several analogies to cancer-related experiences in this book—comparing them to plane trips, snow, and falling ice. After a particularly bad night with my out-of-control five-year-old, I came upon another interesting analogy born of the observation that both cancer and my son had given me bloody noses (Teddy by kicking me in the face with his boot while I tried to buckle him into the car). With a tinge of humor, I couldn't fight the urge to jot down more similarities between coping with cancer and raising children. I made the list mainly to amuse myself, to maintain sanity, and to prove that despite my indescribable frustration with a son who couldn't transition without throwing a complete fit, nothing is beyond words.

I never planned on finishing the list, and I certainly never anticipated publishing it (as a potential adoptive parent, it may be best *not* to reveal how much I fail at the role sometimes). However, that night after my nose stopped bleeding and Teddy hugged me at bedtime with more love than he had ever hugged me before, I changed my mind and finished my list.

25 Similarities Between
Coping with Cancer and Raising Children

(1)   Both experiences can give you nosebleeds.

(2)   Counting slowly to 10 becomes an extremely helpful coping mechanism.

(3)   When something new and different happens (for example, your toes go numb or your three-year-old blurts out "Shit!" when his favorite team screws up), you react, then you wonder if you overreacted or under-reacted.

(4)   Both make you appreciate any help you can get, especially if it involves food or babysitting.

(5)   Both make you want each day to slow down *and* speed up simultaneously.

(6)   Taking a shower becomes a huge accomplishment.

(7)   A plan becomes nothing more than a starting point—you need to be ready to adjust and adapt at any moment.

(8)   Both make you appreciate your parents more than ever before.

(9)   For many, both lead to the need for a great plastic surgeon.

(10) Both can make you start to pull your hair out.

(11) All those people who had cancer or kids before you had either of the two...they become your heroes.

(12) If you haven't already, you find out who your real friends are and you cherish them forever.

(13) When you look like a wreck, you don't care like you used to.

(14) You feel love and gratitude like you've never felt them before.

(15) You feel anger, fear, and frustration like you've never felt them before.

(16) You learn that it's possible to feel love, gratitude, anger, fear, and frustration at the very same moment.

(17) Both experiences make you reflect on so much that you previously took for granted.

(18) Both completely change your life in ways you never could expect no matter how many books you read on the subject.

(19) Both experiences make your weight and your mood fluctuate like never before.

(20) Both seriously screw with your sleep habits.

(21) If you don't let go of your pride, you're doomed.

(22) If you're surrounded by wonderful people, things are exponentially easier.

(23) Both experiences make you realize how very fragile—and how very precious—life can be.

(24) Both teach you the deep power of hope and faith.

(25) Both teach you that shit happens, but miracles do too.

What it Means to Win

Despite my lifelong love of the Olympics, I felt differently when the Winter Games rolled around in 2014. It wasn't because of my fear of bombs made from toothpaste, or because I'd been busy and distracted by work. I felt differently because the Olympics were, for me, when it all began: August 3, 2012 while watching the Summer Games—when I found the lump. Back then, I wondered if I would see another Olympics.

A year and a half later, when the Games in Sochi arrived, I was still alive. Physically I felt great, and mentally I was in a pretty solid place too. It had been weeks since I felt any pain that I had twisted into a cancer recurrence, and that break allowed my anxious mind some much-needed respite.

Still, it was hard for me when I saw news coverage about the Olympics, even when it was my man-crush (Bob Costas) at the desk. For a short time, I wondered if cancer had ruined the Olympics for me forever.

Ultimately, I decided that it hadn't. Cancer had *not* ruined this event that I loved so much. Because if I let cancer do that, I would've let cancer win.

* * *

Given my emotional struggle with the Olympics, by the start of the 2014 Winter Games, I decided it was time to examine what it meant to "beat cancer." What did it mean to win against the disease? My thoughts on the topic had evolved a lot since the summer of 2012. Back then, the meaning was simple—*Don't die from cancer.* The URL of my blog—www.tarabeatscancer.com—came from that sentiment and that sentiment only. *Cancer would not kill me.* I still liked to believe that cancer wouldn't kill me, but things had changed since I picked that web address.

Since then, I had seen how relentless the disease can be, even on young and able bodies like my own. I had seen so many different forms of the disease—from rare sarcoma to lymphoma to glioblastoma to breast cancer exactly like my own. I witnessed the havoc wreaked by those cancers and by the medications used to treat them.

Meanwhile, I arrived at a whole new understanding of what it meant to beat cancer. And it had nothing to do with cancer. I wouldn't give the stupid disease such satisfaction.

* * *

To me, someone can beat cancer and die from it, too. In fact, my concept of beating cancer is indescribably more difficult to achieve than the traditional concept which, for most, involves getting all the cancer cells to go away. Because to me, beating cancer—like *really* beating it—takes more courage and love than I could ever explain. It takes more than sitting through a whole bunch of treatment, and trust me, that isn't easy.

I've seen with my own eyes several people who have done it and are doing it—who have won and are winning over cancer in the way that I mean *win*. One of those people was Mary. Yes, Mary died of breast cancer, but breast cancer did not kill her spirit. Even in her last days, with the help of her loving family, Mary kept her dignity, her grace, and her inner strength. Even when she couldn't sit up, she somehow exuded beauty and peace. She loved her children, her husband, and her God, and she cared for all of them in the most loyal of ways. Mary beat cancer, even if her obituary says otherwise.

I have seen other people beat cancer, too. I have seen a twenty-something cancer patient become an oncology nurse practitioner on the floor where she was treated. I've seen two young mothers battle metastatic breast cancer while lighting up every room they enter and comforting those who are upset around them. I've seen a young mother adopt a third child and power through treatment for a recurrence. I made a incredible friend who had cancer while continuing to work full time and make sick kids' wishes come true (literally). I met a fellow blogger who told me that his cancer will come back and when it does, he will beat it again. And I became friends with a young woman battling Stage 4 triple-positive breast cancer who told me that in a most unexpected way, she had never been happier than she was after her diagnosis.

Some people may misinterpret this chapter's theme to be that age-old saying, "It's not whether you win or lose, but how you play the game." But that isn't what I mean at all.

What I mean is that even if my cancer were to return and, heaven forbid, if it were something that my body ultimately couldn't handle, I'd still expect to win. Call me stubborn or naïve or just plain crazy. But even if cancer took my life, I have hope that I could nevertheless save my spirit. *That* is what I think it means to beat cancer.

Part Eleven

My Ship

I have hated the words and
I have loved them, and I hope
I have made them right.

Liesel Meminger
(protagonist in *The Book Thief* by Markus Zusak)

Never Undone

On the day before Valentine's Day 2014, I realized that the holiday was fast approaching. After a minute or two of thought, I had a novel idea for how Brian and I could celebrate.

"We should go out to dinner!" I suggested with great enthusiasm as Brian left the house for work on February 13. He laughed like I was nuts, but he agreed that dinner sounded great.

When I got to my office and clicked to my trusty restaurant-reservation website, I realized why Brian had laughed at me—my idea wasn't so novel after all. There were no reservations to be had for Friday February 14 unless we wanted to eat at 10 PM and by then, I would have gnawed off my jacket and fallen asleep with an upset stomach. When I also realized that all of our babysitters would be booked, I accepted that dinner out with my Valen-time (as Annabel called it) wasn't going to happen.

"Takeout and TV?" I asked Brian while following up. He thought that sounded great too, so Thai food and the Winter Olympics it would be.

After the kids were in bed, Brian left to pick up the take out. I hadn't finished my work for the day, so his trip was the perfect opportunity for me to log back in and wrap it up. When he texted me that the Thai place was packed, I was selfishly relieved because I needed more time.

An hour and a half later, Brian still wasn't home.

"You find a hot date?" I jokingly texted him.

He never responded.

I started to worry, and peered out the front window. Brian's truck was parked in the driveway, still running.

I figured he was talking to one of his fellow coaches about hockey, and I was relieved that he was back safe. I decided to leave him be. If I got hungry, I could go out to grab the food and get started on our romantic meal.

A few minutes later, the front door opened. Brian came in, put down the paper bag of Thai food, and burst into tears. Brian doesn't cry easily or often so the next five seconds were some of the scariest I've ever experienced. *What had happened? What awful news had he heard?* Forever scarred by the tragic death of one of Brian's former players, my first thought was that another one of his players had been in a car accident. I had the split-second thought, *Oh God, how will everyone get through that again?* But it wasn't that.

My mind raced a bit more until he was able to get the words out.

"It's Kristin," he said.

He didn't need to say anything else. I knew. Our friend's cancer had returned.

For a moment, I felt relief that everyone was still here. Relief that Kristin was still here. But that relief was fleeting.

Brian sobbed something about her liver. I could barely stand up.

Brian carried me over to the sofa, the place where we had cried together several times about my own cancer. We sobbed some more, Brian somewhat in control of his tears and me not at all.

For the next few minutes, I wailed like a maniac—a crazy person I never knew was inside me. "No! No! No! This can't happen. This didn't happen. Noooo!"

I kicked and shook and cried some more. "Why? Why? How? No! It can't be right! This can't be happening!"

Brian just let me throw my fit. I don't think he had the strength to do anything else. So he just hugged me tight.

A few minutes later, he told me to stop. "This isn't about us," he explained. "This didn't happen to you. You know that, right?" I thought I did, but I wasn't sure. Kristin had been a special friend to me throughout my treatment. It was because of her that I found my tumor, and after my diagnosis she mentored me through surgery and chemo.

But Brian was right. In my instinctual effort to try to process what had happened to Kristin, I started to get my situation mixed up with hers. Brian helped bring me back. This *wasn't* about me. This was about our friend and what she and her family were going to have to endure.

* * *

I have debated whether or not to write about Kristin's recurrence in this book. On one hand, part of me feels that it's useless to tell the small fraction of her story that I know; that telling just a piece of that reality is somehow disrespectful to the other parts that remain untold. Part of me worries that if I focus on my own perspective—if I write about Valentine's Day in *my* house and how *I* felt since hearing that her cancer had metastasized—that I am putting my far less significant experiences before Kristin's far more important ones.

On the other hand, Kristin and I have a lot more in common than a family that we love and a brutal kind of breast cancer that we hate. We both believe in facing the truth no matter how hard that can sometimes be.

The truth is that even now, over a year later, I still don't know what Kristin is going through. Just before this book went to print, I wholeheartedly celebrated that Kristin's most recent scans showed specks where the metastatic tumors used to be. But I don't pretend to fully comprehend her journey, or that of other friends with metastatic disease. I do remember, however, the five weeks I spent wondering how far my cancer had spread inside me—feeling it in my head, my neck, my lymph nodes, and even my knee. I will never forgot those excruciating days prior to my first surgery—the diagnostic tests and the torturous sound of the phone ringing with news of a result. I can still feel the pain of how hard it was to face my own mortality so abruptly, and how much it hurt to consider losing the people I loved. I don't know what Kristin is going through, but I have tasted a fraction of it and it's indescribably awful.

At the same time, I worry about the harm that writing about Kristin could cause. Maybe this chapter crushes a patient who is peeking out of his or her cancer cocoon, or maybe it causes panic in survivors who dread facing the reality that the war they thought was over may need to be fought again. If nothing else, I understand because since I heard of Kristin's recurrence, I've often felt crushed and panicky too.

Nevertheless, if there's one foundation this book is built upon, it is the truth. And the truth is that no one's individual story exists in a vacuum. Each one of our stories is intertwined with someone else's story—at times fleetingly, and at other times so much so that they could never be undone.

Entitled

The news of Kristin's recurrence had a profound effect on me. The subsequent months were hard on so many levels—I felt deep sympathy for my friend and her family at the same time that I felt a sheer stubbornness that they could find a way to defy all odds. I felt sorry for Brian, who was a loyal friend to Kristin's husband and lived their nightmare up-close. I felt sad for my family because I wanted them still to believe that my treatment had been able to cure my cancer. And most of all I felt pain for Kristin who, once again, had her hope and faith shaken. I knew how difficult it was to do so much as breathe when that happened.

After Kristin's cancer returned, I sought respite in my writing. A week after that awful Valentine's Day, I wrote the following piece about a concept that hung heavy on my mind—entitlement.

Excerpts of a blog
published February 22, 2014

There are places in the world where people don't feel entitled to anything. They don't expect to be able to drink clean water or use a toilet. If they can't see, they don't expect eyeglasses; if they get sick, they don't assume there are medicines to treat them. In many of these places, people don't feel entitled to write or speak or even think freely. They don't assume they will grow old or die peacefully. Unfortunately, they know better than all that.

I've seen a few of these places in person, worked with men and women who have lived there, read about them in books and in newspapers, and learned about them on television. For good and for bad, I've found that unbelievable people and stories are born in such places.

Fortunately, I happen to have been born in a place where people *do* feel entitled to these types of things—where people feel entitled to life, liberty, and the pursuit of happiness. I grew up thinking (albeit, subconsciously) that I was entitled to safety, to love and companionship, to children, and to growing old. How lucky am I to live in a place where I grew up expecting these things and assuming I would have them?! How very, *very* lucky.

Cancer, however, has a way of instantaneously altering all expectations and assumptions. A diagnosis can hit us smack in the face (or the breast, or the liver, or anywhere really) with the reality that we're crazy fools to feel as though we're entitled to anything in this world…especially time.

Detoured

Weeks prior to Kristin learning that her cancer had metastasized, I called my doctor to complain of pain in the left side of my chest. I had felt the pain intermittently for months, although it wasn't the pain that bothered me—it was the fear of the pain. After Kristin's news, the pain worsened and I became convinced that my cancer had returned too.

I thought about the pain all the time, wrote about it in several blogs (most of which I never published), and talked to my oncology team about it twice. Sydney put in an order for a chest X-ray, but I decided to take ibuprofen on a routine basis for a week and see if it still hurt after that. It didn't, and for a short time my fear subsided.

Then came February 14—the night the pain returned with a vengeance. From that point on, I was scared. Actually, I wasn't just scared—I was absolutely terrified. I knew why, yet I didn't know why. I knew what helped, yet I couldn't help it. It felt like a full-time job just to stay in control of my fear, and although I managed to do so, it wasn't easy.

I understand now that it was so difficult because I vividly remembered August 3, 2012—drinking a glass of water in Kristin's kitchen and telling her how strong she was; watching our boys play together and peeking in on her newborn as she slept comfortably on the bed; later thinking to myself, *Why her?* and facing the honest truth—*If it could happen to her, it could happen to me.*

* * *

There's no doubt—the news that Kristin's cancer had metastasized to her liver crushed me. It crushed me as a friend, a mother, a sister, and a wife. It crushed me on an unselfish level and it crushed me on a completely self-centered one. In some ways, Kristin's recurrence strengthened my faith, but in other ways it leveled it. Somewhere near the leveled end of the spectrum existed that nagging pain in my chest.

The logical part of me knew what others were thinking—*If the pain returned when you heard Kristin's news then obviously the pain is all in your head.* I must have told myself that two million times. But fear is not rational, which is partly why it's such a cruel and nimble enemy.

So for months my mind wandered to dark places—places that paralyzed me for moments when I least expected it. Places that made me quiver.

One night a few weeks after that awful Valentine's Day, I broke down to my mom. I cried like it was August 2012. She listened and told me she understood. It always amazes me how much those two words—*I understand*—can comfort me.

My mom also told me that I should get the pain checked out.

"I'm too scared to," I explained.

I fell asleep that night with puffy eyes and a deep sadness that cancer was able to torment people like it did.

By the next morning's commute to work, I was so sick of being worried that I decided it was time to take action. I got to my office, shed my winter layers, and immediately called my oncologist's office to take Sydney up on her X-ray offer.

Sydney spoke with Dr. Denver and called me back a while later to tell me that Dr. Denver thought an MRI would be best. The first available appointment was the next Monday at 4 PM. Six days away. Shaking, I put it on my calendar.

* * *

Before my diagnosis, I knew that my life could change in an instant. But cancer showed me just how that could all play out. I felt and I saw how quickly one path could morph into another. It was that knowledge and experience that made the thought of the MRI so absolutely terrifying. Because more than I could ever rightfully explain, I wanted a clean result on that test. But so had my friend, and she didn't get it.

The MRI

When my mom and I approached the elevators in the Dana-Farber parking garage the afternoon of my MRI, she asked me a question with upbeat energy that I knew she had dug deep to find.

"Should we go to the third floor and cross over the bridge or just walk outside?" My mom was referencing the footbridge that crosses over Jimmy Fund Way connecting the older Dana building to the newer Yawkey building.

On a normal day, I make that decision in a split second based on whatever I'm feeling at the time—the need for fresh air or perhaps the desire to stay dry and warm. But that day, it seemed like the most difficult question I'd ever had to answer. In fact, I couldn't even muster up a decision.

I muttered to my mom that I didn't know and I fought back tears. By my response, she knew that her simple question had overwhelmed me and I'm sure she wished she could have taken it back. But my mom didn't flinch—she chose the footbridge and we kept moving forward.

I lost my composure in the waiting room of the imaging center. Weeks worth of fear, anxiety, anger, and frustration (both for myself and for others who had been there) erupted out of me in the form of tears, boogers, and maybe even drool—all before I could fill out the first question on the clipboard the receptionist had given me. My mom took the clipboard and filled it out for me while I sat in the chair next to her, holding onto a paper cup of water as if it were an oxygen mask on a rapidly descending plane. A few minutes later, I signed the paper where my mom told me to.

It's impossible to explain how scared I was while I waited to enter the room with the MRI machine. I took an Ativan as instructed and that helped, but my mind still conjured up all sorts of awful scenarios. For instance, the cabinet in the prep room was labeled "Contrast Reaction Medication." As I stared at the IV in my left arm—the passageway through which they would feed the solution to make the images possible—I hoped to a higher being that my body would not react to that solution as it had reacted to the Taxotere. I wondered if the team of angels from the Yawkey building could make it to Dana in time to help me like they did last time. I prayed that they could, or that the Dana building had its own team of angels.

The MRI itself wasn't as bad as I thought it would be. Since the techs were imaging my breast (or rather, the tissue around it), I lay face down with my numb boobs positioned in two openings and my head resting through a hole like I'd seen on massage tables. It was by no means comfortable (I had to keep my arms raised above my head) but it was most certainly bearable.

I held the alarm that the tech told me to use if the contrast caused me any pain. "But if you use the alarm," the tech warned, "we have to stop the test and you would need to come back another day for a new test." (Apparently they can't insert the contrast twice.) That warning was all the motivation I needed to stay completely still for the 30 minutes of banging and clanging.

In the brief periods of quiet respite, I heard music through the earphones the hospital provided. The tech had even asked which Pandora station I wanted him to play over the earphones. I chose Bruce Springsteen (obviously), but "Dancing in the Dark" was the only Bruce song that came on in that 30 minutes. I found the chorus ironic as I stared into the darkness and tried with all my might not to move.

When the MRI was completed, I realized how tired the Ativan had made me. I remember only bits and pieces about the rest of the night— being really hot after the test, trying to put on my jewelry again as my hands shook. I remember waiting for our car in the valet area as I sat upright with my eyes closed. I remember an older woman next to me explaining to her companion that she only tips the parking attendants at places that she plans to return to. "I worry they'd remember me if I didn't tip them and they'd do something to my car next time." In my dazed and exhausted state, this lady's musings caught my attention. *What a miserable way to live life*, I thought to myself, too tired to say anything to the woman about how ridiculous she sounded.

*   *   *

I didn't go to work the next day because I was sure that the results were going to show cancer. I didn't want to be in the office when I heard this devastating news. So I waited at home for the phone to ring from *Blocked*.

In the meantime, a partner with whom I worked scheduled a call with me. She was unhappy with the way I had approached an assignment and wanted to tell me so. I tried to listen while Barbara voiced her opinion on my alleged mistake, but despite the law-firm hierarchy that everyone else seemed to respect, I couldn't keep my mouth shut.

Barbara knew why I was home that day, but if she cared she sure didn't give that impression. At one point in our heated conversation, I told her that I could never forget how she insisted on having that conversation at that particular time. I doubt that any junior lawyer had ever spoken to Barbara like I did that morning, but I didn't care. Convinced that I was about to hear that my cancer had metastasized, even my job felt insignificant.

Blocked called not long after I hung up with Barbara. My stomach dropped, my adrenaline rushed, and I answered. Slowly and seriously, an older-sounding woman asked to speak with Tara Shuman. *Gulp.*

"This is she."

The woman's tone appeared extremely serious as she said, "Good morning," and gave her name. She sounded like she had bad news to deliver. I almost threw up.

"I am calling from the Democratic…"

I snapped out of my panic.

"Do *not* call me!" I screamed, unable to contain myself. "I'm waiting for very important test results and I thought you were my doctor and you just scared the hell of me! Do *not* call me again!" I had never screamed like that into the telephone.

"Should we try back later today?" she asked politely. She couldn't be serious.

"No! Don't call me back today or ever! I told you that already!" I clicked the phone off with force, and perhaps a tinge of guilt as well.

A few hours after that, while my mom and I anxiously waited on the sofa and watched movies, the real *Blocked* rang through to the cordless phone.

I picked up.

It was Sydney, Dr. Denver's physician assistant.

"The MRI was clean," she explained with a smile in her tone. I started to cry, which probably terrified my mother until I gave her a thumbs-up to indicate it was a happy cry. She started crying too. I fell to my living room rug and sat there shaking and trying to listen to everything else Sydney was telling me. But I don't remember anything she said after that.

Clean. No word had ever sounded more important.

There is no doubt that the clean MRI was a wish come true. But I should've known by then that cancer is not usually so black and white. Sydney explained that the MRI looked at the tissue in the breast. "But I don't have any breast tissue, right?" I asked once I had collected myself.

"Right. So it looked at everything around the left implant. And we didn't see any nodules or any evidence of cancer. That's a very good thing." I wished she could have stopped there, but there was a bit more.

Sydney explained that an MRI provides excellent images of tissue, but this one didn't look at my chest wall or the bone. I had been under the impression that the test would tell us everything about the pain in my left breast area, but I was wrong.

"If the pain persists for another few weeks, we can do a CT scan or an X-ray and see if there's anything in the chest wall or anything wrong with the bone." My chest ached as she spoke.

* * *

Most of us—particularly those in the Kingdom of the Ill—crave clear answers. We want a *Yes* or a *No*—*Positive* or *Negative*. Something definite—a *plan*. But for good or for bad, we often don't (or can't) find such certainty.

Even after the clean MRI, I knew that no matter how many tests I underwent to try to relieve myself of the anxiety of feeling cancer, I would never know for sure whether those deadly cells lurked inside me. I would never know how or when I would die, and that wasn't because of cancer. That was just because I'm human.

I also happen to be a total control-freak, so after the somewhat incomplete test result, I needed to focus on a few things that I *did* know. And I knew that I was surrounded by people who gave me hope and faith in the human spirit—family and friends who showed me by example what it meant to be resilient and strong. I had a mother who told me, "We will get through this together," and instinctively took the clipboard from me when I was too weak to fill out the paperwork myself. I had a husband who kept things at home normal even when we both felt like we were living a nightmare.

Life and death are undoubtedly and unavoidably full of unknowns. But there are some "knowns" too. For instance, even in my exhausted and dazed post-MRI state, I realized with great clarity *this*—that every time I left Dana-Farber, it was with someone who overtipped the parking attendant because even after a long and difficult day, it made him or her feel good to smile and be kind to another human being. I love those kinds of people and I am blessed that a few of them love me.

What's Inside

Some women love being pregnant and some women hate it. I was somewhere in the middle. I enjoyed certain parts of my two pregnancies— for instance, feeling the baby kick and seeing him or her squirm on an ultrasound. I hated other parts—for instance, how immobile I became. But the part I disliked most of all was the stress that I felt as the carrier of a precious little person. All of a sudden, I stopped jaywalking and became a better driver. I also started to pay much closer attention to my body. For a person prone to anxiety, it wasn't always fun.

I remember being pregnant with Teddy and my doctor telling me that if I didn't feel the baby kick in some number of hours, I should call her. What a terribly frightening instruction! How was I supposed to monitor the baby's movements? At the time, I was working full-time and going to law school at night. What if I got distracted and failed to report a period of stillness? Would I have missed my chance to save him from whatever harm had caused him to stop kicking? Of course, Teddy was Teddy from the start, so it turned out that being-too-still was never an issue.

Being pregnant was good training for being a parent because it was the first time that I consciously struggled to determine how to react appropriately to something unexpected. I never knew if I was underreacting or overreacting when something in my body changed. For instance, I remember one afternoon when suddenly my ankles tripled in size. It was horrifying, and not only because it looked nasty.

I debated whether or not to call the doctor. *Will she think I'm nuts? I should wait. I did just eat a lot of Cheez-Its. It's probably the salt. But what if it's something worse? Yep, I better call.* So I called.

The doctor told me what doctors often tell me—"Watch the symptoms and if they don't subside, call back."

My ankles never went back down completely until after Teddy was born, but later that night they shrunk enough for me to know that I hadn't come upon a fatal condition that autumn day.

I also must admit another part of pregnancy that I hated—when people referenced my (supposed) instincts with statements like, "You know your own body." Because I didn't. My body was doing crazy things—like gaining 60 pounds and bumping my bra size up to a DD. This definitely was *not* the body I knew.

As you can probably guess, I find a lovely parallel between this state of pregnancy vigilance and the vigilance I still often feel after cancer. The uncertainty, the fear, the body I barely know. I'm supposed to trust something that betrayed me and I'm supposed to know something that has been reconstructed in ways I never could have imagined.

* * *

While my loved ones celebrated my favorable MRI results, my fear nevertheless persisted.

One Friday morning after I got to work I told my mom about the lingering pain. She insisted that I call to schedule the CT scan that Sydney had mentioned when she called with the MRI results.

All day as I tried to work, I knew what I needed to do but I didn't have the courage to do it. I didn't want to go through all of it again—the test, the waiting, the anticipation of the dreaded answer. I just wanted to pretend that everything was okay.

On my walk to the train after work however, something in me changed. Maybe it was the fresh air that felt so much warmer than it had earlier that morning. Maybe it was the realization that pretending wouldn't heal me. Or maybe I was just tired of being scared. Whatever it was, I decided I needed to take the next step. Unfortunately by that time, the Dana-Farber office was closed for the weekend. So I had to wait—again.

I decided that on Monday morning (which happened to be my 34th birthday), I would call Dr. Denver to complain for the fourth time that the left side of my chest hurt. I would rearrange my schedule—fall back on work and laundry and everything else in life—to try and figure out why I was still in pain in the spot where the tumor had been extracted.

In the meantime, I totally obsessed about what I felt (or thought I felt). I wished I were one of those people who "knew her body" but I had absolutely no idea what was going on in there. While part of me wanted more than anything to find out, another part of me couldn't bear the anguish of doing so.

The Intruder

When Monday, March 10 rolled around, I didn't immediately call to schedule the CT scan as I had planned. In fact, three days after that I still hadn't mustered up the courage to do it. For whatever reason, I felt the need to justify the delay—to explain (mostly to myself) the indescribable fear that was holding me back. When I sat down to attempt this explanation, I arrived at a metaphor that clarified so much for me.

Excerpts of a blog
published March 13, 2014

Imagine this…

You live in a house. The house is modest, sometimes messy, but mostly clean. It's nothing special to strangers, but it's special to you and those who love you.

Your family lives in the house. They eat in a kitchen full of fruit, snacks, and memories. They sleep in bright bedrooms with warm blankets, plenty of pillows, and piles of stuffed animals. They watch movies, read books, and play games in the living room. They fill the house with laughter and some tears when they hurt themselves.

Imagine this…

Your house has a basement. You go there sometimes—to do laundry and play knee-hockey. You exercise down there in the early mornings and you store the holiday decorations in the crawl space.

Imagine this…

One night, hours after your family has fallen asleep, you hear a strange noise coming from the basement. You assume it's a mouse because there's no way anything bigger than a mouse could get in. But it didn't sound like a mouse. Some time later, you want to know for sure where the noise came from even though you're too scared to check and too thoughtful to wake your spouse.

You lie awake, listen carefully, and pray the noise stops.

It doesn't.

Hours later, you're shaking.

You know someone is down there.

You find the courage to call the police. They're the ones trained to face intruders. The police arrive relatively quickly. They're strong and kind. They inspect the basement and move straight to the origin of the strange noise.

You wait upstairs. You're not alone, but part of you feels like you are.

After minutes that feel like decades, the police have bad news. They deliver it quickly while your world spins…

An Intruder has been living in your basement, likely for years. The Intruder slept close to where your kids played knee-hockey. He ate breakfast near boxes of Christmas ornaments. He bathed where you washed your family's clothes. The Intruder lived in a dark space beneath those bright rooms where your family snacked and dreamed and laughed and played. You had no idea.

Worst of all, the police inform you that the Intruder is trained to kill. Despite that you never saw anything, the Intruder has been stockpiling an arsenal of weapons—big and dangerous ones. You don't understand how this could happen. You still don't even know how the Intruder gained access.

The police explain that they can't extract the Intruder just yet. Even as you speak with them, the Intruder eavesdrops from beneath the floor planks. "You'll need to live here with the perpetrator for a while," they explain. "When the time is right, you'll help us wage the battle against him. If all goes well, he could be gone forever."

When the time comes, you do as you're told.

There's damage after the battle—some broken windows, holes in the walls, theft of valuable things. But your house is standing and you patch things up and make peace with the absence of what is gone for good.

Unfortunately, you're not the only one. Intruders have lurked in a few of your neighbors' houses too. You watch those neighbors fight and you help each other whenever possible.

Finally, the Intruder is gone from your house and from your neighbors' houses too. The police warn you that the Intruder could return, but the odds are against it.

"If he does return," the police warn, "he's back for good. He'll make his home wherever he wants and he'll rebuild his arsenal." The police tell you in that case they could help slow down his deadly stockpile, perhaps even to a pace so slow that it's barely dangerous for quite a while. But he'll be there—lurking beneath your every footstep while you try to live your life in the house you love.

Nevertheless, you celebrate (quietly). The Intruder is gone, at least for now. Thank goodness you heard the noises.

For a while you're safe. You're scared because it happened, betrayed because you still don't know the Intruder's route in, and thankful because so many good people helped you fight him off.

Time passes. Your house is full of laugher during the days just like it was before. But at night, you lie awake. Listening for noises.

One bright, sunny day a few months later, you receive devastating news. The Intruder is back in the house across the street. There's nothing you can do about it. You're crushed.

You listen at your house more closely than ever before.

One night you hear them—the sounds of an arsenal being assembled. Or maybe you hear nothing. It could be mice. Or it could be the Intruder building an atomic bomb.

You want to call the police again and one time you do. They come and tell you that they checked one corner of the basement. "The Intruder wasn't there," they say.

You want to feel relief. "But did you check everywhere else?" you ask.

"No. Did you want us to?"

"I don't know," you reply. Then for weeks you're frozen, wondering over and over again whether or not you really want them to.

Recurrence Rut

A short time after I wrote the *Intruder* post, I hit what felt like rock bottom of my recurrence rut. The clean MRI did nothing to comfort me. I still felt pain and despite all of my efforts to think more positively, I had convinced myself that the source of the pain was cancer.

Once I had convinced myself that the cancer had returned, symptoms of it surfaced everywhere. Fatigue, nausea, pain under my arm, and even a massive nosebleed. All the while I was too scared to take the next step of scheduling a CT scan to take a look at the parts of my chest that the MRI hadn't been able to see.

I had never been so frustrated or so disappointed in my own inability to be positive and hopeful. No contrived optimism, no quotes, no songs, no blogs, no therapy sessions, no *nothing* was able to lift me out of the recurrence rut in which I was stuck.

Finally, I got so tired of the fear that I decided it was time. I placed a call to my doctor, left a message, and waited for the call back to schedule the CT scan. From the depths of my dark cave, I somehow scraped together enough guts to pick up the phone when *Blocked* rung back to book the appointment.

The CT Scan

On the day before the scheduled test, I woke up early to exercise (as was my routine). But that morning, I felt absolutely exhausted and the exhaustion terrified me. I knew that it was normal to be tired at 5 AM, but it wasn't normal for me (at least not after I had brushed my teeth). I recalled Kristin telling me fatigue was another reason that she had had a feeling something was wrong.

On the drive to the gym, the hair on the back of my neck stood up. I felt cancer inside me. I was so sure of it that I started to think about how I would live my life for the next few months knowing that I was about to die.

I tried to psych myself up. I told myself, *You will do it. You will find peace and you will say goodbye when you need to.* But then I started to cry at the thought of how I wasn't ready to say goodbye—of how much I wanted to remain alive.

When I got to my gym class, I tried to hold it together. But I couldn't. I felt the cancer in my chest as I rolled out my sore legs. I thought about how I wanted to carve out the tumors, but there was no way to. I panicked and almost threw up in the bathroom. I had to leave.

Since I couldn't escape without some sort of an explanation, I approached the instructor, who I consider a friend. I was too upset to temper my delivery, so the truth just poured out in tears. "It's back," I cried. "I know it's back." Kevin told me it was *not* back, that I had done everything I could have done to beat it. But I didn't believe him. I felt so badly that soon, my tragic test results would shock him and everyone else into seeing that they had been wrong about me; that *I* had been wrong about me. That I had not—at least not literally—beaten cancer.

I ran out to my car and bawled my eyes out the whole way home. It wasn't even 6 AM yet, so when I crawled back in bed sobbing, I shocked the hell out of Brian (who usually didn't expect me until 45 minutes later).

"I can't do this anymore," I told him. "I need to figure this out." He agreed, still half asleep and completely confused.

When I had scheduled the MRI a few weeks prior, I had chosen a time that was relatively convenient for my work schedule. I tried to balance a whole bunch of things the week of that first test. But that dark, early morning before my scheduled CT scan was different. That morning I had fallen back into survival mode—the mode I remembered from my surgery and chemo days—where I couldn't focus on anything but figuring out if my body was going to allow me any more life.

I called out of work and sent several messages to Dr. Denver and Sydney. By 9 AM they had rescheduled the CT scan for that afternoon. I knew I couldn't bear the agony of waiting another day.

* * *

The hours home alone before Brian picked me up for the test were dreadful. I felt like a ghost in my own house. I tried to distract myself at my computer but instead I found myself staring at Brian's screen saver (a photo of him with Teddy and Annabel) and wondering if they would be okay without me.

By the time I checked in at the radiology desk at Dana-Farber, it was a struggle to stand up straight. The receptionist asked my name and my birthday. She found me in the computer, and with all good intentions remarked, "Well that's great, you have an easy day today! Just this one test!"

"Easy day" wasn't exactly what it felt like for me, but I was in no position to explain that rationally. I just grunted in response.

Then we waited. I shook and drank water and filled out my own paperwork, despite not even being able to remember the date. Finally a man called my name. I thought I was going in for the test, but it turned out he just had some screening questions. Brian stood next to me as the man rattled off questions with less empathy than someone behind the desk at the RMV.

"Birthday?"

"Three-10-1980."

"You've had CT scans before, right?"

"No."

"Oh."

"Well, I had one before cancer but none after."

"Okay. Have you ever had a reaction to an injection?" I was confused. He repeated the question.

"I don't know. I had a bad reaction to a chemo drug. Is that an 'injection'?"

"No, I mean contrast."

"Contrast? Um, no, I don't think so."

He asked me more questions, kept typing with his back to me, and then sent us out to the waiting room again. I wasn't impressed, and Brian was flat-out pissed. Even one of the best cancer institutes in the world still had room for improvement.

After some more waiting and uncontrollable shaking, it was finally time for the CT scan. A young woman, probably in her late twenties, came to retrieve "Tara S." My heart jumped into my throat. I gulped, then left Brian and my mom behind to venture into the testing area.

From the moment I met her, I liked the nurse who prepared me for my scan. She noticed things—like that I was on the verge of tears—and she so sincerely wanted to ease my pain. When she asked me to take off my bra, explaining that underwire could interfere with the scan, she immediately went to lower the shades to the window that looked into our room (I hadn't even noticed the people behind that glass). The shades were broken, but the nurse insisted on getting them to work so I could have some privacy. I waited while she tugged at the string. I admired her persistence.

"Oh, don't worry," I said a minute later. "Half this place has already seen my boobs." As I joked, I felt deep appreciation for how the nurse showed me respect at a time when I was feeling extremely uneasy.

When I lay down on the table (clothes and shoes on), the nurse explained that another nurse would be helping her because she was new. I had come to love new nurses. They seem to try harder to do well than the more experienced ones, and I've always been one to judge people largely based on effort.

As the new nurse prepped the IV gear, she explained that they would run contrast into the IV at one point during the test.

"You will feel a warm flush and you'll probably feel like you peed on the bed even though you didn't." Lovely (and ultimately very true).

She then explained what would happen during the test. The table would move me in and out of the thin tunnel a few times and a voice inside would tell me when to hold my breath. It sounded simple. Still, tears fell onto my pillow.

As the team prepared, I felt as if my spirit was separate from my body.

The nurse reiterated that the test would not be as scary as I thought. "It's not the test I'm afraid of," I explained. "It's the results." The nurse looked at me. She saw the sheer terror, and I could tell how much she wanted to make it better. At one point, the young woman almost started crying too, which made me want to hug her and tell her I would be okay, even though I thought that was a lie.

Then the new nurse rubbed my arm and told me that her mom was a breast cancer survivor of several years…that she can only imagine how scary this must be…that I will get through it. She told me that I was brave.

That last part made me laugh out a "Yeah, right." I had never felt less brave in my entire life.

It all sounds simple now, what the nurse said to me. But the power of her kindness was indescribable. She took the weight of the world and made it lighter.

Soon it was time to place the IV into my arm. (After one year of infusions, my veins were tired and inserting an IV was not an easy task.) The new nurse went to fetch her mentor—a more experienced nurse—and they stood on either side of me.

The new nurse attempted to insert the IV. She dug around in my stubborn vein for a while, apologizing for causing me pain. "It's nothing," I explained. "I really don't mind."

Eventually both nurses realized that the IV wasn't going to flush correctly and we would have to try again. I couldn't even really see her, but I could tell the new nurse was disappointed in her apparent failure. She apologized some more. I tried to convince her that I didn't mind at all. "It took five times at my last infusion," I assured her. But neither of the nurses saw that as an excuse. They clearly did *not* want to stick me four more times, and I appreciated that.

The expert nurse—a woman equally as kind and comforting as her mentee—started to assemble the materials to insert the IV on my other arm. I knew that she would get it in on the first try—she had that sort of calmness and confidence. But I had another idea.

"She can try again," I told the mentor nurse, referring to the new one. They both froze for an instant, confused. "I know she can do it, so let's have her try again."

What happened next was so awesome, probably because I think that education is the key to all progress in the world. I watched the experienced nurse teach the new one. The woman on my left explained to the woman on my right how deep she enters the vein with the needle before she "threads the catheter" (only a quarter-inch in). She asked the new nurse to describe what she felt as she tried to hook into my vein.

For a minute, it wasn't about me; it was about teaching and learning, about an expert passing on her wisdom to someone who so badly wanted to gain it. Despite the fear that had minutes prior (and minutes later) overwhelmed me, I was able to escape into those few moments and see the real beauty in them.

We all celebrated quietly when the new nurse got the IV into my arm on her second try. I was so proud of her and she was proud of herself too, which made it even better.

The test came next and both nurses continued to guide me through it like angels who had swooped down to Earth just to rescue me.

When we were done, I could see the experienced nurse's name stitched into a patch on her white coat. I locked her name into my memory so I could thank her one day. The new nurse's badge was flipped backward, however, so I couldn't see her name. Once my legs stopped shaking violently (no doubt, at the thought that a radiologist was somewhere viewing the inside of my chest that was riddled with tumors), I asked the new nurse her name.

"It's Kristen," she answered.

I smiled to myself and knew I would never forget it.

* * *

Sydney had told me that I could get the results as quickly as the night of the test, but I figured Dr. Denver would call the day after. Even if he saw the bad news that night, he would want to give me one more night of peace before he broke it to me. Nevertheless, I gave Brian my cell phone for the evening because I didn't want to have such horrible words etched in my brain forever.

When, just before dinnertime, Brian answered the call from *Blocked*, I was in the basement crawl space digging out a box of old baby shoes at Annabel's command.

"It's Dr. Denver," I heard Brian say from upstairs. I dropped the box of shoes, nearly collapsed, then leaped up the old wooden stairs two at a time.

Brian was listening carefully and after what felt like an eternity (it was probably five seconds), he smiled.

"Good news."

I fell to the kitchen floor, with so much relief and thankfulness that I could barely catch my breath. Teddy and Annabel came running over, scared and confused. I had to explain to them that sometimes people cry because they are so happy. They didn't understand and I had to keep repeating to them I was crying because I was happy. Eventually, they believed me and they were sincerely happy too.

I couldn't compose myself enough to talk to Dr. Denver, but he gave Brian all the important information. *The results are preliminary. Protocol dictates that two radiologists review the scans, and although only one has reviewed them so far, I wanted to call.*

I could never explain the relief that those results brought me. I still didn't know why my chest hurt all the time, but with a clean MRI of the soft tissue and a clean CT scan of the lungs, chest wall, and lymph nodes, I felt confident that my pain was what my oncology team had suspected all along—post-surgical musculoskeletal pain. I felt confident that the Intruder had not returned, and the sense of relief was so powerful that I felt like I could float away.

The Bone Scan

March 26, 2014. I first heard the date six months prior, on the day of my last infusion. At the time I remember thinking that March seemed impossibly far off—to such an extent I couldn't even comprehend it. As I clicked forward five times on my smartphone calendar to enter the appointment, I felt the ironic emotion with which I was so very familiar— desperately wanting the future while simultaneously being terrified of it.

When my six-month follow-up appointment rolled around I wasn't nervous, mostly because I figured I couldn't possibly receive any bad news as a result of it. Still I knew I would have to talk to Dr. Denver about the pain that persisted in my chest, and I wasn't looking forward to that conversation.

I hated talking about it for several reasons, including because I could never sufficiently describe the actual pain (which frustrated me to no end). It was a deep pain—sometimes so deep that I could feel it behind my shoulder. Sometimes the pain was dull, and at other times it was sharp. Sometimes the pain burned and sometimes it ached. With all my breast tissue long gone and the superficial nerves still not functioning, it was a strange sensation to feel something beneath where I felt nothing.

I tried to pay particular attention to the pain for several days leading up to my appointment. I avoided the gym in order to determine if additional rest would alter my pain threshold (it did, though not by much).

When at my appointment we got to talking about the pain, Dr. Denver explained his confidence that it wasn't due to the reemergence of cancer. Still, after I answered all of his questions, he ordered a bone scan. It was the last of his attempts to confirm that my pain was not caused by a recurrence. "After that," he explained, "we'll have looked everywhere we can."

On my way out, I scheduled the bone scan for the next day. The scheduling lady explained that three hours before the scan, I would need to receive some type of injection. "Three hours?" I asked her, surprised. "That's a long time!" Sometimes a job and cancer can be tricky on the schedule.

For a whole host of reasons, the next day wasn't a convenient time for me to spend over four hours at Dana-Farber, and I knew it wasn't convenient for my mom either. Nevertheless, knowing that Brian wouldn't be able to take me, my mom never hesitated.

"I can do this alone," I assured her, trying to pretend somehow that it were true.

"Absolutely not!" she insisted. She wasn't going to budge, so I didn't bother arguing. Plus, I really wanted her to be with me.

* * *

The bone scan is a blur in my memory. I was exhausted—physically and emotionally—and every available bit of energy I had at the time was earmarked for hope. It wasn't hope that the scan would come back clean; more than that, I hoped that even if it didn't, there'd be something they could do to give me more time.

A few minutes after I emerged from the bone-scan machine, the nurse who had injected me with radioactive dye told me that my scans were clean. I hadn't expected the results until later that day (at the earliest), but the nurse had already spoken to the doctor who reviewed the scans on-the-spot—thus ensuring no other pictures were necessary.

I couldn't believe the news, or that I had received it then and there.

"Is this a dream?" I asked the nurse.

"No," she smiled.

But I couldn't process it; I was so sure they were going to find cancer in my bones. The news to the contrary brought me a sense of relief that was, once again, indescribable.

As I prepared to leave, the nurse asked me if I had young children. I said that I did.

"You can hug them, but you shouldn't sit next to them for an extended period of time tonight. There are still traces of the radioactive material inside you."

"Um, okay. Is that really safe then?" I inquired, thinking back to the metal container from which she took the dye before she inserted it into my vein (it looked like something from the Manhattan Project).

The nurse assured me that I'd received a very small dose of the radioactive material. That didn't make me feel better, so I refocused my attention on the good test result. As I exited the room, I was so excited to share the news.

When I found my mom in the waiting room, I tried to play it cool since we weren't alone.

"It was clean," I told her. She was as shocked as I was to get the results so soon. She started crying. We hugged. The sense of relief was palpable.

To this day, my mom says the craziest thing regarding her role in my treatment. She says that it was (and is) a *privilege* to be able to help me. I laugh at her whenever she says that. "A privilege that you get to help me though all this shit? Oh yes, you're one lucky lady!"

"I mean it," she insists, smiling at my sarcasm. And the craziest thing is that I really think she does.

Musing on the Planets

While conversing with other young-adult cancer patients during a Dana-Farber web chat in the summer of 2014, I heard two men give very different perspectives on the question of whether cancer had changed them. One participant explained that his diagnosis of Stage 4 gastric cancer had changed him profoundly—that he would never be the same again. The other participant explained that his diagnosis of Hodgkin's lymphoma had *not* changed him—that he was proud to be the same person that he was before cancer.

I appreciated these two perspectives and could have provided examples from my own life to prove the truth in both of them, but all of a sudden, I felt desperate to find an answer that better suited me. On a work call a few days later, I got some unexpected help.

I was speaking with an experienced consultant hired by my law firm to help lawyers develop their business. Ken and I had a good relationship, and he knew that I had cancer.

In this particular conversation that touched upon my professional goals (which goals did *not* involve being a lawyer), Ken told me that he didn't claim to know what it was like to have gone through what I had gone through. Ken told me, "It's as if you've been to another planet and now you're back." He admitted that he, like many others, hadn't seen that other planet and thus couldn't fathom what it was like to have returned from there.

Ken's acknowledgement of the depth of my experience meant a lot to me. As I processed it for a second or two, I almost broke my no-crying-at-work rule.

"I love that analogy," I responded. "But the thing is, you never really get to go back." I really don't think I do.

* * *

I still find myself pondering the other-planet analogy, perhaps because the thoughts and emotions that cancer continues to evoke are at times so dark, isolating, and foreign that I often feel like they could have only come into existence by way of forces entirely alien to me. Most days it's as if I have a commuting relationship between the two planets; one minute I'm lying on an ultrasound table wondering if the technician has found cancer in my liver or my pancreas, and an hour later I'm riding bikes with my kids. Well that's one real-life example anyway.

I've come to believe that perhaps I'm someone who will float in a strange space between the two planets for a while longer, or maybe even forever. I've met too many awesome people on the foreign planet to ever want to leave its atmosphere altogether, even if I were blessed with that choice. At the same time, I still can't seem to plant my feet back in the world I inhabited before August 8, 2012—a world where things like growing old were assumptions I made without any conscious thought.

I've thought a lot about how different people respond to a cancer diagnosis—how some people write about it for all the world to read while others tell only a few people. I've thought about how some people change lots of things after a diagnosis—their home, their spouse, their job, or their hobbies—while others hold on tighter to what they already have.

In the end, I believe that cancer can profoundly change us by forcing us to move in the direction of who we really are and who we really want to be. For the lucky ones who were already there or headed in that direction, the world doesn't change much. But for those who had veered off-course, cancer somehow brings us back.

My Ship

I have a ship—not a literal one of course (that would be way too expensive and I don't know a thing about ships) but a figurative one. Usually I'm uncreative and I call my ship "My Ship." Sometimes I call it "My Life Boat," and that's barely witty.

Let me tell you about My Ship.

First, I get to pick who travels on it with me. No one else's opinion matters. I decide. Just me. After all, it's *my* ship.

Lest I be rude, let me assure you that you have a ship too. You really do, even if you don't know it. You can fill that boat with whomever you want, you can paint it any color, and you can name it something completely ridiculous if that makes you happy. After all, it's *your* ship.

You may ask, "What exactly does this ship do?" That's a good question. Ultimately, what the ship does is simple—it sails. Sometimes there's no wind and everyone grabs a paddle and keeps the ship moving forward. And sometimes there are monsoons and everyone takes a bucket and helps scoop water out of the hull. But even the paddling and the scooping is all part of the sailing.

You may then ask, "Where does the ship go?" That's a good question too, and the answer depends on whose ship it is. Because ships set sail in many different seas and travel to countless foreign ports. Those many routes and all the different-colored sails help make the ocean beautiful.

Another thing about My Ship is that I'm the captain of it (and you're the captain of yours). But first, let me back up…

As babies and as kids, we aren't ready to captain our ship. So others steer it for us. Sometimes they teach us exactly how to sail, for when it's our turn. Sometimes we need to learn from their mistakes.

As adults, we take over at the helm. Sometimes we need to call in relief, but still, as the captain, we choose who will sail our ship when we're too tired or too sick to do it ourselves.

The best part about being the captain of our own ship is that we pick our co-captains, our crew, and all of our guests. Sometimes we allow someone onto our ship and later realize that he or she is far too much like a pirate—he or she would be better off on someone else's ship or maybe floating in the ocean alone. If we're brave, we kick those people off our ship (with a life jacket, of course). Because there is no room for pirates where we're going.

* * *

It wasn't until after I was diagnosed with cancer that I recognized My Ship for the amazing vessel that it is. I have no idea what made me see it, but over the last two years, I've thought a lot about who I want on My Ship. Who is a disguised pirate, dragging the boat down or slowly poking a hole in its bottom? Who would help me paddle or scoop or raise the sails high to catch the wind? Who would I ask to help me navigate? Who would make my trip more joyful? More purposeful? More…full? I have a list in my head.

Here's another thing—some people care a lot about what their ship looks like. In some ways, I do too. I want my boat to be clean and strong, safe and comfortable. But I don't want a yacht. I just want a ship that can weather great storms and still be full of laughter and peace. I want My Ship to travel far and still come back to the harbor in which it was built.

I love to think about My Ship. I make decisions about how to spend time based on My Ship. My Ship has brought me clarity and comfort. It's a very beautiful thing.

My Ship—like all ships that leave port—has sailed through rough seas and alongside spectacular sunrises. My Ship has dents and patches and parts that creak, as those things happen to any ship that heads out into the open, unforgiving sea. Which is why we better load our ships with loyal co-captains, a great crew, accurate maps, and the right motivations.

Because we only get one ship.

And one awesome journey into the sunset.

Epilogue

Hope is a waking dream.

Aristotle
(philosopher)

Hope Is a Book

Long before cancer, I wanted to write. In fact, about five years ago, I had a clear vision of the book I would author—a novel based in South Africa. The book would explore themes that had always fascinated me including truth, fear, courage, love, and loyalty. I researched the time period in which the story would be set and I planned to draw on lessons I had learned about South Africa's people and its history in my time studying abroad in Cape Town over a decade prior. I scribbled down an outline, shaped the main characters in my head, and named the heroine. Even though the characters were fuzzy, I fell in love with them.

But I wasn't a writer.

I was a public-high-school-teacher-turned-corporate-lawyer. I worked in a behemoth law firm from which I desperately wanted to escape.

On my commutes on the train to and from Boston, I often dreamed about dumping the Firm and spending my days as an author. Those dreams included a pace of life that was much slower and more purposeful than the pace that left me physically and emotionally empty at the end of each day. The visions included office windows that opened to welcome in fresh air and they included enough sleep so that my right eyelid wouldn't twitch all the time as it did when my lawyer job (coupled with my desire to tuck my two young kids into bed at night) allowed me a daily average of four hours' sleep.

In my life-as-an-author vision, I spent my days typing away in natural sunlight at the local library or at home. I would read as much as I could about the fall of apartheid and I would carefully place my characters into that complicated history. Once published, my novel would not only entertain people, but it would *matter* to them.

However, my dream to become an author had one big glitch: a paycheck (or better yet, a lack thereof). Pouring literary brilliance (or literary crap) onto my computer screen wasn't going to pay the bills and Brian and I sure as shit didn't have much money saved. So the book that I dreamed about writing went unwritten; my vision became little more than unspoken thoughts and unshared scribbles.

When I couldn't take it anymore, I left the Firm for a smaller firm. I was infinitely happier after that move, particularly because, every now and then after my kids went to sleep, I had actual *free time* on my hands. I slept more, started to exercise again, and paid more attention to being well. I even dabbled in my town's annual writing contest. My poem won third prize for my age category. Not exactly the Pulitzer, but I was writing and it felt good.

Years later, the novel still remains unwritten, but not in a way that makes me feel unfulfilled or anxious. Because one day, I will write that book. Before I do, however, I had to write this one.

* * *

I planned to write *this* book as much as I planned to get cancer, which is to say, *not at all*. When I was diagnosed, my vision of the South Africa novel died—so quietly that I barely noticed, but I buried it nonetheless.

My dreams became hopes and prayers to see my kids grow up. No fresh air. No natural light. No library.

Still, there was fire in me that I had never felt before. With that fire, I started to write.

I wasn't writing a book at the time, but rather a blog of medical updates and random reflections on life-with-cancer. My writing was often born from fear so powerful that my hands and knees shook as I typed. The blog wasn't necessarily a choice, but rather an instinct. Nothing that I put down onto my screen felt like brilliance. It just felt like therapy—like what I needed to do to keep breathing. I had no idea that those thoughts and reflections would one day form the foundation of this book.

* * *

In its preliminary stages, this book grew in 20-minute spurts whenever I could find the time—mostly on the train to and from work. I wrote in bed after my husband fell asleep, until I could no longer keep my eyes open. I wrote on the sofa between snack requests from my children, and their subsequent apologies for having spilled everything I'd just prepared. I worked on this book from the passenger seat of the car and from the rink during Brian's hockey games. I never wrote at the library, but I wrote in waiting rooms and infusion suites at the Dana-Farber Cancer Institute. Even when I wasn't sitting at my keyboard, I still wrote on pages in my mind.

Writing this book was—at times almost simultaneously—an extremely painful and deeply fulfilling process. As the pages took shape, I became entrenched in the memories, some of which I'd already blogged about and others that I'd only then recalled. A few times, the recollections made me so anxious that I needed to stop and walk away. But I always returned, even if my writing was crappy and my hands still shook on the surface of my keyboard.

* * *

Some people believe that everything happens for a reason. Personally, I don't think that. I believe that life and death happen and we have an infinite number of ways to react to the glorious, the tragic, and the everything-in-between. Everything-happens-for-a-reason makes me feel like a pawn in someone else's game. Instead I would like to believe that I can shape my life based on how I choose to react to what is in my control, and more importantly, to the countless things that are out of it.

I started to write when I was diagnosed with cancer—not because of any dream or vision, but because I had something to say and I felt better when I said it. I don't think God gave me cancer so I would write. However, I *do* think that in a dark, treacherous alley, I came face-to-face with a chance. Maybe that chance was from a higher being, or maybe it just bad luck. I really have no idea, and that's not what matters anyway.

What matters to me, in this very moment, is that as much as I despise so much of what accompanied my cancer diagnosis, I choose to consider it as something more than just bad luck. Because in a crazy, unexpected, and awesome sort of way, cancer helped make a dream of mine come true…

I wrote a book.

Acknowledgements

Hope is...

...my Grandma and Grandpa, who loved books with a passion I found wonderfully contagious.

...my Dad, who built our family and raised me to believe that I could achieve anything.

...my sister Rachel, who grew up reading encyclopedias with me in our bunk beds and who gave me my first taste of real hope.

...my brother Sean, who is the most vital of passengers and who did a million little things on this wild ride that eased my pain.

...my brother-in-law Matt, whose remarkable work ethic and determination helped inspire me to finish this book.

...my soon-to-be sister-in-law Lauren, who is a perfect model of what all health care providers should be.

...my best friend Brianne, who taught me that worry's like a rocking chair—it keeps you going but gets you nowhere—and who nevertheless understands me when I worry.

...Brianne's family, including her husband Seamus and their boys JJ and Maccus, who arrived on my doorstep when I needed them most.

...my selfless mother-in-law Janice and father-in-law Paul, who held down the fort more times than I can count and who kept it a fort full of reading, coloring, knee hockey, and baseball.

...my brother-in-law Greg, who wrote a book years ago and proved to me it's possible.

...my cousin Kirsten, whose heart is made of gold and who knew (and delivered herself from New Jersey) exactly what my family and I needed before we even knew we needed it.

...my Aunt Helen, who gave me dozens of butterflies and big hugs that helped me believe that everything was going to be okay.

...Kathy, Carole, Katie, Kristen, Karen, Colleen, Jill, and the other clinicians at the Brigham and Women's Faulkner Hospital, Dana-Farber Cancer Institute, and Brigham and Women's Hospital, who brought me fresh air when I desperately needed it.

...Christine, Pat, Dr. Lui, and Paula B, who in my darkest time gave me the most precious gift of hope.

...all of the other amazing men and women at Winchester Hospital who supported my mom while she cared for me.

...my core medical team—Dr. Bunnell, Dr. Nakhlis, Dr. Chun, and Danielle—who not only saved my life but who did so with the intelligence, empathy, kindness, and humility that every patient deserves.

...Dr. Fasciano, who is so much more than my "therapy lady," and who handed me tissues while she listened to me and helped me become stronger than before.

...the Dana-Farber Cancer Institute and Brigham and Women's Hospital, and the life-saving work that is done there every day.

...Amy and Rebecca, who showed me what reconstruction of the body and the soul looks like.

...my cousin Tara, one of the funniest women on the planet, who dreams big, works hard, and inspires me to do the same.

...my cousins Kyle, Susan, and Kenyon, who continuously support me with the utmost generosity and enthusiasm.

...my other cousins, aunts, and uncles (by blood and by marriage), who always seem to say or do something wonderfully helpful and kind when I need it most.

...Grandma Kosta, whose smile and laugh is ingrained into my memory forever.

...my childhood friends, including Mike, Jillian, Kara, Mikaela, and Kate, who came out of the woodwork after my diagnosis and reminded me that bonds we make when we're young can last forever.

...my friends Amy and Tom, whose love and generosity may never be surpassed.

...my friends who inspire me, keep me laughing, and remind me every day about the importance of family—the Wood, McCready, DiFiore, Marcone, Connor, and Connolly families.

...my friends and neighbors Amy and Jess, who dedicated their skills to helping make this book successful.

...the Herr family, whose love, loss, and strength I think about every day.

...the Bowdoin basketball girls, who kept me as one of their teammates even after I turned in my uniform.

...my other Bowdoin friends—Carrie, Sara, Nathaniel, Eben, Mike, Kevin, and Conor—who I far-too-rarely get to see but who I know are always there.

...my HomeBase friends, with whom I start most of my days and continue to strengthen my hope muscles.

...Monique, Angela, Helen, and their co-workers, who helped me believe that bald is beautiful.

...those who give so much of themselves to cancer patients—Susan and the staff at the Kraft Family Blood Donor Center, the Schwartz family, the volunteers at Dana-Farber including my friends on the Patient and Family Advisory Council, the Jimmy Fund Walk staff, and the We Beat Cancer crew.

...Joy and Ashley who I wish more than anything I could bring together again.

...the one-of-a-kind Canton hockey community which continues to teach me about the grit, unselfishness, and lasting camaraderie that is "to fight like a bulldog."

...my dearest Wildewood and Old Meadow friends—some of the most sincere, generous, and fun people on Earth—with whom I am blessed to share the streets we call home.

...my kids' teachers and my friends at the Blue Hill Montessori School, who have made this journey infinitely easier for us.

...my former teachers and coaches, who continue to teach me years after I left their classrooms or their practices.

...my former students, who taught me more than I ever taught them.

...my mentor and friend Mark, who taught me that a blessed soul is not complete without creating something beautiful (and that billable hours ultimately mean nothing).

...my brave friends who bring light to darkness and choose to live strong—Maggie, Sara, Katie, Marisa, Meghan, Kathy, Jean, Becky, Michael, Devon, Debi, Cathy, Jillian, Tara, Jack, Julie, Elinore, Anne, Lisa, Kim, Carol, Rosey, Paula, Marissa, Amanda, Sarah, Meliss, Lia, Linda, Marie, Raquel, Michelle, Kristi, Holly, Laurie, Irene, Maureen, Mireille, Sebastien, and Jerry.

...Billy and Annabel C, who delivered me pink envelopes full of strength, laughter, and hope.

...Payton, Shaye, Griffin, Selena, and other young leaders who are the future of our fight against cancer.

...my friend Heather, who warmly welcomed my kids into her house during our toughest times.

...the loyal members of Team Tara, whose miles walked bring us closer to a cure.

...Mary, Ngan, Hy, and Cong, who force-fed me dim sum and taught me that with enough love and hard work, sometimes the impossible *is* possible.

...my fellow bloggers, who understand what it feels like to hit *Publish*.

...Kristin and Corey and their beautiful children, who are the reason I found my cancer when I did and who inspire me to live every day to the fullest.

...the town of Canton, Canton High School, and all the good people there, who provide unwavering support to me and my family.

...the amazing crew who filled the cooler on our doorstep with meals during my treatment.

...our friends at First Parish Unitarian Universalist, who welcome us with open arms on the rare Sundays that we actually get to church.

...friendships that began at work but live on away from the office—Marylana, Kate, Joyce, Emma, David, Hannah, Colleen, Sarah, Jenny, Dani, Jill, Liz, Braden, and Beth.

...friends and colleagues at Ropes & Gray, who taught me priceless lessons about what is truly important in life.

...my friend Lynne, who graciously printed out all of my blog entries and in doing so was the first person to show me that there was a book hidden inside.

...my colleagues at Verrill Dana, who generously allowed me time away from the office after my diagnosis and who graciously supported me upon my return.

...my friend Andy, who always stopped to talk to me (despite that he had work to do) and who taught me the power of meditation (despite how much I suck at it).

...my friend Keri, who doesn't notice hills when we run up them but with whom I will nevertheless keep running until I can't run any farther.

...my other friends at Harvard Medical School, who supported me in the months during which this book finally came together.

...the Spruce Point Inn and our friends and family who made it possible for us to go back there.

...Oprah Winfrey, for the stories she told and the perspective those stories gave me.

…Bruce Springsteen, for the hopeful words he sings, and my friend Danny for giving me the gift of the Boss when I needed it most.

…my Facebook friends, who moved this book forward with their constant feedback, encouragement, and support.

…my blog readers, who are the foundation of these pages.

…Herceptin, and every person who played a role in bringing it into both existence and my infusion suite.

…the loved ones of cancer victims, who give me the precious hope that were cancer to take me, my family and friends would still laugh, smile, and find beauty in the world.

…every cancer patient, caregiver, survivor, and "aliver" (to quote the amazing Dr. Mandy Redig), who I pray have felt the precious comfort of hope, and of being here now.

…my friend Leonard, whose honest feedback encouraged me to edit this book in the way that it needed to be edited.

…my friends Jennifer, Mark, and Erica, whose artistic talents and skills, as well as amazing generosity, made this book look like the dream-come-true that it is.

…my friend John, for spending countless hours copyediting, fact-checking, and improving on every single line of this book (thus treating my work as if it were worthy of such attention).

…my friend and editor Kendra, who loves books as much as I do and who kept my house, my family, and my dreams for this project from falling apart.

…the Writing Saves Lives board—Bill, Joanna, Caitlin, and Peter—with whom I can't wait to build something truly great.

…my mom, who is and forever will be my brightest guiding light and the most brilliant, caring, and all-around amazing woman I know.

…my husband Brian, who falls asleep almost every night to the light of my laptop and the sound of my typing, and whom for that reason and countless others I will love and appreciate for the rest of my life.

…my children Teddy and Annabel, who I love as big as the sky. You are my lucky day and the most important reason I never lose hope.

Thank-You Note

A cave, a light, a purpose,
a place to breathe and cope;
blank pages, crumbs of clarity,
a sanctuary of hope.

A blog, a book,
a ship, a chance;
a search for peace
in fighting stance.

These pages are
a shining sea—
my own idea
of victory.

Thank you all
for I've been blessed
to rise upon
this hopeful crest.

Thank you truly
for all you've done;
for all your stories,
of which I'm one.

Cover Credits

Mark Abair (cover design) has raised thousands of dollars and run hundreds of miles for the Leukemia and Lymphoma Society (LLS). After learning in 2008 that his friend had been diagnosed with acute myeloid leukemia, Mark became actively involved in LLS (he ran the Boston Marathon in 2011 and 2014 for the organization). Mark is now training for another marathon, and continues to volunteer for LLS.

Jennifer Davidson (front-cover photograph) is an attorney, photographer, and angel to countless people far and wide. Jennifer has witnessed great loss in her life, including the unexpected passing of her sister Jessie in 2012. Jessie couldn't walk or talk due to significant mental and physical disabilities and her death inspired Jennifer to run the Boston Marathon to raise money for Technology for Autism Now. Jennifer had never run more than a few miles but in April 2014, she ran 26.2 miles for Jessie. Five months later, Jennifer walked the same Boston Marathon route for The Jimmy Fund, joining Team Tara and inspiring us for many miles.

Erica Shea (back-cover photograph) was diagnosed with Stage 3 Hodgkin's lymphoma when she was 22 years old. Four years later (and just two days after bringing home her newborn son), Erica experienced shortness of breath and severe chest pain. She was rushed to the hospital and subsequently learned that she had congestive heart failure, mostly likely as a result of her chemotherapy. In December 2013, Erica was placed in a medically induced coma after she was diagnosed with sepsis—a critical condition that can precede organ failure. Erica underwent open-heart surgery in January 2014 so that doctors could insert a ventricular-assist device that supports heart function and blood flow. Erica survived this grueling ordeal, although at the time this book went to print she still desperately awaited a heart transplant. *Please encourage organ donation. It's the last and most-valuable gift we could ever give.*

About the Author

Tara Anne Shuman is a health care attorney who aspires to teach literature and writing to high-school students. She already has begun writing several other books, including a children's book and a novel set in South Africa. Tara volunteers at the Dana-Farber Cancer Institute and speaks to many different audiences about her cancer experience. She is the proud founder of the non-profit organization, Writing Saves Lives, and a true believer in the healing powers of writing. Tara lives in Canton, Massachusetts with her husband Brian and their two children, Teddy and Annabel. She is grateful for each day and believes deeply in the value of truth, humor, hope, love, and hard work.

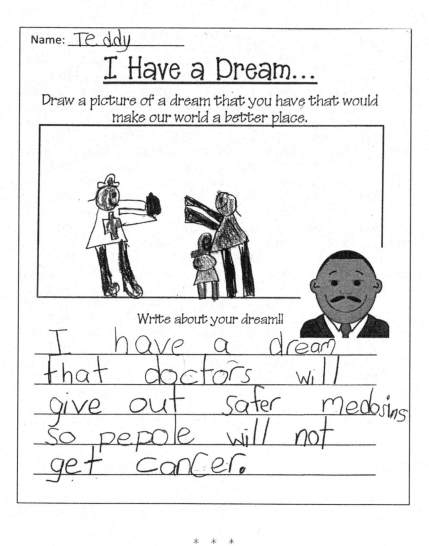

Name: Teddy

I Have a Dream...

Draw a picture of a dream that you have that would make our world a better place.

Write about your dream!!

I have a dream that doctors will give out safer medosins so pepole will not get cancer.

* * *

For more information and to contact Tara,
please visit www.hopeisagoodbreakfast.com

~~The End.~~
The Beginning.

CPSIA information can be obtained at www.ICGtesting.com
Printed in the USA
LVOW04s1744300415

436767LV00011B/144/P